T0306194

THE SLOW BOIL

JONATHAN SHAPIRO ANJARIA

THE SLOW BOIL

Street Food, Rights, and Public Space in Mumbai

STANFORD UNIVERSITY PRESS

STANFORD, CALIFORNIA

Stanford University Press
Stanford, California

Printed and bound by CPI Group (UK) Ltd, Croydon, CR0 4YY

Library of Congress Cataloging-in-Publication Data

Names: Anjaria, Jonathan Shapiro, author.
Title: The slow boil : street food, rights and public space in Mumbai /
    Jonathan Shapiro Anjaria.
Other titles: South Asia in motion.
Description: Stanford, California : Stanford University Press, 2016. | ©2016
    | Series: South Asia in motion | Includes bibliographical references and
    index.
Identifiers: LCCN 2015042394| ISBN 9780804798228 (cloth : alk. paper) | ISBN
    9780804799379 (pbk. : alk. paper) | ISBN 9780804799393 (e-book)
Subjects: LCSH: Street vendors—India—Mumbai. | Vending stands—Political
    aspects—India—Mumbai. | Public spaces—Political aspects—India—Mumbai.
    | Streets—Political aspects—India—Mumbai. | Civil
    rights—India—Mumbai. | Urban policy—India—Mumbai.
Classification: LCC HF5459.I4 A55 2016 | DDC 647.95/54792—dc23
LC record available at http://lccn.loc.gov/2015042394

Typeset by Bruce Lundquist in 10.75/15 Adobe Caslon

For Ulka

CONTENTS

ILLUSTRATIONS

ACKNOWLEDGMENTS

This book was realized with the generous help of many people. I am especially grateful to Sharit Bhowmik, whose assistance in the initial stages of my research in Mumbai was absolutely vital. Without his generous help, this project would not have been possible. As the project got off the ground, the faculty at the University of California, Santa Cruz provided indispensable intellectual guidance. Triloki Pandey's mentorship from the beginning enabled me to carry out research in Mumbai, Anna Tsing showed me the expansive possibilities for ethnography, and Lisa Rofel demonstrated what a fine-tuned approach to political economy looks like. A decade later, their comments and critiques continue to reverberate. I also thank James Ferguson for facilitating discussions on neoliberalism that profoundly shaped this project, Amita Baviskar whose research and writing inspired my interest in urban space, and Akhil Gupta for discussions at the Interrogating Modernity and Postcoloniality seminar, which shaped my approach to the state. I am forever indebted to Steve Caton for introducing me as an undergraduate student to anthropology and its wide-ranging possibilities.

Research and writing for this project was made possible by generous funding from the American Institute for Indian Studies; the American Council of Learned Societies/Mellon Foundation; the University of California, Santa Cruz Department of Anthropology; and the Department of Anthropology at Brandeis University. Hindi language training was funded by the American Institute of Indian Studies Summer Language Fellowship. I especially thank Purnima Mehta and Elise Auerbach at the American Institute for Indian Studies for tirelessly providing essential assistance with research logistics.

I have been fortunate to finish writing the manuscript among tremendously supportive colleagues at Brandeis University. I especially thank

Sarah Lamb for her inspiring mentorship and intellectual guidance. I am extremely grateful to Laurel Carpenter, Elizabeth Ferry, Charles Golden, Anita Hannig, Janet McIntosh, Rick Parmentier, Ellen Schattschneider, and Javier Urcid for fostering a uniquely vibrant and nurturing intellectual environment. Without them, I would not have been able to complete this book in a timely manner.

Over the years, the ideas contained in this book benefited from conversations with a number of friends, interlocutors, and colleagues. I thank Nikhil Anand, Zainab Bawa, Lisa Björkman, Lawrence Cohen, Kushal Deb, Naresh Fernandes, Maura Finkelstein, Curt Gambetta, Ashner Ghertner, Nandini Gooptu, Inderpal Grewal, Akhil Gupta, Andrew Harris, Douglas Haynes, Ayesha Jalal, Rutul Joshi, Naveeda Khan, Nida Kirmani, Shekhar Krishnan, Ratoola Kundu, Omar Kutty, Genevieve Lakier, Moises Lino E Silva, Mark Lytle, Reema and Renuka Mavlankar, William Mazzarella, Caroline Melly, Lisa Mitchell, Aniruddha Paul, Sarah Pinto, Smitha Radhakrishnan, Nikhil Rao, Ursula Rao, Zeb Rifaqat, Sharmila Sen, Gavin Shatkin, Rob Shields, K. Sivaramakrishnan, Harris Solomon, Tulasi Srinivas, Phil Steinberg, Paromita Vohra, and Neha Vora. I also thank Melissa Hackman and Caroline Melly, colleague-comrades from the very beginning, and Jennifer Derr, Allison McKim, and Lucinda Ramberg, for the many spirited and delicious evenings; Liza Weinstein, for astute readings of parts of this manuscript; and Colin McFarlane, for being an inspiring and fun interlocutor over the years. And finally, I thank Shilpa Phadke, whose scholarship helped inspire this project in the beginning and whose warm hospitality in Mumbai made it come to fruition at the end.

I have been fortunate to work with a number of students who have compelled me to see the city differently. Experiencing Mumbai with Bard College students Ella Belensky, Rosemary Ferreira, Logan Hollarsmith, Yinan Hu, Ava Jewett, Ethan Midlin Jones, Shivalika Kalra, Marnie MacGregor, Elias Moose, Anar Parikh, Rachael Scheibert, Lia Soorenian, and Sarah Stern, as well as the students at the Kamla Raheja Vidyanidhi Institute for Architecture and Environmental Studies, including Ashwini Kamath, Ruchitra Hemani, and Apeksha Gupta, was especially enlightening. Conversations about cities and public space with Josh Berman,

Charlotte Erb, and Alina Pokhrel were very instructive. I am grateful for the thorough archival and library research assistance by Jara Connell, Ariel Meave, Aneil Tripathy, and Ysabel Yates. I thank the archivists at the fabulous Centre for Education and Documentation, Mumbai as well.

Audiences at various presentations provided invaluable insights and critiques, much of it incorporated into this book. These include presentations at the Center for the Study of Social Sciences, Kolkata; the Center for Environmental Planning and Technology, Ahmedabad; the Cornell University; Durham University; Irmgard Coninx Foundation, Berlin; Lahore University of Management Sciences; Max Planck Institute, Halle; National Institute for Advanced Studies, Bengaluru; Oberlin College; Oxford University; Stanford University; Tata Institute of Social Sciences (School of Media and Cultural Studies), Mumbai; Tata Institute of Social Sciences (School of Habitat Studies), Mumbai; Tufts University; University of California, Berkeley; University of Leipzig; University of Oregon, University of Pennsylvania; and Yale University.

It has been a delight to work with Stanford University Press. I especially thank Jenny Gavacs for her support and diligent editorial assistance, the anonymous readers for their truly inspiring comments and suggestions, and Thomas Blom Hansen for his encouragement at all stages of this project.

It is a rare pleasure to express gratitude to my family, the people who provide the most but get thanked the least. Having kids of my own has made me ever more appreciative of my loving parents, Terry and Steve, who have encouraged all the personal journeys I have taken, however surprising they might have seemed at the time. I have also been very fortunate to have deeply caring parents-in-laws, Nishigandha and Shailendra, to whom I owe a special debt of gratitude for making life in Mumbai so comfortable. My children, Naseem and Rehaan, were born at the start of this project and have shaken things up ever since. Without prodding, they have turned into shrewd cultural critics, and I shudder at the thought of their review of my work. I am grateful to them for keeping things in perspective, as all kids do, and, more important, for showing me how to see the world in different ways. And finally, my partner, friend, and collaborator, Ulka, is the person who makes everything possible. Not a sentence of this book has been left untouched by our conversations and debates, as well as by the dreams, academic pet peeves, and flights of fancy we've shared over the years.

And most important, although I cannot thank them by name, I am deeply indebted to the many people in Mumbai who showed me how the city, its streets, its networks of authority, and rights-claims work. The people discussed in this book offer a model of patience, care, and generosity that I can only aspire to. There is truth behind the cliché that Mumbai and its residents are an inspiration.

A version of chapter 4 appeared as "Ordinary States: Everyday Corruption and the Politics of Space in Mumbai," *American Ethnologist* 38, no. 1: 58–72. Other early versions of parts of the book appeared as "Street Hawkers and Public Space in Mumbai," *Economic and Political Weekly*, May 27, 2006, 2140–46; "The Mall and the Street: Practices of Public Consumption in Mumbai," in *Lived Experiences of Public Consumption: Encounters with Value in Marketplaces on Five Continents*, edited by Daniel Thomas Cook, 203–20 (New York: Palgrave Macmillan, 2008); "Guardians of the Bourgeois City: Citizenship, Public Space, and Middle-Class Activism in Mumbai," *City and Community* 8, no. 4 (2011): 391–406; "The Politics of Illegality: Mumbai Hawkers, Public Space and the Everyday Life of the Law," in *Street Vendors in the Global Urban Economy*, edited by Sharit Bhowmik, 69–86 (New Delhi: Routledge, 2010); and "Is There a Culture of the Indian Street?," *Seminar* 636 (August 2012): 21–27.

THE SLOW BOIL

CHAPTER 1

INTRODUCTION

WHILE IDLED IN TRAFFIC ONE AFTERNOON, an elderly driver of an autorickshaw, the affordable, three-wheeled, motorized taxi ubiquitous in Mumbai's northern suburbs, leaned back to strike up a conversation. He had a speckled beard and a broad smile, and he seemed to enjoy his job and the conversations with strangers it offered. After asking where I was from and what I was doing in Mumbai, the conversation took an unexpected turn.[1] "What's the famous monument of New York?" he asked rhetorically. "It's the Statue of Liberty, right?" Without waiting for my response, he continued: "What's the monument of Mumbai?" I stumbled while searching for an appropriate answer. I proposed the Gateway of India, the arch overlooking the Arabian Sea, completed in 1924, an icon of city promotional materials and popular tourist spot. He shook his head. If this was a test of my research credentials, I had failed. "No, no, it's the *vada pao!*" he said. And with that, he turned again to face me and took a hearty bite out of an imaginary sandwich.

Vada pao consists of a fried ball of battered mashed potato, the *vada*, crushed within a sweet and spicy chutney-soaked bun, the *pao*. It is Mumbai's most popular snack. There are others that are famously associated with the city, such as *bhel puri* and *pao bhaji*, but no other food is as ubiquitous and passionately consumed. Vada pao hawkers can be seen in front of train stations; near schools, colleges, and hospitals; at

1

busy street corners; and near the entrances of parks. They prepare the snack on makeshift metal tables perched on the curb. The vadas are deep fried in well-used black pots. The chutneys are stored in small metal tins. The sandwiches come wrapped in recycled newspaper, accompanied by a green chili pepper. They are cheap and filling and consumed by a broad spectrum of the city. To some, eating vada pao is a guilty pleasure—a quick bite on the way home from work. To others, it is a means of surviving in an expensive city. However its role is conceived, the humble vada pao was an unlikely object to elevate to monumental status. Monuments, write Wohl and Strauss (1958), are "symbolic representation[s]" of a city. They produce images that circulate, shape, and, their creators hope, elevate a city's global status.

Monumentalizing street food was surprising in other ways. To many political leaders, journalists, and residents, hawkers represent a "symbol of metropolitan space gone out of control" (Rajagopal 2001). They are often described as a "'menace' [and] a 'problem' that needs to be 'addressed'" (Patel 2013). On seaside boardwalks, signs such as "Do not patronize hawkers and beggars," make avoiding street food into a civic duty. Alarmism over the hawker "menace" is seemingly everywhere. One day while waiting for the elevator in my Mumbai apartment, I noticed a flier freshly posted to the foyer wall. I looked closer. It was an article, titled "Hawker Proliferation—Economics and Impact," that listed the inconveniences to drivers and pedestrians that hawkers cause. "Hawker encroachment [is so pervasive]," the article explained, because of corruption and the fact that "people do not care enough to protest." Taking up the provocation, a neighbor had scrawled a message above the title: "WHY WE SHOULD NOT DO BUSINESS WITH HAWKERS." Writings like these are commonplace. Two years earlier, Citispace, a civic group, distributed a pamphlet with a similar message. If you want "clean and orderly surroundings," you should "play the role of 'watch dog'" and "complain about persistent illegal hawkers" (Citispace 2004).

Local newspapers display a similar perspective on hawkers. Every week newspapers report on hawker trouble spots and the efforts by the state to deal with them. Articles with titles such as "Keep Vendors away from No-Hawking Zone" (Verma 2005), "Download an App, Take an

Illegal Hawker to Task" (Subramanian 2013), and "Hawkers Look to
Take over Rs 4 Andheri Auto Deck" (Rao 2015) depict Mumbai's streets
and public spaces as conflict zones consisting of pitched battles among
residents, state functionaries, and a ragtag army of encroachers. Newspapers regularly describe "pedestrians [who] have been battling for two
decades to reclaim their streets from encroachers" (Subramanian 2006) in
neighborhoods "worst hit by [the] hawker invasion" (Bhatia 2007). "The
hawker issue is important for citizens, who are used to fighting—most
often, a losing battle—for space" ("Times View" 2015), says another. Articles describe the feeling of disempowerment among residents living in
areas where hawkers have "laid siege" (Baliga 2013) to the roads. Says one
resident, "We have been fighting this battle for many years now but over
a period of time the number of hawkers have [sic] actually increased"
(quoted in Bhatia 2007).

The vada pao is an unlikely "monument" for other reasons. To civic
activists frequently quoted in the media, hawkers are often a symbol
of poor governance, an indifferent bureaucracy, and broken democracy.
Unlicensed vada pao vendors and hawkers like them are thus not only
physical annoyances but understood to be part of a larger problem of encroachment enabled by corrupt officials. Hawkers are understood to be a
manifestation of a nexus with state functionaries fueled by a mix of retail
corruption, unofficial compromises, and dubious appeals to social welfare.
While unlicensed, they appeal to the state on the basis of entitlements
owed to particular disadvantaged groups. They mix rights claims based on
individual citizenship with belonging in a larger collective. They are said
to blur the boundary between private subjecthood and public practice.
In this discourse, the mere presence of hawkers signals the failure of the
state to abide by the principles of liberal citizenship and the rule of law.
To them, hawkers not only obstruct pedestrians; they also obstruct the
flourishing of political modernity itself.

In 1998, the Citizens' Forum for the Protection of Public Spaces (later
renamed Citispace) brought their campaign against encroachment to
the Bombay High Court. To Citizens' Forum activists, not only was the
Brihanmumbai Municipal Corporation (BMC) failing to fulfill its obli-
gations to regulate public space, but its ad hoc practices gave unlicensed

hawkers "rights" to the street. By 2003, the case went to the Supreme Court of India, which issued a groundbreaking ruling in Citispace's favor. In addition to instructing the BMC to implement a hawker regulation system, it issued new guidelines restricting hawking. Among them was a ban on curbside cooking. And yet following the 2003 ruling, vada pao vendors and other hawkers were as visible as before. Few hawkers, or state functionaries, were aware of the ban. Implementing the law was complicated by another factor: most hawking was already criminalized. If Mumbai's street food vendors already lacked licenses, how could they be banned? In a telling sign of this legal confusion, Mumbai's hundreds of thousands of hawkers continued to work on the street following the ban as before.

Monumentalizing the vada pao was also ironic in light of the new "global city" discourses circulating in Mumbai at the time. To those who aspired to transform Mumbai into an international business hub modeled after Shanghai, the city's street economy represented an impediment—a problem of world becoming. By the early 2000s, the effects of India's economic liberalization, a process that had begun a decade earlier, started to be visible. New shopping malls, office complexes, luxury apartment buildings, and elite spaces of leisure and consumption such as cafés, nightclubs, and grocery stores, all rare in the late 1990s, became commonplace. To many, this new landscape of consumption offered hope of transformation. The fact that many of the first new symbols of globalized Mumbai, such as shopping malls and clubs designed with an international aesthetic, appeared in former textile mills facilitated a narrative of a city in transition. A report produced by Bombay First and McKinsey & Company, "Vision Mumbai: Transforming Mumbai into a World-Class City" (McKinsey & Company 2003), spurred dreams of a transformation of the city's image; the once gritty city of mills and slums might soon give way to a proud global metropolis with a slick, international aesthetic. As a headline at the time put it, "From Mills to Malls, the Sky Is the Limit" (Bharucha 2003).

A devastating flood in July 2005 tempered some of this euphoria. Cheeky billboards appearing on the streets in 2006 asked: "Shanghai ya Doobai?" (Shanghai or Doobai?) playing off of the Hindi word *dubna*, which means to drown. Nevertheless, with multiple billion-dollar infrastructure projects built up in subsequent years, such as the Worli-Bandra

Sea Link, the Mumbai Metro, and a stylish new international airport terminal, the dream to remake the city through dramatic aesthetic and architectural intervention reemerged. Amid these urban transformations, important questions arose: Can Mumbai's landscape of squatters, slum settlements, and vibrant but visually chaotic street commerce be reconciled with transnational aesthetic ideals? What is the place of the poor in this story of transition? Or, put in another way, is there a place for the vada pao in globalizing Mumbai?

CONTRADICTIONS OF THE STREET

The hundreds of thousands of hawkers that line Mumbai's streets are emblematic of the city's compelling—and to some, frustrating—contradictions. Although most are unlicensed, they profoundly shape the appearance and feel of the city.[2] They are subject to periodic raids but are also essential providers of services who distribute nearly all of the city's fresh fruits and produce while providing affordable meals to its millions of working-poor residents. This book explores the meanings of these incongruities. I show how this criminalized street economy is not just a space of exclusion, but also a space for active engagement in the political sphere; spatial contestations are characterized by violence as well as dynamic negotiation, debate, and compromise over political form. Whereas much writing on squatters, hawkers, and slum demolitions sees them as instances of elite appropriations of space, I show how tensions surrounding evictions are also a way in which crucial questions of rights, citizenship, and global belonging are worked out—for instance: How might universalizing ideas of citizenship be reconciled with a heterogeneous political sphere? In a democracy shaped by political liberalism, can rights claims be context specific? And can participation in global modernity emerge in coordination with, rather than only as a negation of, local context?

The Mumbai hawker controversy parallels transnational trends; however, it diverges in significant ways from these trends on account of hawkers' vital place in public debates over the city and its future.[3] Through ethnography and historical analysis, the chapters in this book highlight how the mundane question of street vending speaks to broader issues about space and rights in the city. The evidence shows

FIGURE 1.1 *Arranging vegetables before the evening crowd of commuters arrives*

that everyday conflicts over encroachment and corruption constitute a critical discussion over how to inhabit and make claims on the city. In Chapter 2, I begin with the question: Are we witnessing a new moment of spatial contestation and exclusion of the poor? I show that for over two centuries, the authorities in Mumbai have struggled to control a landscape of encroachments and illegalities. Moreover, the municipal government has dealt with the "hawker nuisance" at least since the 1880s. And yet scholars often treat demolitions, dispossessions of the poor, and elite-oriented development as effects of a new logic of urban governance associated with neoliberalism. I provide an account of the history of informality in Mumbai to challenge this assumption of novelty. Drawing from various historical documents—including official publications, travelogues, and early twentieth-century newspapers—I show that for over a century, people's encounters with state functionaries have been characterized by compromise, co-option, and negotiation rather than anonymity and discipline. What is new about the contemporary urban moment is not spatial contestation itself but its broader significance as a site for negotiating the form and content of rights.

What does it mean to work on the side of the road without a license? Is it a result of urban exclusion or an act of rebellion? Writings on informal economies typically fall into one camp or the other. In Chapter 3, I offer a different approach; I provide an account of hawkers' life histories and their relationships to the street, work, and the city's recent dramatic transformations. I show how hawkers occupy a contradictory existence, inhabiting a precarious legal status while deeply enmeshed in the daily life of a neighborhood. I argue that this space between precarity and possibility offers a model for urban ethnography: attention to political economic processes and affective experiences is not mutually exclusive—with one more "real" than the other—but exist in a generative tension that is constitutive of urban life.

Hawkers' spatial claims are secured through cultivating relationships, sometimes intimate ones, with state functionaries, often through unofficial payments called *hafta*, but also through countersurveillance, social interactions, and public protest. Chapter 4 examines these encounters with the state. I show how, despite being unlicensed, hawkers' everyday experi-

ences are marked by proximity to the state rather than distance. Hawkers'
protracted encounters with BMC officials, clerks, workers, and the police
challenge the language of abandonment and abjection that informs much
scholarship on urban marginality. As I demonstrate, the street is not only
a product of the disciplinary techniques of rational governance but an
outcome of a negotiated process: in the eyes of the everyday state, unlicensed hawkers are not outside the law but more or less illegal (Björkman
2013). This spectrum of illegality opens up possibilities for negotiation.
As a result, what is otherwise called corruption is also, in a practical sense,
a space for the negotiation of rights claims—claims that ironically might
otherwise not be recognized.

When civic activists brought new attention to the "hawker problem"
in the 1990s, they raised new questions concerning urban citizenship, corruption, and the proper form of democratic politics. This activism demonstrated that the question of whose voice is heard in urban governance
was inseparable from the question of how to speak to the state. Chapter 5
shows how middle-class residents' engagement with the informal life of
the street produces what I call a sensibility of the "estranged citizen" that
reflects a feeling of alienation from traditional circuits of power. To civic
activists, hawkers symbolize state corruption and inefficiency, but also
powerlessness in face of the illiberal rights claims of the poor. However,
I argue that as a sensibility, the subjectivity of the estranged citizen is irreducible to a single political position or political economic process. This
ambivalent subjectivity has the potential for open-ended politics that
goes beyond efforts to appropriate urban space from the poor.

Whereas to civic activists, Mumbai's fluid streetscapes represent a
problem, these features are increasingly celebrated as a virtue by architects, designers, students, and writers around the world. Chapter 6, the
concluding chapter, examines the new place of the ad hoc streetscape
within transnational architectural discussions on the megacity. Thirty
years ago, Mumbai's landscape of squatters, slums, and informality was
seen as an embarrassment; now these characteristics are often celebrated
in exhibits, blogs, and films as signs of innovation, ingenuity, and small-
scale entrepreneurialism. Resignifying "underdeveloped" urban landscapes
as instances of "makeshift" or "tactical" urbanism raises a new question:

How does informality figure in the branding of cities? How is this new way to read urban landscapes recalibrating the relationship between the universal and the particular? And more important, this perspective on informal urbanism puts ethnography itself in critical crosshairs, with the geographer Ash Amin (2013), for instance, arguing that the trend toward narrating cities through affective experience, strategies, and maneuvering precludes attention to structural inequality.

This book documents a long-simmering tension over the street consisting of a mix of violence, subversion, shifting illegalities, ambiguous regulations, and flexible state practices. A hawker once summed up these everyday processes as producing a long simmering "boil" on the street. Seeing the city as a slow boil introduces a perspective absent in urban studies writing that so often rests on either dystopic or celebratory narratives. This perspective highlights the small maneuvers and negotiations that produce the city. It also highlights the generative element of spatial conflicts—for instance, how hawker demolitions are inextricable from long-standing debates over the content and meaning of rights, citizenship, and political modernity. Swirling alongside moments of exclusion are other symbolic processes and imaginative work that are remaking the physical and political spaces of the city.

The arguments contained in this book emerge from nearly a decade of research in Mumbai, the most intense period taking place in 2004, 2005–2006, and intermittently between 2008 and 2012. A central aspect of the research was conversation with hawkers as they worked on the street. When it was possible and welcomed, as it often was, hawkers generously enabled me to get a firsthand sense of their spatial practices, allowing me to sit with them on the street and observe their interactions with customers, passersby, and the small army of government functionaries who visited each day. Our conversations took place during their brief breaks from work or during downtimes, such as the early afternoon. I also conducted semiformal interviews with dozens of hawkers and hawker activists in a variety of locations throughout the city—in tea shops, parks, quiet spots amid construction sites, in their homes, while on casual walks, and in more unusual locations such as police stations, the foyers of municipal offices, and the spaces in front of municipal warehouses.

Mirroring hawkers' own experiences, my fieldwork on their entanglements with the state would often occur unexpectedly. Casual afternoons talking with hawkers while they worked would often be disrupted by the arrival of a BMC truck or police jeep and the subsequent scattering of people and their goods. On other occasions, conversations would be interrupted simply by the rumor of a municipal truck heading our way. Within moments of these rumors, the street would be abuzz with people scanning the road, ready to flee at a moment's notice. At these moments of crisis, a hawker leader would be summoned via cell phone. Arriving at the scene, at times he or she would see me and request that I join their entourage as they met the relevant authorities. In this manner, I would accompany hawker activists to BMC ward-level offices, godowns (warehouses), and police stations as they dealt with the fallout of the raids.

The goal of this research was to understand how the street functions as a locus of political contestation. Toward this end, I interviewed people actively involved in the campaign to reorder Mumbai's streets by regulating hawking. This research with civic activists, leaders of citizens' groups, and organizers of residents' associations was conducted under very different conditions from fieldwork with hawkers. These conversations were held in private settings and in English rather than on the street and in Hindi. We met in offices, homes, and community meeting rooms—settings that encouraged more formal conversations. Whereas on the street I kept note taking to a minimum—because the sight of pen and paper usually attracted a crowd, as well as suggestions of official connection—in more formal settings, note taking was expected, if not encouraged. While lacking in spontaneity, these interactions enabled detailed, on-the-spot recording of people's words that was not possible in my work with hawkers, which I reconstructed as soon as I was alone, such as on train platforms, in buses, at cafés, or at home that evening.

In the following sections, I outline the Mumbai hawker controversy, as well as how three themes in urban studies and related fields speak to it. First, I focus on political economic approaches to spatial conflict. Second, I examine transnational processes and concepts of public space. And third, I show how conflicts over urban transformations must contend with the state's incongruities and the varied forms of political recognition it offers.

THE MOMENT OF WORLD-CLASS CITY MAKING

Demolitions of street markets in Mumbai present ritualized scenes of terror, chaos, and confusion. They start with a murmur. Hawkers' stalls quickly shut down one by one as news of an impending raid ripples down the street. The market comes to a standstill as hawkers flee with what they can—a pot, a scale, a bundle of coriander, a basket of bananas. Customers unexpectedly caught in the frenzy look on as municipal workers swoop down from gray trucks to tear down stalls and grab equipment. Wooden poles, scales, pots, blue plastic tarps, tables, chairs, wicker baskets, broken sign boards get thrown into the cargo bay. As the trucks roll down the street, they crush tomatoes, spraying red juice and seeds on the pavement. The demolitions end as abruptly as they begin, leaving shards of wood, the refuse of vegetables, and stunned men and women in their wake.

A few hours later, the markets often come back to life. People emerge from the anonymity of the crowd to start rebuilding. The process is calm. There is no bickering over spots or attempts to gain more territory since the markers of ownership—paving blocks, trees, street signs, utility boxes, and garlanded images of gods—remain in the aftermath of a demolition. Bricks are restacked, a table rebuilt, canvas spread on the ground, and tarp tied to a tree. Merchandise hastily hidden in advance of the raid is retrieved from a gutter dried out in the post-monsoon aridity. A man lifts a canvas cloth, revealing piles of fresh eggplant and cabbage hidden behind a fence. Others carry tables of merchandise that had been hidden behind a sympathetic shopkeeper's store. Back at their spots, someone is seen restacking fruits in neat pyramids, or rearranging garlands of flowers in tight concentric circles, or starting up a gas stove for tea and waiting for customers to return.

How can we make sense of this ebb and flow of street life, markets, and violence? Why do these demolitions happen? Why are people able to reoccupy space so easily? And what is the relationship between these spectacles of eviction and moments of return? Many scholars have used the economic reforms in India in the 1990s as a starting point to understand related conflicts over space. India's metropolises are commonly deemed neoliberal, meaning that they are newly "opened to global investments by an entrepreneurial municipal body" and characterized by processes of

FIGURE 1.2 *Preparing paan before the evening commute*

"'creative destruction,' where livelihoods and landscapes are destroyed to make room for those that can efficiently fix capital" (Chatterjee 2009, 147). Gavin Shatkin (2014, 3) argues that the politics of space in India are simultaneously products of "resistance to a state-led modernist ideology" as well as effects of Indian cities' "integration into international networks of production and exchange." If we followed these writings, we might interpret hawker demolitions as manifestations of two interlinked phenomena: (1) the disciplinary state exercising power through spatial intervention and (2) restrictions on the "right to the city" (Harvey 2003) of the poor resulting from linkages with transnational political economic processes.

This reading of Indian cities reflects a larger trend in urban studies, including city-oriented work in anthropology, sociology, and geography, that emphasizes how power and economic processes manifest in space.[4] Marxist-inspired scholars building off the work of David Harvey (1989) have shown how spatial contestations are manifestations of a new logic of development, such as "entrepreneurial governance," that focuses more on creating consumer-oriented and corporate-friendly cities than on providing for social welfare (Smith 1996, 2002). Echoing this view, in the literature on the politics of urban development in South Asia, infrastructure is seen as increasingly fragmented (Gandy 2008), development policies elite oriented (Banerjee-Guha 2007; Dupont 2011; Anwar and Viqar 2014), and urban politics increasingly aligned with middle-class "lifestyle" needs (Fernandes 2006; Nair 2005). The effects of metropolitan India's new global linkages, many argue, is a severe reduction in the poor's quality of life. According to Sharma (2010, 71), for instance, "such an urbanisation under global forces . . . [is] dividing city dwellers into great 'consumers,' living in gated neighbourhoods and separated from the unprivileged 'others,' whose rights to the city are denied or infringed upon."

In this way, scholarly critiques of urban spatial processes in India since the 1990s often hinge on a direct link between economic liberalization and restrictions on rights. Many authors argue that postliberalization policies, court cases, and development practices fundamentally changed whose voices get heard, whose rights count, and on what basis those rights get recognized. For instance, Gautam Bhan (2009, 2014) analyzes how, in cases related to slum clearance in New Delhi in the late 1990s and early 2000s, the Supreme Court of India established a new precedent of differentiating rights based on class. According to the Supreme Court's rulings, the legitimacy of one's claim to urban space hinges on how that person inhabits the city, that is, whether one lives in a "housing colony" or slum (Bhan 2014, 5). The court determined legitimate occupation of space based on the physical appearance of buildings rather than their legal status in a formal sense (Björkman 2015; Ghertner 2011b). Bhan thus argues that as a result of this new juridical stance, "the very citizenship of the urban poor began to be called into question" (2009, 135). Goldman's (2011) study of new urban development practices and institutional shifts in Bengaluru also emphasizes the link between marketization and restrictions on poor people's rights. Like Bhan, he emphasizes how neoliberal-sounding discourses manifest in the city's institutional structures. By examining what bankers, civil servants, and consultants say in public meetings and other fora, he provides an account of the discursive logic of elite imaginations of the future "world-class" city that is "creating a new art of 'speculative government'" (Goldman 2011, 556). The effect of this new form of governing, argues Goldman (2011, 577), is a "redefining [of] state relations, urban citizenship, rights and rules of access" that threatens to thrust the poor into a condition of "'bare life,' no longer covered by legal or civil rights that once guaranteed them some access to the city and its resources."

Considering the massive slum evictions in India in recent years carried out in the name of urban improvement, one cannot deny the importance of these critiques of urban discourses that naturalize the exclusions of the poor. However, in focusing on one question—How are large-scale evictions of the poor justified in the name of development, profit accumulation, or world-class city making?—this approach overlooks other equally important ones. For instance, how do people remain where they are between evictions? How do the poor engage with state practices that are, especially in India, heterogeneous and often in competition with one other? How do globally circulating development and governmental discourses work through the varied and often competing political forces within the state? And finally, what are the historical genealogies of contemporary spatial contestations? Indeed, the problem with the dominant critical framework in urban studies is that it tends to reduce the entirety of urban politics to singular rationalities of governance or effects of transnational political economic processes. It assumes an uninterrupted trend toward greater marginalization of the poor, dispossession, fragmentation, and commodification. This analytical framework tends to portray city processes unidimensionally as products of power, whereas spatial contestations are interpreted as straightforward signs of class-based conflict, elite assertion, and a state captured by capital. In sum, Marxist-inspired critiques of urban development mix a dystopic vision (e.g., cities consisting of a dispossessed poor and all-powerful corporations) with nostalgia (e.g., substantive citizenship is linked with class *now* and urban development is *no longer* inclusive). These critiques paint a picture of straightforward struggles between globalizing forces and local resistance, between the powerful and the powerless, suggesting a flattened and misleading "opposition," in the words of Hansen and Verkaaik (2009), "between the spontaneous fullness and anarchy of life . . . [and] the impoverished, grey and disciplining forces of society, city and state" (19).

Recent ethnographies by anthropologists Lisa Björkman (2015) and Ilrena Searle (2014) and the sociologist Liza Weinstein (2014) offer important alternative perspectives to the politics of urban development in India. Rather than start from the premise that cities are on a trend toward greater exclusion, they emphasize the contestations within projects to remake the city. Searle's ethnography of real estate and value making in New Delhi reveals the mutual incomprehension, frustrations, and failures at the heart of spectacular accumulation. Indeed, rather than a neat story of foreign investors lining up to link with local investors, Searle shows the "frictions" (Tsing 2005), failures, and compromises at the heart of the globalized real estate sector. Liza Weinstein's (2014) ethnography of developers and housing rights activists in Mumbai similarly shows the competing state forces and democratic processes that undermine narratives of total urban transformation. And finally, Lisa Björkman's (2015) ethnography of Mumbai's water politics shows that neoliberal infrastructure policies and programs exist as unactualized projects rather than as new forms of governance. When read together, these studies show that neoliberal ideas get refracted through a dense terrain of already existing political practices, resulting in physical landscapes and a corresponding terrain of rights that do not correspond with the "world-class vision" of its proponents. "Accumulation by dispossession" (Harvey 2006), like the hawker or slum-free city, is more accurately the stuff of developers' dreams than a reality.

The critical Marxist perspective either takes these dreams at face value (by saying, for instance, that dispossession is happening and the city is captured by neoliberal forces) or dismisses them as obvious assertions of wealth and power. What this perspective overlooks is how these dreams act as unactualized projects enmeshed in the city's existing political, social, and imaginative worlds. This critical perspective also often encourages a tautology—for example, that evictions of the poor show how the poor are marginalized—that overlooks the contingencies, incongruities, and unevenness associated with spatial conflict.[5] It also ignores the symbolic and imaginative processes that swirl alongside the evictions, squatting, and everyday tussles over space. As I argue, the hawker controversy in Mumbai, like spatial conflicts elsewhere, is not only a story of inequality (even if, surely, the actors have unequal access to power); it is also a story of how ordinary spaces of the city get made. Furthermore, I show how urban transformations are always mediated by historical legacies of rights claims, political practices, affective relations, and urban aspirations. Thus, rather than see spatial contestations as manifestations of larger political economic trends, this book sees contestations as crucial sites where we can witness implicit debates over the content of rights and the promise of citizenship, along with the shaping of subjectivities—for the poor and the elite alike—that go beyond an either-or story of inclusion and exclusion.

The complications around Mumbai's street contestations exist partly because globality and political modernity in Mumbai are unfinished projects that, in their partiality, also contain a potential for productive negotiation and imaginative exchange. Surely the word *globality* has wide-ranging connotations, variously understood as a set of policies or linkage with transnational circuits of capital, goods, and people (Tsing 2000), and the project of modernity is unfinished everywhere (Gaonkar 2001). But here I specifically refer to the experience of modernity as "a question of difference" (Ferguson 1999) and the related sense of globality as an (often illusory) "transcendence of place" (Mazzarella 2003, 55). Consider Jumbo King, the restaurant chain that hoped to modernize the vada pao by taking it off the streets and giving it a sheen of international respectability. Dozens of Jumbo King restaurants opened throughout Mumbai (Shanbaug 2014) in the mid-2000s. Their innovation was to sell vada pao but without its associated street sociality. Moving away from the bustling street corners where vada pao are usually sold, Jumbo King situates its vada pao in the sanitized aesthetic of international fast food chains. These small storefronts are brightly lit and have big signs clearly displaying menu items and prices. Whereas street vada pao come wrapped in recycled newspaper, Jumbo King's vada pao are served in waxed paper printed with company insignia.

When the first Jumbo King stores opened, they introduced themselves to the city with billboard advertisements saying: "We aim to make the vada pao world class." Borrowing the language of civic boosters and international consulting firms such as McKinsey & Co. was significant: Jumbo King was not only transforming a popular snack; it was also transforming the image of the city. But as I argue, we need to explore the symbolic and imaginative worlds that swirl alongside seemingly obvious political economic processes. Urban interventions like Jumbo King do not simply reflect a trend toward corporatized and sanitized public space but also link street vending, and the humble vada pao in particular, with a desire for world belonging that has had a long historical legacy in India. Jumbo King's billboard thus "offers a solution to a puzzle," as Mazzarella (2003) discusses in the context of the Mumbai advertising industry, of how to reconcile the culturally embedded, intimate sphere with outward aspirations for globality.

Thus while this book focuses on street vending, it also addresses the larger question of how we read everyday engagements with the street, the city, and globality. We might interpret other city phenomena similarly, whether middle-class civic activism or even BMC evictions and police hafta, or negotiated bribe demands—as phenomena linked with powerful forces remaking the city, but also enmeshed in conversations, ideas, and imaginaries that exceed political economic explanations and exist in the realm of desire. Consider, for instance, the civic activists who have protested against hawker encroachments since the mid-1990s. Do they represent an embourgeoisement of urban politics (Chatterjee 2004; Fernandes 2004; Arabindoo 2011)? Perhaps. However, this would overlook the link between their struggles to reshape the meaning of rights and the content of citizenship and their aspiration to achieve the universality of the liberal subject, an effort that does not always coincide with specific class interests. Or consider municipal workers who recognize the legitimacy of hawkers' place in the city despite the latters' illegality, thereby contradicting policies made at the upper levels of bureaucracy. Or the police, whose overlapping social worlds with hawkers at times explain their cursory law enforcement and willingness to negotiate illicit payments in return for permission to stay on the street. And, of course, consider hawkers' own complex engagements with public space, the state, and the globalized landscape of consumption around them, which are irreducible to a logic of insurgency against powerful forces of urban restructuring.

The transformations of Mumbai associated with neoliberal globalization, once touted by critics as foreboding signs of the future, remain incomplete. Gated community-style enclaves for the rich are common but still not quite the norm. Big box stores run by multinational corporations have recently arrived, but only on the city's outskirts. Air-conditioned supermarkets continue to be a rarity patronized by a small elite.[6] Despite eager pronouncements in the media of the mall replacing the street market, the ubiquitous cycle of hawker evictions and reoccupation of space does not correspond with critics' narrative of expanding urban exclusion. The demolition trucks that crush vegetables, the men who tear down stalls, and the officials who threaten fines do not index completed projects of urban transformation. Likewise, while hawker evictions at times mirror neoliberal-sounding development narratives, they are also enmeshed in ongoing, contested, and at times internally contradictory city-making processes. These processes brim with incongruities and contradictions that writers have yet to fully grapple with: the generative mix of hope and despair; state functionaries' central role in sustaining slums *and* hawker markets; civic activists who campaign against hawkers and wealthy developers; unlicensed hawkers who advocate for enhanced regulation of space; municipal officials who advocate for street regulations they know won't work; and middle-class professionals who rely on street markets even as they support their removal. And then there are hawkers' complex uses of the street, its infrastructure and associated regulatory apparatus: the unlicensed *dosa* vendor who places his griddle just to the left of a "no-hawking zone" signpost pointing to the right (and in the rain, using the sign to support a plastic tarp to keep his customers dry); a fruit vendor who builds a table out of sidewalk paving bricks abandoned on the side of the road (hoping that the municipality will not confiscate its own property in a raid); constables waiting on a street corner while a hawker makes *paan* for them; and finally, the dozens of unlicensed hawkers hiding in plain sight, it would seem, on the streets in front of BMC offices.

Mumbai's street vendors represent many contradictions: beloved nuisances, legitimized criminality, streetwise futurity, and precarious persistence. Their relationship with the state is characterized simultaneously by violence, predatory extortion, intimacy, collaboration, and hope. Or consider the street itself. From one angle, Mumbai's streetscapes represent the slow violence of socioeconomic inequalities; from another, they provide astonishing opportunities for small-scale economic enterprise.

This precarious condition may not last; however, at the moment it suggests that analyses of spatial conflict need to address how people stay in place as much as how they are forced out. It also suggests that we need to understand urban life in terms of productive incongruities rather than inexorable forces.

SPATIAL CONCEPTS

The scene of women or men standing behind baskets of fruit, tables piled high with vegetables, or carts loaded with household items has been understood as a problem for nearly two centuries. The problem of the messy visual aesthetic of informal street economies goes beyond the late twentieth-century "world-class-city"–making moment. The spatial practices of hawkers, and especially hawkers of food, have represented danger and disorder in cities around the world at least since the early nineteenth century, if not earlier.[7] Colonial authorities in particular have historically perceived hawkers as "a problem—obstructive, noisy unhygienic individuals—[rather than] . . . a constructive element, contributing to the effective functioning of the city" (McGee 1973, 22). The increased emphasis on the regulation of street practices in late nineteenth-century Mumbai echoed increasing hostility toward street commerce in London and throughout the rest of the British empire. In Durban, South Africa, harassment of vendors was so great that Gandhi, a young lawyer at the time, stepped in to their defense (Vahed 1999), while in Singapore, a heated battle over the use of public space by vendors raged in the 1880s and 1890s (Yeoh 2003). The perception of hawkers as a problem is certainly linked with the political economy of space—for instance, the visible presence of the poor may be linked with property values; however, the traction of this discourse is a function of particular concepts of space that have emerged out of India's colonial and precolonial history. Conflicts over hawking are as much about ideas and imaginaries of the city as about power.

Thus, we cannot understand the "problem" of street trade in India without an understanding of the "conceptual mapping" (Kaviraj 1997, 83) of open, nondomestic space into the framework of modern governance. Certainly, prior to the colonial era, access to streets was shaped by relations of power. What changed with colonial rule was the conceptualization of open spaces as *"civic* spaces" (Kaviraj 1997, 98), owned by none but the responsibility of all, and therefore subject to municipal regulation. As Sudipta Kaviraj argues, in late-nineteenth-century Calcutta, as elsewhere in colonial India (Glover 2007), a bureaucratized notion of public space encountered, if not quite replaced, vernacular notions of the outside. In the Brahminical cultural milieu, for instance, city spaces were mapped in terms of "inside" and "outside" rather than "private" and "public."[8] Whereas the inside represented the ordered domestic sphere, the outside connoted "intrinsic disorderliness" (Kaviraj 1997, 99; see also Chakrabarty 2002). By the late nineteenth century, this vernacular "conceptual mapping" (Kaviraj 1997, 83) of space mingled with—although certainly was not replaced by—ideas of public space subject to shared responsibility and municipal control. One of the most important transformations occurred in the 1880s, when changes in criminal and property law in India concretized the distinction between public and private space (Anderson 1992) through public nuisance crimes: crimes causing "any common injury, danger or annoyance to the public" (Cutler and Griffin 1871, 268).[9] As elsewhere in the British empire (Anderson 1992, 22), this category of crime acquired unprecedented prominence in late nineteenth-century Mumbai. The effects were profound. Activities that were previously tolerated on the street, such as "urinating in public and selling wares on the street" (Anderson 1992, 11), now became punishable offenses in the eyes of colonial authorities.

The impact of this new spatiolegal regime on hawking was especially significant. Hawkers have existed in Mumbai since its emergence as a modern metropolis in the early nineteenth century.[10] However, a significant change occurred in 1882 following the Bombay Municipal Corporation Act, when "street trading and hawking were brought under the regulatory powers of the Municipal Corporation" (Jumani and Joshi 1984, 18). While street commerce had previously been tolerated, it had not been singled out as a practice subject to rigorous governmental control. Thus in 1882, "for the first time in the history of Indian cities," write Jumani and Joshi, the "legality of hawkers . . . [hinged on] holding a license" (18).

The transformation of hawking in open space into the transgressive act of hawking in *public* space was an effect of colonial rule. But more precisely, it was a product of a set of transnationally circulating discourses: legal, urban, and symbolic. The remapping of urban space in India occurred alongside similar changes elsewhere. In Victorian England, for instance, a new emphasis on "bodily propriety" transformed the cultural meaning of eating in public. Because of its "capacity to embarrass or revolt others forced to witness the spectacle of this intimate, embodied activity" (Valentine 1998, 195), a formerly tolerated practice became similarly understood as "out of place" (Kass, quoted in Valentine 1998, 195), further hardening the public-private distinction.

This sudden "out of place"-ness (Herzfeld 2006) of practices associated with "private" activities such as eating, drinking, working, and trading is also linked with transnational shifts in the symbolic meaning of the street. First, an important shift occurred in the late eighteenth century when architects and engineers, borrowing ideas from the medical sciences (Vidler 1978), "conceived of the city as a place of flows, movement and circulation" (Joyce 2003, 66). The new understanding of urban landscapes as "bodies, healthy or sick" (Vidler 1978, 28), reflected a shift in governance from "persons to places" (Joyce 2003, 67), so that slums and crowded, narrow streets became signs of poor health literally and metaphorically.[11] Second, by the late nineteenth century, streets acquired important new economic significance. To the late colonial state, having shifted its focus to promoting market efficiency (Birla 2009), blocked streets prevented profit accumulation. And third, during this time, congested streets were increasingly understood to pose a problem for political subjectivity. By the late nineteenth century, writes Patrick Joyce (2003, 11), "danger, darkness, traffic, [and] the very mundane impediments of unpaved roads, mud and horse droppings" became interpreted as curbs on freedom. As a result, the construction, maintenance, and governance of streets were guided by a need to "remove all impediments" to the imagined liberal subject—that "freely choosing, responsible and therefore self-monitoring [person]." Thus by the late nineteenth century, the street was transformed from leftover spaces between buildings to parts of a vast circulatory system (Sennett 1996), promising swift passage through space as well as the flourishing of a new kind of person: individuated, unencumbered by social ties, and disconnected from the past—"an agent who was set free from constraints imposed by tradition to pursue its own private ends" (Gaonkar 2001, 2).

The concretized difference between public and private spaces was also assumed to depend on concretized differences between public and private selves. This produced a new mapping of spatial value, characterized by the "interiorization of social life" (Holston 1989, 107). Franco Moretti argues that despite the tumult of public life described in classic accounts of the modern city (Simmel 1950[1905]), the "great novelty of urban life" lies not "in having thrown people into the street, but in having raked them up and shut them into offices and houses. It does not consist in having intensified the public dimension, but in having invented the private one" (Moretti 1983, 127). Indeed, with "visibility" on streets representing backwardness, a remnant of "life in the provinces," continues Moretti, the defining effect of urban modernity was to have "drastically and irreparably devalued [the street] *as a place of social experience.*"

Although the intention here is not to describe spatial concepts as neatly unfolding in Europe and then traveling around the world, it is important to historicize the close association of modern streets with ideas of subjecthood. This in turn highlights how the "problem" of hawkers in Mumbai goes beyond the technical issue of walkable sidewalks or the denial of citizenship to the poor. It is also informed by transnational historical processes and conceptual, legal, and political genealogies. As scholars of colonial urbanism have shown (Glover 2008), concepts of urban space, governance, infrastructure, and modernity are not bound to one context but are produced through a global conversation in what Saunier and Ewen (2008) call the "transnational municipal moment."[12] It is my contention that the significance of Mumbai's streets, as well as the ideas that shape what count as appropriate and inappropriate activities on them, are inextricable from this transnational traffic in meaning. Categories such as the "modern" and the "vernacular" do not simply index discrete cultural practices but animate local contestations, anxieties, and aspirations.[13]

Indeed, if the demise of "visibility," as Franco Moretti puts it, defines urban modernity, than how do we account for Mumbai, a city that has not fully shunted work, play, and bodily practice from the street? Early chroniclers of the city, such as Govind Narayan Madgavkar (Rangana-than 2009), read Mumbai's streetside spectacles as a sign of entry into the modern world. To him, "the visual medley and the intense stimuli in the crowded bazaars of Indian neighborhoods were captivating" (Prakash 2010, 56). Implicitly comparing the bustle of the city with the languid life of the countryside, Madgavkar produced a "rapturous representation of the kaleidoscopic but orderly city" (ibid.). The subjective experience of Mumbai's street spectacle is also brilliantly captured in Hindi films such as *Shri 420* (dir. Raj Kapoor, 1955). In an opening scene, *Shri 420* shows the Mumbai street through the eyes of Raj, a newly arrived migrant to the city. We see him standing amid traffic, awestruck by the eclectic bustle of people and activities swirling around him. In this representation, Mumbai's streetscapes conform to neither a modernist ideal nor its vernacular inverse. Instead, it shows Raj navigating a hybrid world. In one instant, Raj is shown in the alienating "moving chaos of everyday life in the modern world" (Berman 1982, 160) and a moment later is immersed in dense webs of sociality and community, navigating an urban modernity that is "part village community, part cosmopolitan street" (Mazumdar 2007, xx).

To many other observers, however, Mumbai's streetscapes represented a troubling muddling of the public and private. To Sidney Low, a British journalist who visited the city in 1907, the visibility of everyday life signaled cultural otherness. After strolling through the "native" town, as the neighborhoods beyond the historically European areas were called, he observed that people

> do all sorts of things in public which to our thinking should be transacted in privacy. . . . As you pass along the streets of the bazaar you can look right into half the houses. The shops are simply boxes, set on end, with the lids off . . . [where one can] stand and watch the baker rolling his flat loaves, the tailor stitching and cutting, [and] the coppersmith hammering at his bowls and dishes [while all around people can be seen] dressing, shaving, washing, and sleeping, and, in spite of the caste rules and religious restrictions, even a good deal of eating. . . . The Indian townsman does not mind being looked at. He is accustomed to it. He passes his life in the midst of a crowd. (Low 1907, 23–24)[14]

But it was not just the "imperial flâneur" (Prakash 2010, 63) who read the dense streetscapes and heterogeneous public practices as a sign of incompleteness. Mohandas Gandhi's disdain for the Indian city is well known. On one occasion, for instance, he called India's metropolises "poor editions of [those in Europe]" (quoted in Jodhka 2002, 3347).[15] To social scientist N. K. Bose, Calcutta, with its "goats grazing on the Maidan . . . [and] herds of buffaloes on Shakespeare Sarani" (Sen 1975), was a "premature metropolis" (Bose 1965). Indeed for over a century, officials and local elites expressed the view that even though they may live in the city, Indians were not truly urban. "[Indians] are not yet accustomed to confin[ing] themselves to . . . footpaths" ("Native Papers" 1890), declares a late nineteenth-century account. Another noted that "Indians persist in using the road in the manner of their forefathers in rural towns and villages" (Edwardes 1923, 95). To another, only the threat of bodily harm would transform Indians' spatial practices: "The motor car has succeeded where even the tram car has failed, for it is teaching the native to look ahead and to perceive that the middle of the road is not the place for an aimless saunter" (quoted in Hazareesingh 2007, 66).[16]

How should we interpret this seeming clash of "concepts . . . implicit in [the] social practices" (Kaviraj 1997, 83) of the city? Dipesh Chakrabarty offers one possibility. He argues that over the past century, colonialists and nationalists alike have attempted "to make the bazaar, the street, the mela—the arenas for collective action in pre-British India—benign, regulated places, clean and healthy, incapable of producing either disease or disorder" (Chakrabarty 2002, 77). To him, this represents an encounter between vernacular and modernist ideas of space. However, unlike Low, who reads the vernacular as a sign of backwardness, Chakrabarty sees it as a potential sign of rebellion: "People in India, on the whole, have not heeded . . . [elites'] call to discipline, public health and public order. Can one read this as a refusal to become citizens of an ideal, bourgeois order?" (Chakrabarty 2002, 77). It is important to note that Chakrabarty presents insurgency as a question rather than, as many others do, taking it for granted. The problem with the latter view is that insurgency conjures a binary world: a world of vernacular/local/cultural practices, on the one hand, and modern/universal/official practices, on the other. But spatial contestations do not entail carving out a space of autonomy outside the modern; they concern how the modern should be "configur[ed]" (Kaviraj 1997, 92). The "refusal" Chakrabarty points to might be better understood in terms of compromise, negotiation, and maneuver; modernist spatial concepts are not just a bludgeon against the vernacular but offer a diffuse "language" (Kaviraj 1997) through which power is executed and spatial claims are made.

REGULATING THE STREET

Certainly space is regulated not only by concepts and cultural codes, but also by formal state institutions. Understanding the state's role in the regulation of space requires two perspectives. The first is empirical, focusing on questions that address how the judiciary has regulated the use of the side of the road in India. The second is analytical, focusing on questions of how these regulations are related to negotiations over rights to public space. In other words, what is the relationship between court judgments and state practices on the ground, as well as the important public debates on the city that they spin off? To put it another way, the courts have had an active role in adjudicating hawking, as well as other spatial practices labeled encroachment; however, the question remains whether its judgments have mattered. And if so, how?

When the Mumbai hawker controversy became litigated in the Supreme Court in the early 1980s, it revolved around two questions: Do people have the right to occupy the side of the road to sell goods and services? and, Are municipal demolitions of street markets constitutional? The Bombay Hawkers' Union (BHU) took the BMC to court in the early 1980s in response to violent evictions and the impossibility of getting new licenses. It called attention to a troubling pattern of "arbitrarily refusing to grant or renew licenses for hawking" (*Bombay Hawkers' Union and Ors. v. Bombay Municipal Corporation and Ors.* 1985). It argued that the 1888 BMC Act, which provided the commissioner legal cover for demolitions, contradicted Articles 19 and 21 of the Indian Constitution granting all citizens right to life, as well as the right "to carry on any trade or business." This act was antidemocratic in spirit, the petitioners argued, because it "confer[ed] upon the . . . [authorities] unguided power to refuse to grant or renew licenses for hawking and to remove the goods without affording to the hawkers an opportunity to be heard." In its final decision, the Supreme Court upheld the constitutionality of the 1888 BMC Act, arguing that there is only a tenuous connection between the right to a particular trade and the right to livelihood (Mahalwar 1990). The decision stated that while people have a right to hawk in the abstract, "they do not have the right to [hawk] on any particular place" (Mahalwar 1990, 251). However, the court also ruled that "if the circumstances are appropriate and a small trader can do some business for personal gain on the pavement to the advantage of the general public and without any discomfort or annoyance to others there cannot be any objection" (Mahalwar 1990, 251). The court ultimately instructed the BMC to create a hawker regulation system with this principle in mind.

BHU v. BMC, and especially *Olga Tellis v. BMC*, a concurrent case, marked the beginning of an unprecedented juridical involvement in urban affairs not just in Mumbai but around India.[17] *Olga Tellis* was a landmark case in the 1980s that dealt with the right of squatters to resist evictions. Initiated by a journalist working on behalf of laborers whose street-side shanties were destroyed without notice, *Olga Tellis*, like *BHU v. BMC*, highlighted two significant problems: (1) municipalities guided by colonial-era laws, such as the 1888 BMC Act, routinely contradict constitutional guarantees, and (2) the "rule of law" ideal is often at odds with the state's official commitment to social welfare (specifically, its "Directive Principles") ("Street Vendors" 2000).[18] In 1985, the Supreme Court attempted a compromise in a simultaneous ruling on *BMC v. BHU* and *Olga Tellis*. On one hand, it argued that colonial laws giving the municipal commissioner power to demolish structures are constitutional; on the other hand, it argued that because people encroached on sidewalks due to financial compulsions, not criminal intent, the municipality must provide proper resettlement following evictions.[19]

In the subsequent decade and a half, the Supreme Court took a more hard-line approach. In 2000, judges famously said in *Almitra H. Patel Anr. v. Union of India and Ors.* (2000), "Rewarding an encroacher on public land with a free alternative site is like giving a reward to a pickpocket" (quoted in Ramanathan 2006, 3195). Whereas *Olga Tellis* permitted the principle of social welfare to blunt the hard edge of the rule-of-law ideal, as well as the inviolability of private property, subsequent rulings did not allow such compromise. Juridical interventions into the hawker matter reflected this shift as early as 1989. In *Sodan Singh v. New Delhi Municipal Committee* (1989), the Delhi High Court ruled that constitutional rights to life and livelihood are inapplicable to the hawker controversy: "The petitioners do have the fundamental right to carry on a trade or business of their choice, but not to do so on a particular place," declared the final ruling, effectively delegitimizing hawkers' and other unauthorized squatters' spatial claims (Mahalwar 1990, 253–54). This trend continued through the 2000s, culminating in the 2003 Supreme Court decision that sided with civic groups and called for severe restrictions on where, what, and how people can hawk.[20]

This new legal discourse on squatters occurred alongside an important shift in urban politics in India: the unprecedented involvement of middle-class urban professionals in city politics. The Seventy-Fourth Constitutional Amendment, passed in 1992, decentralized urban governance, while giving new voice to residents' welfare associations and nongovernmental organizations (Ghertner 2011). In the 1990s, Indian cities witnessed the emergence of what Janaki Nair calls "more muscular middle-class resident's associations" (Nair 2005, 345). These groups started "a concerted attempt to clean up the Indian cities, to rid streets and public lands of squatters and encroachers and to reclaim public spaces for the use of proper citizens" (Chatterjee 2004, 171). An editorial written in 1998 by a lawyer named Raju Moray demonstrates the language of this newly invigorated middle-class political consciousness:

> The plight of the pedestrians in Mumbai is pitiable. Most roads in Mumbai (including newly laid Development Plan roads) do not have footpaths. And footpaths, wherever they exist, are encroached upon by hawkers. So walkers, joggers [etc.] . . . [are] constantly at risk of being knocked down by passing vehicles. The right to life of such citizens (a fundamental right guaranteed by Article 21 of our Constitution) is jeopardised daily.
>
> Who is responsible for this? Though it is easy to blame hawkers, the real culprit is the Brihanmumbai Municipal Corporation (BMC) which is duty

bound under Section 61 (m) of the BMC ACT, 1888, "to make adequate provision . . . for the construction, maintenance, alteration and improvement of public streets." (Moray 1998)

Whereas 1980s litigation against the BMC was framed in terms of access to space and freedom from state violence, the new legal discourse, as Moray's editorial shows, is framed in terms of quality of life, access to good governance, and freedom from governmental inefficiency. The pedestrian is a particularly apt figure to reflect this political shift. By moving through, rather than dwelling in, streets, the pedestrian potentially embodies the normative subject of the public sphere as well as public space. "Pedestrian," unlike the hawker, is a category that potentially includes all city residents. Thus this defense of pedestrians' rights—and the Bombay High Court's acknowledgment of them—also represented a victory for the idea of nondifferentiated rights claims over forms of citizenship shaped by difference, rootedness, and entitlements.

Moray's editorial signaled the ascendancy of a new kind of legal discourse in public interest litigation (PIL) in which the "injured party" was not a specific group of people but the "citizen" in a generic sense. At the time of Moray's editorial, for instance, activists from residents' welfare associations were arguing in the Bombay High Court that the BMC's failure to keep sidewalks hawker free was hurting all residents of the city (Balakrishnan 2003). This represented an important shift. PILs—an effect of the "liberalization of *locus standi*" (Baxi 1987, 34) following the antidemocratic measures of the 1975–1977 Emergency (as the twenty-one-month suspension of civil liberties was called)—were originally intended to allow activists and journalists "to address the court on behalf of disadvantaged groups" (Singh 1995). However by the mid-1990s, the beneficiaries of this "movement for 'juridical democracy'" (Baxi 1987, 33) shifted from the poor to a universalized category, the "citizen." The form of the PIL remained the same: an injured party seeking redress from the state. However, the nature of the claim fundamentally changed.[21]

Does this new political discourse, dominated by quality-of-life issues and demands for good governance, represent an embourgeoisement of the notion of the public? In some cases, this seems to be the case. For

instance, Amita Baviskar (2007b) shows how, in a campaign to eliminate cows and cycle rickshaws from New Delhi's streets, the interests of
the wealthy were "normalized and universalized as those of the 'public.'"
However, most literature on the rise of good governance and quality-
of-life politics in major cities is less nuanced, emphasizing not the particularities of place and political context but how spatial conflicts are
manifestations of global processes. For instance, scholars working in
North America and Europe have shown how normativizing elite urban
subjectivity has disenfranchised the homeless and working poor. Writings
on urban beautification campaigns explore how "undesirable" populations
are effectively denied citizenship through spatial practices. To many writers, this "revanchism" (Macleod 2002), or taking back the city from "variously defined 'others'" (Smith 2010, 202), reflects a globally circulating
"S.U.V. model of citizenship" (Mitchell 2005). In these studies, the state's
acceptance of elitist "model[s] of citizenship" (Mitchell 2005, 91) seems
to represent a fait accompli.

By contrast, I argue that assertions of a universalized notion of citizenship often take place on shaky ground. As I show in the following
section, generalization of universalist forms of citizenship (premised on
individuated subjects and abstract rights, for instance) is more of an aspiration than an empirical condition. Indeed, the activists who file PILs
on behalf of good governance, and pressure the BMC to evict hawkers,
position themselves as a third entity separate from both the organized
party politics of the poor and the everyday apparatus of the state. They
call themselves "citizens' groups" as a way to distinguish themselves from
other grassroots political organizations whose work focuses on pressuring
the state for social services. John Harriss, writing on Chennai, argues that
civic activists make a telling distinction between "denizens" and "citizens"
(2007, 2719). What this distinction shows is that what matters is not
only political content but political form: "denizens" make claims on the
state based on entitlements (i.e., for food, water and housing) (Roy 2003),
whereas "citizens" make claims based on abstract rights (i.e., quality of life
and a governing system free of corruption). Rather than NGOs or other
pressure groups such as unions and informal associations, which work
on behalf of specific populations (e.g., slum residents who need water or

better sanitation), citizens' groups claim to work on behalf of a universal urban inhabitant.

Certainly slum residents also make claims based on abstract rights, and middle-class groups demand state services; likewise, both the rich and poor are likely to make demands on the state through liberal and illiberal means, a point that many have made in critiques of Partha Chatterjee's (2004) notion of "political society." However as will be clear in the following chapters, "citizens" and "denizens," like liberal and illiberal politics, are aspirational and partial categories with an uneven and vibrant life of their own. It is the dream of maintaining the difference between the universal citizen-subject and grounded, populist demands, rather than its empirical reality, that animates politics in metropolitan India. Moreover, the restrictive use of "citizen" represents a single voice among a chorus of others. The twin processes of juridical activism in urban affairs and the rise of middle-class politics take place on unstable terrain, making them much more an open-ended, unfinished project than a straightforward process of elite takeover. Thus, the shift from social injustice to governmental inefficiency as the primary mode of politics, epitomized by the pedestrian replacing the squatter as the injured party in PILs, is not only an instance of class maneuvering but part of a contingent negotiation over the meaning of citizenship and spatial claims involving state functionaries, squatters, and civic activists alike.

NEGOTIATING CITIZENSHIP

When I started researching conflicts over public space in summer 2004, it appeared that the Mumbai hawker controversy was coming to an end. The Bombay High Court had recently ordered the BMC to implement a new license and regulation system. These new rules, which included bans on cooking and hawking within 150 meters of train stations, hospitals, and schools, as well as restrictions on what hawkers could sell, portended a dramatic reordering of Mumbai's streetscape. It seemed that the city's freewheeling public spaces were to be replaced by a rigid system of monitoring, surveillance, and control. And yet the dream of ordered streets was short-lived, as the regulations were immediately challenged. Hawker union leaders, BMC officials, and civic activists engaged in a heated debate over the form, implementability, and even necessity of new hawker regulations. What had looked like the beginnings of a harsh new spatio-legal regime instead infused new life into the hawker controversy.

Two years later, the hawker case was adjudicated by the Supreme Court. Again, it looked as if the controversy would come to an end. The discrepancy of governance in the abstract and governance in principle reemerged as a crucial point of debate. Even before the final judgment was made, important questions raised by the BMC, hawker unions, and civic activists threatened to undermine this ambitious project to remake the city's public space: How many hawker licenses should be issued? On what basis should they be issued? Who would be eligible to receive them? And where could they be used? Rather than conclude the decades-long hawker controversy, juridical intervention that promised dramatic restrictions on the use of public space expanded debates over urban citizenship.

Recognizing that civic activists and hawker union leaders were jostling to get their competing views heard, an additional municipal commissioner arranged for a meeting to discuss the impending case. The Supreme Court had just declared that the BMC should issue twenty-three thousand new hawking licenses. However, important questions remained: Who would be eligible to receive the new hawker licenses? Would experienced vendors be given priority, or would a lottery system be more equitable? Who would decide where hawkers could work? If local stakeholders were to determine hawking zones, then who were the "stakeholders" of a public sidewalk: the people who live in the area, the people who work there, or the people who walk through it? In one meeting, for instance, Raj, a civic activist, debated these questions with a BMC License Department official.[22] Raj vehemently insisted that licenses should be granted according to a random lottery. No category of persons should be given preferences for licenses, he argued. But the BMC official took a different view. With the exception of the physically disabled, he said, licenses should be given only to people living in the city for at least fifteen years—only to the "indigent and indigenous," he added, delighted with his wordplay. In encounters such as this, hawker advocates looked on in silence. On one hand, the official's thinly disguised nativist agenda was unappealing to most hawkers (most of whom are from north India), while on the other, a universal lottery system would undermine the logic of "occupancy urbanism" (Benjamin 2008) through which hawkers secure their unofficial spatial claims.

With the debate over a license lottery unresolved, the BMC official redirected the discussion to the question of who should determine the number of hawkers allowed on a given street. The civic activist spoke first. He said that "stakeholders" representing the variety of interests of each street or neighborhood should determine the appropriate number of hawkers. But the official pointed out that that would raise a problem: in their journeys through the city, residents articulate different interests at different moments. An office worker might want a tea hawker near his job but not near his home. His point was that "interests" are not discrete. Those who use streets the most—commuters and workers—are often the most mobile, and thus their formal claims to them are less explicit. Determining "rights" to public space is especially complex because its use is so fluid. Again, this debate was not simply a question of who has legitimate claim to the sidewalk but of what a claim to space means at all. How is such a claim established, and on what basis is it recognized by the state? The debate hinged on broader questions as well: Is urban space inhabited by universalized liberal subjects with discrete, stable, and fixed identities? Or is it more of a negotiated space, shaped by fluid concepts of rights and citizenship?

The literature in legal and political anthropology is especially helpful for making sense of the significance of these debates over hawker regulation. First, work in legal anthropology (Merry 1998; Comaroff and Comaroff 2006) has shown the importance of examining the embedded contexts of laws rather than just their content. This is particularly relevant here since the Mumbai hawker law centered on conversations surrounding its potential implementation rather than its actualization. Second, literature in the anthropology of the state (Hansen and Stepputat 2001; Trouillot 2001; Aretxaga 2003; Das 2007; Sharma and Gupta 2006) has shown how the idea of a state's internal structure and coherence (Abrams 1988; Mitchell 1991) crumbles in the face of everyday encounters with its actual practices. As Veena Das (2007) argues, rather than see state practices as manifestations of a singular logic of rule, we should instead examine the heterogeneity of the state's operations. These interventions encourage an analysis that embraces, rather than shies away from, the contingencies of everyday practice: officials' interpretations of opaque regulatory regimes that might be at odds with the idea of a disciplinary state, municipality workers' negotiation of unofficial payments from hawkers, and limitations on state resources that affect when and where evictions occur. It is in these contingencies that spatial claims get produced and rights are asserted. Indeed, as I argue in the chapters that follow, hawkers' experiences of the state are not reducible to rationalities of rule, but constitute a contested terrain of claim making. Moreover, the spaces that get produced through state practices—the streets themselves—are shaped by government rationalities but are irreducible to them.

These conversations at the BMC office reveal the discrepant imaginaries of the state that circulate in the city. They are animated by a question that echoes the anthropological literature: Is the "state" and its forms of governance an abstract entity really "'above' an on the ground entity called 'society'"? (Ferguson and Gupta 2002, 982), or is the state inevitably enmeshed in the gritty realities of social practice? Regulations proposed by the court assumed a stable understanding of the relationship between "citizens" and the "state" when in fact this relationship, and the meaning of the categories themselves, is fluid. Underlying the court's recommendations to the BMC were universalistic ideals promoted by civic activists: rights granted to abstract, undifferentiated citizens (Subramanian 2009), as well as a state machinery characterized by proceduralism, the rule of law, and a "vertical" relationship to society (Ferguson and Gupta 2002, 983).[23] And yet to hawker union and BMC officials, these concepts and imaginations of governance were very much up for negotiation. As I discuss below, two questions in particular, both of which undermine the premise of political liberalism, were considered valid topics of negotiation: (1) how people can legitimately assert a "right" to space and (2) on what basis the state recognizes people's claims.[24]

In one of the meetings held in the BMC headquarters to discuss the hawker regulation system being adjudicated in the Supreme Court, Raj began with a startling announcement: most citizens' group activists objected to the meeting's premise because it delegitimized the court's orders. A limit of twenty-three thousand new hawking licenses had already been proposed by the court, while a committee had already created a list of hawking and nonhawking zones after surveying the city. So, the critics asked, what is there to discuss? To them, the very fact of subjecting the plan to debate was deeply troubling. They shared their suspicions with the group: Why debate the implementation of a Supreme Court decision that has not even been finalized? What right does the BMC have to host a public debate over proposals that are supposed to be technical? As they saw it, the city's tumultuous street markets were on the verge of being regulated for the first time in decades, and the BMC, the state institution tasked with its implementation, was balking.

Confirming the activists' fears of an unsympathetic state, the BMC official leading the meeting opened with some candid remarks: "This is a meeting to think of solutions to the hawker problem . . . because it is perceived as a problem." With 200,000 to 300,000 hawkers in the city (no one knew the total population for sure), the plan to issue 23,000 licenses had clear shortcomings. What should be done with the rest, he asked? "Do you think it will be possible for us to keep away 180,000 hawkers?"

Alternatives were proposed by various participants. A civic activist said that the remaining hawkers should be given licenses for mobile vending. She justified this by saying that in the past, "all hawkers would roam around. They wouldn't sit on the pavement." A leader of a wealthy South Mumbai residents' association offered a different view. In lieu of a licensing system, she said, local residents' groups could work with local "trusted" vendors to keep public space orderly.

Witnessing the official consider alternatives to the licensing system caused the other activists to erupt with discontent. They had been campaigning for a formal system of hawker regulation for years. Talk of circumventing the Supreme Court's proposal threatened to derail their work. Some turned their backs to the official in a deliberate act of defiance. Others started small side conversations. An elderly man exclaimed that discussing alternatives to the Supreme Court proposal was merely a BMC ruse to avoid doing its job. He then got up from his chair and stormed out of the room in a dramatic exit. In response, a hawker union leader tried to steer the conversation in a new direction. Frustrated by this turn of events, a civic activist interrupted with a startling comment: "We are citizens. Who are you?"

As the tense murmur in the room died down, the additional commissioner presiding over the meeting offered a gesture of conciliation: "On one side, you [can be] happy because the judgment will go in your favor; [on the other side] you [can be] happy because [you] know it is not implementable." Whereas the citizens' groups had the courts in their favor, the official seemed to be saying, hawkers could count on the everyday realities of the city to maintain the status quo. For him, implementing changes on the street required participants to abandon fixed political positions and think in terms of maneuver, contingency, and compromise. As he rhetorically asked at another meeting, "Do we have only two alternatives?—[either] get rid of hawkers [by] call[ing] out the army [or] just let all hawkers go wherever they please throughout the city?" The absurdity of calling the army to deal with hawkers was meant to highlight the inadequacies of thinking in terms of technical solutions alone. In a text message to a civic activist that day, a BMC official reiterated this view: "Come up with a compromise solution to bring to the judges," it said; "otherwise the Supreme Court ruling will have no effect on the ground."[25]

But to civic activists, talk of compromise, contingencies, and the difficulties of implementation were interpreted as proof of state incompetence. They had much evidence to support their view; it was no secret that unlicensed hawkers could be found on nearly every city street. As a result, these meetings consisted of heated exchanges in which civic activists accused BMC officials of neglecting their job. In one instance, an activist demanded, "Why are you not taking any action against hawkers?" "We are. The trucks are out there all day," the official replied. "But," said the activist," I never see a truck in *my* area!" To this, the official explained the limitations of municipal power, the restricted resources at their disposal, and the fact that hawkers, who have numerical advantage, run away when the trucks come.

Amid one such confrontation, an assistant arrived with a tray of tea. As cups were passed around the room, the BMC official turned to the civic activist and said with a mischievous smile, "This is *hawkerwali chai* [hawkers' tea], if you don't mind."

This provocation was meant to unsettle the activists from their moral high ground. It was a tussle, a back and forth, between the official's confident pragmatism and civic activists' indignation. But it was also a commentary on the contingencies of ordinary life and governance in the city. There was an implicit question in this provocation: If hawkers' tea can make its way into the rarefied atmosphere of the BMC headquarters, can anyone escape the informal world of the street? Is it possible to inhabit a city outside the ad hoc world of making do (*jugaad* in Hindi), which hawkers symbolized, state functionaries willingly participated in, and civic activists abhorred?

This provocation also challenged my own assumptions. Looking around as I sat in a plush chair taking in the urgent voices, the cool breeze of air-conditioning, and neat stacks of files, the municipal office seemed to explicitly reject the riotous streets outside, with their traffic, heat, piles of vegetables, and relaxed sociality. However, it became clear that the formal city was not holding at bay the throbbing, informal city that lay outside but was deeply engaged in its management. Rather than a hegemonic "culture of legality" (Comaroff and Comaroff 2006), the juridical push for greater regulation of the street seemed to represent only one among multiple possibilities. As the official's sardonic comments demonstrated, the actualization of regulations can be made possible only through unofficial compromise. At stake here are discrepancies not simply in political content but in form.

The significance of these encounters for understanding the politics of public space is twofold: first, conflicts over public space are often understood as "struggle[s] for inclusion in 'the public'" (Mitchell 1995, 117)—or, alternatively, as part of a process of restricting the public. However, the meaning and content of concepts underlying the Mumbai hawker controversy remain open-ended. Rather than assuming that ideas such as the "public" and the "citizens" who inhabit it are stable—that they precede the spatial conflict—we might instead look at how they emerge through the contestation. Second, these debates over form contain important negotiations over the content of informality, implicitly addressing questions such as: How can ad hoc arrangements be accounted for in a modern city? Are they inherently corrupt? Do they necessarily contradict democratic principles? The appearance of hawkerwali chai amid this space of official decorum signaled what scholars have previously suggested (Roy and AlSayyad 2004; Lino e Silva and Doherty 2011; McFarlane and Waibel 2012): that neat dichotomies between the informal and the formal have a way of breaking down.[26] At the same time, a state official's calling attention to this fact represented something more: that informality—what it is, how to regulate it, and its role in the city—is central to public debate and even to democratic participation. Informality—of laws, livelihood, and institutional process—was thus not simply an a priori condition, an arena through which politics unfolded, but a generative concept in its own right.

The two main strands of contemporary urban studies research—studies of culture in the city and studies of urban space as an effect of power—have not adequately addressed the contradictions, contingencies, and sense of incompleteness that animate the city. In order to understand the politics of public space and the conflicts over land and informality in the Global South, it is necessary to make sense of the way incongruous conditions of the urban inform everyday life. As Hansen and Verkaaik (2009, 12) argue, most writing on cities, with its "preponderance of work on planning and disciplining," has overlooked the "urban as a kind of sociality, a mental condition but also a way of being in the world." One aspect of this condition is the mingling of diverse political, economic, historic, and symbolic processes: illegality *and* proximity to the state, insecurity *and* permanence, normative rights claims *and* embedded practice, popularity *and* political marginality. These should not be subsumed to a larger narrative or analytical framework—what is *really* going on—but explored on their own terms. This is the story of *The Slow Boil*. Perhaps this is also what the autorickshaw driver meant: the vada pao is the city's "monument," it seems, because no other object better embodies its generative incongruities and the heterogeneous imaginative and political worlds it enables.

CHAPTER 2

THE UNRULY CITY

DEMOLITION may well have been the inaugural act of city making in Mumbai. "[In 1675] the first thing we had to do," writes James Douglas in his account of the early years of British control (1893, 93), "was to remove their *kajan* huts which clustered around the Castle like so many wigwams, and provide them dwellings elsewhere. The next thing was to build a street, a mile long, from the Castle gates, of lowish houses, now our Bazar-street." Eviction and resettlement were recurring themes in accounts of the city's development over the ensuing centuries. In the 1760s, the small huts of workers and toddy tappers lining the outside edge of the fort walls were removed in order to build "new fortifications" ("Town and Fort" 1835, 244).[1] These "cadjan huts," as they were called, continued to be "tolerated [elsewhere] until the close of 1802 . . . [when those] were also removed" (Hamilton 1820, 153). Moreover, the Esplanade, an open expanse outside the fort walls, was encroached on by an "encampment of tents . . . canvas dwellings [that were] the sole refuge for the destitute" (Roberts 1841, 229–30). This area too, an observer noted in the 1850s, was "gradually cleared of trees and cottages" (Anderson 1854, 67–68).

The image of the contested and unruly city emerged alongside, rather than followed, Mumbai's emergence as a modern metropolis.[2] As early as the mid-nineteenth century, authorities and urban elites complained of the "defective state of the high roads" (Edwardes 1923, 14) and "the beggar and hawkers' nuisance" ("A Railway Nuisance" 1934), a "long-standing grievance of the Bombay public" ("Hawkers" 1934). And yet one of the dominant views of contemporary Mumbai is that it has only recently become unruly. A widely circulated "fable" (Prakash 2010) of the city is its shift from "tropical Camelot" to the "dysfunctional . . . out-of-control city of the present" (Prakash 2010, 21). Public discussions about the city's current problems often contain "nostalgia for a previous era when urban life was imagined to be more decorous, less congested, and more 'civil' than it is today" (Glover 2007, 221). For instance, one civic activist said he "remembers Bombay (not Mumbai) as it used to be post independence . . . when there were only those hawkers who used to carry their wares (like Channawallas [vendors of chickpea snacks], etc, knife sharpening guys, etc) and Bombay was a great place to walk . . . much like London is today" (Karmayog.org).[3] Newspapers frequently quote residents who speak of streets being newly overrun by hawkers, while journalists invoke an era without slums and broken infrastructure, when the "civic gospel" reigned supreme (Kulkarni 2010).

While it is easy to critique the nostalgia of civic activists and journalists, more surprisingly, this perspective is replicated in scholarly writing as well. Descriptions of "increas[ingly] segmenting, discriminating and for-tressing" (Coutard and Guy 2007, 730) cities produce an idea of the urban past that is more inclusive, less fragmented, and less obviously shaped by the imperatives of capital. The literature on cities and globalization often suggests that we are living in a uniquely contested urban moment characterized by the abandonment of comprehensive planning and infra-structure provision in favor of a more fractured, "entrepreneurial" (Harvey 1989, 3) form of governance.[4] Scholars of urban India in particular often echo this view. They point to municipal crackdowns on encroachments, Supreme Court support for slum demolitions without resettlement, and state involvement in land speculation to argue that "welfarist rhetoric has now been jettisoned and more coercive aspects of state policy towards the poor are surfacing," which is resulting in a "'class cleansing'" of urban space (Whitehead and More 2007, 2433).

This chapter offers an alternative approach. As I show, conflicts over public space, slum demolitions, urban development priorities shaped by real estate speculation, and attempts at the embourgoisement of the public sphere have a long and recurring history. For instance, when the town planner Patrick Geddes visited Mumbai in 1915, he foreshadowed twenty-first-century critiques of developer-oriented urban governance by decrying the view "that a city like Bombay must depend upon its millionaires" (quoted in Hazareesingh 2000, 804). Indeed, critiques of the city's development in the early twentieth century powerfully echo those of the present: the heavy-handed slum eradication drives, the BMC's violent demolitions of street markets, the reliance on the private sector to build affordable housing, new infrastructure development (such as the trams, which only the middle class could afford; Hazareesingh 2001), and land reclamations whose cost was borne by the public but benefited private firms,[5] and even the rise of car-centric urban planning, which marginalized the pedestrian. To early twentieth-century observers, these processes produced a sense that urban priorities were being shaped by commercial interests rather than for social welfare and that the trajectory of urban development was heading toward fragmentation rather than inclusion.[6]

This chapter examines the micropractices and discourses of spatial conflict in colonial-era Mumbai in order to rethink accounts of contemporary spatial contestation. I focus on three historical moments that are characterized by processes central to understanding the present: (1) late eighteenth- and early nineteenth-century efforts by the colonial state to contain a landscape of congestion, blockages, and encroachments; (2) late nineteenth-century spatial transformations in the name of public health; and (3) early twentieth-century middle-class civic activism around the condition and appearance of public space. The phenomena each of these historical periods exhibit—slum demolitions as a form of "spatial cleansing" (Herzfeld 2006, 142), real estate capital pushing urban development priorities, and the embourgoisement of the public sphere, respectively—are processes that scholars of contemporary life often identify as unique to the newly transformed, globalized urbanism of the early twenty-first century.[7]

The focus of this chapter is on the recurring theme of the "out-of-control" city as it was framed by authorities and the relatively well-off. However, it is important to emphasize that what unfolded on the ground did not simply mirror the desires of those in power. Everyday spatial interventions in the nineteenth century were characterized by negotiation, compromise, subversion, and, very often, outright failure. For instance in 1866, the newly formed BMC, while empowered to "remove huts situated so as to be injurious to the occupants of them, or unhealthy to the neighbourhood" ("Dwellings" 1866, 216), found occupants' protests to be a stumbling block to demolitions. The poor residents staged dramatic encounters to fight demolitions. A writer in the *Bombay Builder* describes "the harrowing scene connected with a 'turn-out' of these miserable living people from those wretched looking little huts to be seen at Camateepoora and on the Flats." These scenes, the author said, posed a challenge to the "well-thinking executive employed to put in force the machinery of our municipal law."

The political economic context of Mumbai has obviously changed over the past two centuries. At the same time, historical accounts of evictions, encroachments, and illegalities in the city strikingly echo those of the present. In light of these parallels, contemporary evictions are not only signs of a new era of corporate capital, but are also linked with the authorities' long, and still unresolved, struggle to impose a sense of order over an unruly city. What is necessary, then, is to highlight historical continuity while simultaneously attending to the imaginative and political conditions of new contexts.

REMAKING THE FORT

It was not until Mumbai's transformation into a port and metropolis of global significance in the mid-eighteenth century that authorities began their long struggle to contain a landscape of congestion, blockages, encroachments, and illegalities. Usurping the neighboring city of Surat for commercial primacy in the mid-eighteenth century allowed Mumbai to become the major conduit for the vast quantities of opium and cotton traded across the Indian Ocean, as well as an important center for shipbuilding and finance.

The new importance of transoceanic trade produced an influx of people and capital, as well as new conflicts over space. Cotton, the commodity that linked Mumbai to the world of modern global trade, ironically also produced a new discourse of urban dysfunction; the material goods that enabled the formation of modern urbanity simultaneously stood for its impossibility. As early as 1787, discontent over "the obstruction which arose out of the irregular and uncontrolled manner in which cotton"—whose "bales, which at a distance appear like fortifications" (Roberts 1841, 230)—"was piled on the green and in the streets" (Morley 1859, 489) dominated complaints to the grand jury of the nascent police administration. The city's imbrications with global trade accompanied the arrival of new discourses of disorder in other ways as well. Inadequate streets, congested neighborhoods, garbage, and the presence of unwanted populations became new topics of public concern. The "beggar-nuisance" and, to the early police administration, the "filthiness of some of the inhabitants, being uncommonly offensive and a real nuisance to society" (quoted in Edwardes 1923, 15, 14), indexed the state's struggle to assert its authority over the built environment.

The arrival of town planning practices in the mid 1700s (Chandavarkar 1994, 36) facilitated the narrative of the out-of-control city. The town enclosed by the fort walls was considered to be congested and crowded, with poorly built and unauthorized structures. Eighteenth-century authorities identified poor native residents' shops and workers' huts as the primary cause of these problems: "In contempt of the Government, several of the inhabitants have made encroachments on the high roads by erecting buildings and sheds without license, the President and Governor, by and with the advice and consent of his Council, has thought proper to ordain and direct that all *cajan* and palm-leaved sheds and pent-houses are to be pulled down till the monsoon sets in" (quoted in Edwardes 1902, 188). Day laborers and *hamals*—"that rascal multitude who carried on the business of locomotion" (Douglas 1900, 37)—constructed illegal sheds on the streets; and throughout the town, according to the Rule, Ordinance, and Regulation of 1812 (Masani 1929, 113), "Many persons are seen frequently working and carrying on their different trades in the public roads, to the great annoyance and nuisance of those who are passing by."

By 1787, the problem of encroachment in the Fort was considered so severe that a Surveys and Encroachments Committee (Rodrigues 1994) was formed with the specific task of inspecting native construction

practices (*Materials Towards a Statistical Account* 1894, 491), ensuring they
are not "prejudicial to public works and the general health of the inhabitants" (Edwardes 1902, 227). After a short inspection period, the committee submitted its findings: dense, narrow, and meandering streets were
to be replaced by wide streets that intersected at right angles; the height
of buildings must be restricted; and "the projections of the shops in the
bazár or principal street of the black town are a very great nuisance and
ought all to be immediately removed, as being positive encroachments on
the street, and receptacles for every kind of filth and nastiness" (quoted
in Edwardes 1902, 227). To many of its residents in the late eighteenth
century, Mumbai's status as western India's commercial capital did not
match its physical appearance—"an old and recurring theme in the city's
history" (Chandavarkar 1994, 35). The unruly landscape was considered
to pose a problem to the health and safety of its residents, as well as to the
city's image.[8]

While the centralized municipal authority that would have been necessary to make significant interventions in the built environment was absent, the "improved condition" (Anderson 1854, 67) required by the city's
new global prominence was made possible by a massive fire in the fort in
1803, which "afforded" "an opportunity of introducing wider and more
regular streets, and of relieving congested localities" (Edwardes 1902,
228). While the cause of the fire was unclear, its quick spread, consum-
ing nearly a third of the city, was attributed to congestion, houses made
of flammable material, and a proliferation of "dangerous" occupations
(*Materials Towards a Statistical Account* 1893, 434) in densely populated
areas.[9] Even before the charred remains of destroyed houses were cleared,
a dramatic reordering of urban space ensued. Indian residents, once a
significant part of the population, were relocated outside the fort in the
newly created Native Town (Masselos 2007), while poor people's homes
were subject to new scrutiny. For instance, "demands were made for the
demolition of certain Bhoys' (Bhois or Palanquin bearers') houses" (Edwardes 1902, 229), "built of nothing but wooden frames filled up with
tattys . . . now so very old and decayed that they are actually tumbling
to pieces" (*Materials Towards a Statistical Account* 1893, 434). While the
evictions were done in the name of a concern for public safety, commen-

tators candidly observed that private real estate speculation played a significant role as well: these huts were "surrounded by a number of wealthy Pársis' [sic] houses" and thus "the ground they occupy if exposed to sale would bring a very high price" (ibid.).

Real estate speculation mingled with security concern, resulting in demolitions outside the fort walls as well. In the years immediately preceding the fire, laborers and others unable to afford the fort's high rents lived in an "encampment of tents . . . these canvas dwellings being the sole refuge for the destitute" (Roberts 1841, 229–30) on the Esplanade. Despite persistent demolitions due to the space's military significance, toddy-tappers and workers' small huts lined the outside edge of the fort walls, which the "government began to remove" in 1768 in order to construct "new fortifications" ("Town and Fort" 1835, 244),[10] while "Cadjan huts were still tolerated until the close of 1802, when they were also removed" (Hamilton 1820, 153). After the fire of 1803, land clearances were extended farther, so that "by this time, the more wealthy inhabitants had built houses in a detached irregular manner, throughout the coco-nut woods contiguous to the esplanade" (ibid.). As a result, "the little vacant ground remaining had in consequence risen to an enormous price" (ibid.). The small huts tolerated for decades on the outskirts of the fort were finally demolished. In an analysis of spatial transformation that has remarkable resonance with today's processes of squatting, evictions, and resettlement on Mumbai's rapidly expanding urban frontier, Hamilton observes, "The sufferers by the fire and indigent from the esplanade, had no alternative but to resort to the Honourable Company's salt batty ground, scarcely recovered from the sea, neither had government any ground to give in exchange for the valuable land taken when extending the esplanade."

Despite these attempts to decongest the fort following the fire, subsequent visitors still complained of congestion and the slow pace of reconstruction. Ten years later, the area remained "dirty, hot and disagreeable, particularly the quarter near the bazar-gate, owing to the ruins of houses which were burnt down some time ago, and have never been removed . . . [while the streets are] so uneven as to render it disagreeable, if not dangerous, for carriages to pass through them" (Graham 1813, 12). An effect of spatial reordering following the fire was thus to shift the discursive focus on congestion from the fort to the Native Town that had been established outside it,[11] an area of dense sensory experience and visual confusion where "the streets literally swarm with life—men, women, children, and bullocks, filling them almost to suffocation" (Roberts 1841, 232) and where "only for an hour or two after sun-rise, that horsemen or carriages can pass unimpeded by stoppages of varied character" (Postans 1839, quoted in Edwardes 1902, 253). This commentary on traffic was remarkable considering that the area's bucolic character had barely been erased, with reminders of the coconut plantations still very much present (Masselos 2007, 287), a view echoed by other visitors. One of them, Maria Graham (1813), observed that despite being located "in a coco-nut wood," the density of activity was such that "I could not help remarking the amazing populousness of this small island; the streets appear so crowded with men, women, and children, that it seems impossible for the quiet bullock *hackrays*, or native carriages, to get along without doing mischief" (3–4).

Visual confusion challenged the aesthetic sensibilities of nineteenth-century visitors. The Native Town, wrote one traveler, had a "vista of streets [that] resemble some ancient mediaeval Italian town or a Jewish Ghetto" (Aubrey 1884, 258). Others wrote that they "expect to come to the grand city of Bombay [but are met with] unfinished-looking streets, heaps of unremoved rubbish, bricks, rabble, want of footpaths, want of form, shape, and neatness, [which] impress us with the idea that we are in the outskirts of it. Not a bit of it; we are *in* Bombay, and this rambling, irregular, dirty, insect-pervaded house is the British hotel" (Shepherd 1857, 9–10).

Looking back at this period, an editorial that appeared in 1901 laments that planned interventions in urban space were only partially successful, a sign of the authorities' failure to rationalize space. "But a generation which knew not Sir Bartle . . . permitted the modern city which sprang up on the confines of the Fort in response to the magic touch of industrial development to become an agglomeration of poisonously unsanitary dwellings scantily intersected by a network of devious, narrow streets" ("The New Bombay" 1901). Indeed, the Bombay Municipal Corporation (BMC), as well as the Board of Conservancy, which preceded it, struggled mightily to rationalize the streets by standardizing their width and removing obstructions, but it yielded few results: "Efforts have at times been made to induce the Native owners of ground, to surrender such small patches as may interfere with the symmetry of the streets, but they have manifested very little disposition to yield" (*"Town and Fort of Bombay"* 1835, 244).[12] Large-scale infrastructural interventions such as Elphinstone Circle (now Horniman Circle)—that "range of new buildings encircling the rubbish encumbered *enceinte* in front of the town hall" ("First Impressions" 1865, 5)—and Governor Bartle Frere's construction of broad avenues on space freed up by the destruction of the fort walls were the exception rather than the rule.

EVICTIONS AND URBAN CLEANSING

Paralleling transnational trends, regulation of space in Mumbai dramatically changed following the creation of the BMC in 1865. Urban governance had previously been "in the hands of the Bench of the Justices of the Peace" and "concerned with the police, administration of justice and the collection of taxes" (Ramanna 2002, 83), with sanitation "entrusted to a Board of Conservancy acting under the direction of the Honourable Bench of Justices" (Kabraji 1901, cited in Dwivedi and Mehrotra 1995). The creation of the BMC signaled a shift toward the total management of the built environment and "new regimes of record keeping and surveillance [and] new ways of classifying people and property" (Glover 2008, xiii) throughout colonial India. This new regime, further consolidated by the 1888 BMC Act, which gave the commissioner the right to remove encroachments, ushered in a new era of bureaucratization that ultimately led to the devolution of municipal authority to local populations (Masselos 2007, 46).

Vast increases in wealth and population during this period enabled concrete manifestations of a new ethic of civic duty (Albuquerque 1985). The historian Mariam Dossal argues that the "preaching of civic gospel" that characterized the late nineteenth century has "led to some remarkable standards in civic planning" (quoted in Kulkarni 2010) that continue to benefit the city. Indeed, nineteenth-century planners such as Henry Conybeare (McFarlane 2008; Dossal 2010) transformed the mundane problems of garbage, drains, and sewage into issues of great ethical duty. The 1860s cotton boom helped provide the funds for a newly bureaucratized urban landscape, while the demolition of the fort walls opened up new space on which to build planned roads and boulevards. New municipal administrative headquarters were built along with a train station, central market, and university clock tower. These were architectural reminders of the city's arrival in the modern age (Metcalfe 2002) and instantiations of a new logic of governance through the reordering of space. Indeed, the establishment of municipal authority through symbolic and bureaucratic measures reflected a transnational shift in liberal governance in which law and order, public health, and the imposition of modern subjectivity became spatial problems in the eyes of the state.

This shift toward the spatialization of urban governance was embodied by the Bombay City Improvement Trust (BIT), an entity established in 1898 with "powers . . . intended to sweep away all the slum property of the city" (*Sanitary Record* 1898, 532).[13] Authorities and observers had earlier referred to poor people's housing, but started using the word *slums* only in the late nineteenth century. In earlier accounts of the city, a more diverse language was used to describe housing that would later be subsumed under the monolithic category of "slum." Writes Maria Graham (1813), for instance, "The lower classes content themselves with small huts, mostly of clay, and roofed with cadjan, a mat made of the leaves of the Palmyra, or coco-nut tree, plaited together. Some of these huts are so small, that they only admit of a man's sitting upright in them, and barely shelter his feet when he lies down" (4). Others describe "shelter[s] under a hut [which] costs him but a copper pice [the smallest denomination] or a handful of paddy per diem" (Aubrey 1884, 43); servants' huts "thatched with palmyra leaves" (Douglas 1893, 69); "fetid hovels . . . filthy and haunted by the demons of fever, dysentery and cholera" (Aubrey 1884, 43); and "*zavli* shed[s]—huts constructed of dry leaves of date or coconut palms" (Burnett-Hurst 1925, 152, cited in Chandavarkar 1994, 181).

While the huts scattered around the fort and alongside its walls had represented a potential threat to public safety in the late eighteenth century, a century later, poor people's housing was reframed as a potential threat to public health. Created in the aftermath of a devastating plague, the BIT gave new legitimacy to destruction as an act of urban renewal. An article in the *Times of India* ("The New Bombay" 1901) reflected the authorities' unprecedented focus on slum clearance: "[Neighborhoods such as Koliwada are] in such a hopeless condition from a hygienic point of view that it [the slums] needs to be radically dealt with. On the recommendation of the Municipal Commissioner the whole area, embracing some 36,000 square yards, will be acquired and cleared, and reconstructed in accordance with modern principles." Fusing discourses of town planning and public health, state functionaries charged with renewing cities were envisioned as surgeons (Vidler 1978, 39), curing the sickness of the unsanitary city through direct, physical interventions; opening congested streets, like blocked arteries; and removing slums, like cancerous tumors. In this metaphor of modern urban planning, poor neighborhoods were necessarily assumed to be unhealthy. "Slum" neighborhoods, such as those "deficient in light and ventilation," surrounded by "gullies [that] are open channels for carrying off sullage" and "generally in a dirty and foul condition" (Turner 1914, cited in Baker 1915, 62), were primary areas targeted for removal.[14]

BIT-organized slum demolitions constituted a process of urban cleansing that rivals any that has occurred since. The first wave of demolitions took place in the immediate aftermath of the 1896 plague. The authorities took advantage of the flight of much of the working-class population from the city, so "during their absence the huts in which they lived [were] condemned by the authorities, and in many cases burned down, with the view of diminishing the danger of infection" (*Sanitary Record* 1897, 414).[15] Over the following ten years, BIT demolitions displaced 14,613 families, and of these families, less than a third were resettled (Orr 1914).[16] Moreover, with great frequency "new dwellings . . . provided by the Government" were left uninhabited because "these, the former occupants of the huts have been informed by their friends in the city, will not keep out the rain during the monsoon" (*Sanitary Record* 1897, 414). Other critics observed that land reclamations, "perhaps the greatest favourites with capitalists" (Ducat 1866, 184), contributed to the city's unhealthy conditions as much as slums: "The filling up of the flats with street sweepings and rubbish, which has gone on for years and is mischievously termed 'reclamation' in Bombay, has done much to prevent the surface floods from running off," notes a letter to the editor in *Indian Engineering* ("The Plague" 1897, 130).

The new infrastructure built by the BIT enabled elite interests to assert greater control over the city's spatial landscape. Road infrastructure in particular offered the most compelling logic for evictions and removal of settlements considered dangerous to the city. To open the city was to make it healthy and clean; the sense that disease was spread through a theory of miasma (McFarlane 2008) spatialized the problem of sanitation. Boulevards acquired new symbolic meaning because they acted as both agents of destruction and facilitators of circulation. "Two broad roads, running due east and west, were cut through the worst parts of the city, sweeping away a mass of insanitary property and admitting the healthful westerly breezes to the most crowded parts of it" (Baker 1915, 63). "Not only will these new roads provide a splendid fresh air channel across the island, but the neighborhood of Pattakwady, a dense mass of low class buildings behind the cloth market, comprising one of the most unhealthy localities in the city, will be opened up by the new main thoroughfares and a series of forty-foot cross roads. . . . Substantial progress has already been made with . . . some condemned houses demolished" ("The New Bombay" 1901).[17] Slum demolitions without resettlement shuffled populations around the city, at times worsening housing conditions elsewhere. For instance, a road-widening project "from Carnac Bridge just north of the Fort, to Queen's Road . . . caused large-scale dishousing which led to an increase in overcrowding in nearby Cavel . . . where 'large numbers of insanitary houses' had 'new storeys added to them,' making light and ventilation in neighbouring houses even worse than before" (Hazareesingh 2001, 241–42, quoting J. P. Orr).

To late nineteenth- and early twentieth-century observers, BIT evictions not only served public health needs but altered the class structure of neighborhoods. Spatial transformations promised to transform the image of the city while opening vast new possibilities for real estate profit and speculation. Road widening and the removal of poor neighborhoods, for instance, were considered "material improvements" on the urban landscape that also made land "much more valuable for purposes of business

and of residence" (Baker 1915). These transformations particularly benefited the politically powerful. In one case, "the building in which is located the American consulate at Bombay . . . [is located] on land which
had been redeemed by the trust from an especially plague-stricken slum
area of the city" (Baker 1915). Reflecting this elite-oriented urban vision,
proponents of these new spatial interventions spoke of an imagined man
"[who could] leave his office in the Fort and starting from the western
end of the Colaba Reclamation, motor up the magnificent central avenue
through the park at the north and along the Sea Road already under construction as far as Chowpatty. . . . Except along the latter part of his drive
[Sewri-Wadalla Scheme] he would see nothing in the slightest degree
sordid or repulsive, but houses of the best class in a city which ought to be
the most beautiful in the world" (Curtis 1921, 579).

However, the elite-oriented logic of urban governance did not quite
correspond with the city it produced. The BIT's development projects
may have often been guided by profit, but that does not mean the entire
city was remade in the image of capital. Similarly, class-informed practices of "spatial cleansing" (Herzfeld 2006) took place, but the city was
never quite "sanitized"; the modernist metaphor of the city as a sick pa-
tient in need of the surgeon's scalpel (Vidler 1978) was more of an ideal
than a vision put into practice. As the early twentieth-century battles
over the use of the street discussed in the following section also suggest, municipal interventions were often thwarted and often had effects
in excess of authorities' intentions; city making, then, as in the present, is
better understood as a contingent process open to compromise and negotiation than as a grand transformation.

STREET SKIRMISHES
The authorities' tenuous grasp over the urban landscape in the late nineteenth century was especially evident in the great variety of ways streets
were used. Municipal visions of a clean and orderly city were frequently
contradicted by the spatial practices of the "human tides which roll
through the streets" (Edwardes 1912, 6). A series of essays published in
1880 and 1882 describes a vibrant streetscape put to use by a wide diversity of people. In these accounts, Mumbai's streets consisted of beggars—

"the lame, the blind, the deformed, the leper and the decrepit"[18]—as well as the "young and old, the poor and some that are well off, the diseased and sturdy, impudent, stout healthy fellows who follow this miserable profession with great pride" (Raghunathji 1880, 248, 249). This author also observed people who "hawk about the town or squat by the wayside" (Raghunatji 1882, 44) selling leeches, lemonade and soda water, coconuts, bangles, pistachios, and ice.

Sporadic efforts to regularize and centralize trading, such as the construction of Crawford Market in 1865 (*Gazetteer* 1910), ironically resulted in a proliferation of informal trade. On streets adjacent to this "central market, of an up-to-date character, and aesthetically constructed" (Wacha 1920, 338–39), "vendors of sugar-cane, plantains, or sweetmeats, squat before their wickerwork baskets after taking up their stations under porticoes, shady trees, or bright glazed umbrellas" (Aubrey 1884, 35), while others, taking advantage of the crowds of potential customers attracted to the new markets, "sit in tailor fashion before their modest stores spread on the ground, sugar-cane, glasses, gaudy gewgaws, satin scarves" (255).

While efforts to regulate street commerce began in 1812 (Masani 1929), it was not until the expansion of municipal authority in the 1860s, followed by the 1888 BMC Act and the 1902 Police Act, that the authorities seriously focused on "street nuisance, street obstruction and squatter cases" (quoted in Kidambi 2007, 150). For instance, a police report celebrated a reduction in the "nuisance crime" rate in 1884 due to "accommodation for these petty traders in the several markets of the city and of stricter supervision by the Police" (*Annual Police Return* 1885, 2)."[19] By the early twentieth century, the BMC took over much of the work of street clearing by deploying vans to fight encroachment. And yet periodic raids, demolitions, and arrests seemed to have had little effect on the city's thriving street economy. Officials noted that hawkers frequently "engaged in a running battle" with the police and municipality over the use of the street (Kidambi 2007, 152), with more victories for hawkers than the state. Writing in 1909, the municipal commissioner observed that "at frequent intervals throughout the day the whole street is occupied by petty hawkers, [and yet] these men do not wish to go anywhere else and could not be induced to squat in special stands" (quoted in Kidambi 2007, 152).

Despite the authorities' efforts to control hawking, street commerce expanded throughout the early twentieth century. Raj Chandavarkar's account of Mumbai's working-class neighborhoods in the 1930s notes "a large number of workers [who] were occupied in various forms of petty trading and production, hawking and peddling. [During this time] everything could be bought and sold on the streets of Bombay" (Chandavarkar 1994, 81). This thriving street trade was a result of limited municipal resources, as well as unofficial spatial claims negotiated with the authorities. Hawkers, knowing the police's limited ability to monitor the streets, went "back to their perch to repeat the offence the minute they get away from Court" (quoted in Kidambi 2007, 153). State functionaries also colluded with hawkers to circumvent regulation. S. M. Edwardes (1912, 119), a former Bombay police commissioner and amateur historian, noted that coffee vendors were "experienced in the wiles of the urban population and sometimes perhaps a protégé of the local police." Likewise, women fruit sellers, for instance, were "fully capable of conciliating the Lord of the Bombay pavements, when he somewhat roughly commands her to move on.... 'Jemadar Saheb' she calls him; and if this flattery is insufficient she offers one of her ripest mangoes with a glance that he cannot resist. It is too much for the sepoy: he smiles and tramps off, and she holds her position undisturbed" (116).

Authorities' new, although often ineffectual, focus on the micropractices of the street was a product of a new emphasis on free-market liberalism. The colonial state's self-fashioning as the facilitator of market efficiency in the late nineteenth century (Birla 2009) resignified old problems of congestion, blockages, and encroachments. Formerly understood as a threat to law and order, these were now understood to "be doing harm to the trade of the city" ("Cancellation of Hawkers' Licenses" 1934). Can early twenty-first-century processes marginalizing the poor—whether due to efforts to attract global capital or to create an environment more suitable to middle-class consumerism (Fernandes 2004)—be disentangled from these earlier processes? Can we speak of a transformed relationship between citizens and the state in the context of neoliberalism, when even by the late nineteenth century, policies and spatial interventions were shaped according to a logic of profit maximization? Moreover, what can we make of the relationship between logics of governance and the everyday life of the city when the effects of laws, framed to directly facilitate capital accumulation, were profoundly uneven? Efficient streets were framed as an imperative for efficient commerce, and streets had to be transformed to fit Mumbai's image of a center for global trade—and yet, as we will see, the transformation of the city remained an incomplete project. Indeed, much to the frustration of the local elites increasingly clamoring for a voice in municipal governance, government rhetoric about the need to control the streets did not correspond with realities on the ground.

THE "HAWKER'S NUISANCE" AND
THE RISE OF THE BOURGEOIS PUBLIC

By the turn of the twentieth century, there was an important shift in the social imaginary of hawkers and the out-of-control city they represented. In Emma Roberts's 1841 account of Mumbai, for instance, hawkers are elements of a spectral urban landscape: "Sometimes in the evening a sort of market is held in the native town beyond the Esplanade, and every stall is profusely lighted; the hawkers, who carry about their goods in a more humble way upon their heads in baskets, have them stuck with candles, and the wild shadowy effects produced, amid the quaint buildings thus partially lighted, afford a continual phantasmagoria." However, by the early twentieth century, hawkers were considered to be an obstacle to the smooth flow of pedestrian traffic and economic efficiency—and ultimately a sign of municipal incompetence.

The shifting signification of hawkers followed the changing political contours of colonial rule in Indian cities. The most important shift was the decentralization of municipal governance in the 1880s (Aijaz 2008). The devolution of power in Indian cities led to significant changes in local involvement in urban affairs. The emphasis on spatial control that dominated colonial urbanism in the nineteenth century gradually gave way to an increased sense of local "autonomy" (Beverley 2011, 483) in the early twentieth.[20] The "Indianiz[ing] of municipal power" (N. Rao 2013, 16) that was evident in Bombay of the 1920s produced an increasingly vocal middle class. Their critiques reframed the symbolic significance of the unruly city. To them, the problem of hawkers and the dense streets they produced contributed to a failure of representative municipal governance and representative democracy.[21] Discourses of public health and fears of the unruly crowd became overshadowed by the new ideas of good governance and the estranged middle-class citizen.

Newspapers such as the *Bombay Chronicle* vividly reflected the new imaginary of streets as manifestations of good governance. This nationalist newspaper, founded in 1910, was "designed, not only to awaken civil society into a more critical disposition vis-à-vis colonial authority, but to directly engage with the Bombay government itself" (Hazareesingh 2000, 805).[22] By the 1930s, it regularly included editorials and letters from readers criticizing the BMC and the police for failing to control the street. Readers described streets overrun by hawkers, impassable sidewalks, violent demolition raids, systematic municipal incompetence, corrupt practices, and elite blindness to the problems of the "common man" who neither owned a car nor used the street to make a living. Readers frequently complained of streets, train stations, and open spaces being in a "hopeless state of affairs" ("Is Bombay Clean?" 1933). They described roads lined with the "excreta of animals, bullocks, horses and dogs" (ibid.), "lepers" ("Bombay's Lepers" 1933), "loafers" (Horniman 1933), rubble left by contractors ("Pedestrians Combine!" 1933), stalls whose "cupboards" and "chairs" "block the whole footpath" ("Hawker Nuisance" 1933), and "small stands" from which vendors sell "uncovered" food that "constitute a menace to the health [of their customers]" ("In and Around Bombay" 1934). Nearly everywhere, walking was made difficult by "the beggar and hawkers' nuisance" ("A Railway Nuisance" 1934), that "long-standing grievance of the Bombay public" ("Hawkers" 1934). Other readers complained about "hand carts with dry fruits, toys, vegetables [that are] allowed to stand for hours together at the same place" ("Hawkers and Footpaths" 1934) and a street "occupied by the vegetable and fruit-sellers who squat on it from one end to the other" ("The Grant Road Nuisance" 1933).

The problem of hawker encroachments in particular was considered to be pervasive. In an assessment of the city's infrastructure, a municipal official observed in the 1930s that for the most part, "the pedestrian prefers to use the carriageway [or, the street] because the footpaths [sidewalks] are either occupied by hawkers or are . . . otherwise uninviting to pedestrians" (Modak 1935, 66). Hawker-lined streets could be found "in Girgaum Tram Terminus [where] the hawkers have occupied one half of the footpath" ("Pedestrians' Trials in Bombay" 1933), while the "native" neighborhoods such as Bhuleshwar and Null Bazaar, Grant Road and Girgaon Road, Grant Road and Bhendi Bazaar were rendered especially congested by vendors ("Hawkers and Footpaths" 1934; "Hawkers" 1934).

As a result of growing public outrage, the BMC started a department dealing with encroachment removal whose initial work focused on the eradication of the city's thriving street economy. Street clearances were violent events that often came without warning. Sympathetic witnesses called the "brutalities toward poor hawkers . . . an outrage on common humanity" ("Pedestrians Combine!" 1933) and a form of "terrorism on poor people" ("Harassing the Poor and Needy" 1933). One man witnessed a "sturdy Maratha with a basket full of mangoes . . . sitting on the footpath at Thakurdwar Road when all of a sudden he was pounced upon by the raiders of the Encroachment Department" ("Hateful and Degrading" 1933). Another reader, who identified himself as S. N. Nanavaty, an attorney, "saw the Municipal Encroachment Car coming and suddenly stopping [at the Grant Road vegetable market]: some men climbed down from it, ran here and there, snatched some things from one hawker and the other and got in the car again. . . . [A] poor Hindu hawker was driving a small hand car [sic] containing brass and copper vessels. They [the Municipal Encroachment car] also took up something from [him]. . . . The poor man stood aghast. It was a most pitiable sight" ("Harassing the Poor and Needy" 1933).

Hawker unions mobilized against the BMC's violent tactics. Rallies and protests were organized against the canceling of licenses and against "harassing the hawkers day and night" ("Sort of Municipal 'Loot'" 1931).[23] Union leaders wrote letters to the editor describing "the high-handed manner in which the staff of the Encroachment Department" work and called for the end of "this most harsh and inequitable system" ("Bombay Fruit Merchants Meet" 1933) and of "the 'looting' of the articles by some members of the Encroachment Department" that resulted in "terrible hardships that entailed upon the hawkers" ("Sort of Municipal 'Loot'" 1931).

However, to middle-class observers of the city's transforming public spaces, it seemed that street vending was growing alongside expanded efforts by the state to control the use of the street. Reports of repeated raids on hawkers (who would return a few hours later) reinforced the sense of the ineptitude of the municipal authorities. Lacking a systematic approach to dealing with street obstructions, the "much-maligned Encroachment Department" seemed "absolutely blind to the hawkers who spread their wares to the full length of the pavement," focusing instead on "snatching away articles kept in front of shops and knick-knacks which slip on to the pavements" ("The Hawkers" 1934). Other letters suggested that significant corruption might be fueling municipal incompetence. A lengthy plea for improved governance over the use of sidewalks mocks the "lorries of the Encroachment Department . . . [who] parade the streets of Bombay" unable to "effectively check this evil" because hawkers' informants previously alert them to the impending raids ("Hawkers and Footpaths" 1934).

PEDESTRIANS AND THE MIDDLE-CLASS POLITICAL SUBJECT

These letters reflect the emergence of a powerful new political voice in urban affairs: the middle-class professional. Letter writers described themselves as tax-paying citizens living in comfortable neighborhoods such as Peddar Road. They directed their critiques at the municipality for its failure to regulate the street. To them, the informal city of hawkers, beggars, and slums indexed the particular problem of inefficient governance and corruption. Periodic violent demolitions merely reflected the incompetence of the municipal authority and its desperate attempts to control a city beyond its grasp.

While these critiques contain a class-based assertion over public space, it is an ambivalent one. On one hand, the letter writers were engaged in a political act to reframe the "public" and the normative urban resident to exclude the poor. Indeed, despite claiming universality, "pedestrians" in letters to the *Bombay Chronicle* were framed through class-specific spatial practices; they represented the subjectivity of people who use the street primarily for walking rather than working. The condition of these streets was a matter of quality of life rather than survival in the city. Letters with signatures such as "Yours, etc . . . 'Pedestrian'" ("Hawkers and Footpaths" 1934) also referenced the ideal of an abstract public that was a product of educational and linguistic privilege. At the same time, these letters can also be seen as attempts to reshape the content of urban citizenship. "Pedestrians" in these letters were city residents with the free time to appreciate a casual stroll, but they were also a group not rich enough to own a car. They were, in this sense, as distinct from the poor who work on the street as from the rich who fly past it.

The pedestrian, as symbolically loaded a figure in contemporary urban politics in Mumbai as it was in the 1930s, signals anxiety over the middle class's place in city politics.[24] Then, as now, the struggles faced by the pedestrian stand in for the middle class's larger struggle to find a voice in municipal governance seemingly dominated by the wealth and clout of the elites, on one hand, and the populism of the poor, on the other. The *Bombay Chronicle* letters with cheeky titles such as "Pedestrians Combine!" (1933) reflect this political subjectivity by merging commentary on municipal incompetence with a critique of the state's own class bias and the ambiguous basis of spatial claims: "The Encroachment Department whose brutalities toward poor hawkers are an outrage on common humanity . . . [tolerates] any sort of encroachment on the foot-paths by shopkeepers, contractors and others who can spend a few annas for the privilege." Benjamin Horniman, editor of the *Bombay Chronicle*, echoed a similar sentiment, describing how the pedestrian, that "long suffering, down-trodden, neglected creature," inhabits a city in which "there is no sidewalk where he can take refuge or if there is, the police and shopkeepers, hawkers and loafers are in a conspiracy to make sure that he won't get the use of it" (Horniman 1933). Horniman focuses his criticism at the misguided concerns of political elites—those who focus on the "grievances of motorists . . . owning expensive cars" and who complain of "the stupidity of pedestrians and their want of road sense." By contrast, he speaks on behalf of the middle-class pedestrian, caught between the interests of the rich and poor.

The *Bombay Chronicle* readers' grievances varied widely. Some complained about the poor taking over the city, while others grumbled that the municipality was neglecting to do its duties, or of broken sidewalks and wasted tax money. Some complained of violence against hawkers, while others of car-centric planning and elite-oriented development priorities. What is striking across these accounts is that, as in the contemporary moment, middle-class critiques of public space were irreducible to capital. These letters and editorials generalize middle-class experiences as they criticized the elitism of municipal governance. However, in their ambivalence, they open a space for the reevaluation of the basis of urban citizenship.

As I discuss in Chapter 5, critiques of municipal governance within Mumbai's contemporary public sphere similarly concern the ideal form of political engagement. In the 1930s, as now, a lack of civic mindedness became the primary explanation for municipal officials' and politicians' neglect of sidewalk conditions. Contemporary civic activists argue that those in power have "chosen politics for the wrong reasons" ("Vote, for Yourself!" 2004). Likewise, the *Bombay Chronicle* critiques municipal corporators' disconnect from city life. At stake here is less the role of corporate and industrial interests than the content of governance. Consider, for instance, a 1933 cartoon printed on the front page of the *Chronicle* titled, "What Do They Know of Beggars."[25] Sketches of men relaxing in a luxuriously appointed apartment are accompanied by the captions, "Our municipal corporators . . . Enjoying comfortable homes/Always at clubs/ Going about in private-cars and taxis/A happy family amongst themselves . . . how can they be expected to sympathize with our beggar-pest." The last frame, the punch line, depicts a male "taxpayer" reading a newspaper with the headline: "Corporation Shelves Beggar Question," accompanied by an image of a pedestrian engulfed by beggars on a Mumbai street. This image makes the message clear: the victims of the state's ineffectiveness are not the poor but those whose journeys through the city are impeded by them. Here, the failure to control the streets is framed as a manifestation of urban authorities' disconnect from the everyday life of the city.

As I show in the ensuing chapters, these critiques of municipal incompetence and the unruly streetscapes it produces resonate strikingly with the present. While this continuity can be framed in terms of the state and industry's need to control the working poor, this tells only part of the story. The persistence of hawkers and squatters as a "problem" also reflects the persistence of a political subjectivity, anxieties over political participation, and conversations over the content of citizenship and proper spatial practice that emerged in the early twentieth century. Then and now we see a political subjectivity framed around a spatial imaginary and the ideal of political participation it is seen to foster—a forging of modernist urbanism and liberalism so that the removal of physical obstacles is seen as equivalent to removing obstacles to an ideal civil society. Moreover, in these invocations of an abstract public, we can see attempts to establish the importance of a universalized political subjectivity; the "pedestrian" is presented as the ideal citizen on whose behalf the state should act because it is the generalized urban inhabitant—a constituency supposedly unmarked by ethnicity, community, or gender. Hardly triumphant, these critiques of the municipality's complicity in the unruly city contain a tone of exasperation. Rather than signs of a class-based takeover of space, we should instead interpret them as engagements in an ongoing conversation over the content and basis of spatial claims themselves.

CONTINUITIES AND RESIGNIFICATION

Writings on spatial contestation often suggest that we are living in a unique urban moment. Cities are said to be neoliberal because of state efforts to remove the visible presence of the poor. Urban governance aimed at attracting global capital and maximizing profits from real estate speculation are said to be unparalleled historically. It is not that these processes of marginalization and elite-oriented development do not exist, but their critics often assume them to be entirely new, suggesting that the city of the past was more equitable and less contested. Nineteenth- and twentieth-century struggles over space in Mumbai challenge these assumptions. Thus we can conclude that the city's early development was "driven by a host of select, private and often competing considerations" (Hazareesingh 2001, 254) and that its "government and municipal infrastructure expenditure . . . directed more readily towards the development of its commercial infrastructure than the improvement of its social conditions" (Chandavarkar 1994, 38).

Certainly the urban scenes I describe took place in a significantly different political economy and social context than today. Nineteenth-

and early twentieth-century "slum" demolitions took place in a context of colonial governmentality, rapid industrialization, and the emergence of a new indigenous public sphere, whereas contemporary evictions and elite efforts to remake public space take place in a postindustrial economy shaped by new discourses such as "good governance" and the fight against corruption. And yet in terms of the everyday life of the street, there are powerful parallels with the present. Across different political economic contexts spanning two and a half centuries, we see continuities of state practices, discourses, resistances, and critiques of the basis of urban citizenship. As I will show in the chapters that follow, we also see continuities in the frictions of urban transformation, as well as in ordinary encounters with state power—encounters characterized by compromise, co-option, and negotiation rather than the rational machinery of an anonymous bureaucracy. This raises important questions: How do we account for these continuities across different historical contexts? How much do theories of city making depend on assumptions of historical novelty? And, what are the implications of histories of spatial contestation for our understanding of the contemporary city?

Thinking about historical processes and contemporary contestations together challenges widely accepted accounts of city formation. It suggests that Mumbai's development is less a production of linear transformation and rupture—for instance, from colonial to postcolonial, welfarist to neoliberal, popular to elite—than a process of reappearance, slow accretion, and partiality.[26] Everyday urbanism is less a product of the grand transformations that dramatically remake the city than of the unactualized projects that represent historical continuities. Moreover, the emphasis on the novelty of evictions of the poor overlooks how spatial contestations today have been shaped by historical processes. Contemporary spatial conflicts in Mumbai should be understood in conversation with urban authorities' long, and still unresolved, struggles to impose a sense of order over an unruly city. Certainly spatial politics are informed by India's two-decade experiment with economic liberalization, but they are also shaped by the rise of Mumbai's linkages with global finance capital and trade in the late eighteenth century, the emergence of municipal governance in the mid-nineteenth century, and a prominent local bourgeois public sphere in the early twentieth. Contemporary processes are also shaped by significant moments left unexplored in this chapter, such as the 1975–1977 Emergency, early 1980s juridical activism, and the mid-1990s decentralization of urban governance in India.

The implications of the historical continuities of spatial contestations are threefold. First, the idea of the out-of-control city has persisted for over two centuries, and yet its meaning has shifted significantly. In the nineteenth century, Mumbai's problems of congestion, encroachments, and illegalities stood for colonial authorities' anxieties over tax collection and public health. In the twentieth, these same problems stood for middle-class anxieties over their lack of voice in municipal governance. The point is not that one replaced the other, but that new social imaginaries emerged to give what many considered the empirical realities of the city's unruly streets new meaning. In light of its historical antecedents, contemporary middle-class civic activism looks less like a process of transformation than a reemergence, and one that is informed by past practices as much as it seems to reinvent them. Rather than see contemporary middle-class frustrations and the authorities' inability to restrict unlicensed hawking, which I discuss in Chapter 5, as a new "assertive claims on public urban space" (Fernandes 2004, 2416)—for instance, linked with transnational trends toward gentrification of the urban core—we can instead see them as engaging in a conversation over how to inhabit and make claims on urban space that has spanned a century.

Second, as much as historical accounts challenge notions of neoliberalism's radical rupture, the unactualized plans of the politically dominant to remake the city—from colonial authorities' efforts to rationalize space to middle-class civic activists' efforts to control the streets—refuse explanatory frameworks premised on totalizing transformation. State efforts to reorder streets, remove slums, and control hawkers, like middle-class efforts to dominate the debate over urban affairs, were partial projects. Colonial municipal governments operated on uneven ground. Armed with the justificatory logic of modern public health, the nascent municipality was unable to transform the city in its image. Likewise, the persistently exasperated tone of letters to the *Bombay Chronicle* demonstrates that the vision of an ordered city was an aspiration rather than a fact. Reducing these interventions to a question of class position-ing overlooks the tenuousness of their claims, just as an emphasis on the rationality of governance rather than on its unactualized plans overlooks negotiations, compromises, and unevenness that characterized people's encounters with the state, the focus of Chapter 4.

Third, and perhaps most important, the historical continuities I de-scribe continue to shape contemporary experiences of the street. It was hawkers themselves who showed me the need to think in terms of a long slow boil of small conflicts rather than narratives of rupture and radical transformation. The incongruous legal, political, and social space hawkers inhabit—criminalized, yet a vital part of the city—highlights the partial-ity of the state's century-and-a-half-long effort to reorder and regulate the streets. Likewise, the persistence of the street as the primary space of trade despite the arrival of a globalized consumer aesthetic contradicts assumptions of the inexorable logic of neoliberal urbanism. Hawkers are concerned less with the imminent arrival of Walmart than with the operations of the municipal government and its effects on their ability to exercise citizenship rights and with their caricature in the press and by middle-class civic associations as an impediment to well-functioning public spaces. They understand their marginality to be a product of lay-ered phenomena. Nineteenth-century ideas of the city as a landscape of circulation (Vidler 1978) and streets as a clearly delineated domain of public practice have contributed to their marginalization as much as new phenomena such as the marketization of the state and emphasis on the city's global image. In other words, hawkers situate their precariousness in the lingering effects of modernist spatial imaginaries rather than in the doctrine of neoliberal globalization. I explore in the next chapter how hawkers make meaning of this urban palimpsest and how they navigate Mumbai's rapidly changing present.

CHAPTER 3

OCCUPIED STREETS

A RED UTILITY BOX and a crumbling boundary wall delineate Aamir's spot on the side of the road. He makes a living by reselling the old newspapers, books, bottles, and electronic items he purchases from residents of nearby apartment buildings. When people want to get rid of their recyclable material, they call him to their homes. Laden with big plastic bags on his bicycle handlebars, he returns to his spot on the side of the road, picks through old electronics for valuable parts, arranges bottles, and sorts newspapers by language—English papers here; Hindi, Marathi, and Gujarati ones there—getting them ready for resale to a trader who trucks the material out for processing. At the end of his workday, Aamir bundles the large objects under a tarp and walks to his home in a nearby *jhopadpatti* (slum settlement) where he stays with wife and three children.

Aamir is the neighborhood *raddiwala*, or scrap collector. He is a big man with a thick mustache and a vicelike handshake. He talks in a low rumble. He is also a fixture on the street. I am unable to walk by without offers of tea and gestures of invitation to sit on the ledge next to his work space; our conversation is sparse, but he is enormously generous with his time. I first met him in 2004 when one of his brothers, a vendor of breakfast snacks, introduced us while walking through the neighborhood. As I write this ten years later, Aamir occupies the same spot. Every evening he is there, sorting paper and bottles, taking apart electronics,

65

talking with friends, drinking tea, or watching the throb of traffic—cars, buses, autorickshaws, tow trucks, schoolchildren, office workers—go by. The best time to catch him is just after dusk, that time between dinner and the end of the workday when Mumbai's streets are at their liveliest. This is when children play outside, middle-aged men and women shop for the day's vegetables, and the elderly go for brisk walks. This is also the time when Aamir finishes his daily routine of buying waste and turning it into a commodity.[1] I had my camera with me one afternoon and took a picture of him posing with stacks of paper. Later I gave him a copy. He flashed his mild-mannered smile and displayed it on the brick wall behind him. Later that week, it was gone. I asked where it went, and he said it had vanished with a sudden gust of wind.

This chapter is about people like Aamir and the streetscapes they produce. It focuses on three questions: How should we interpret public spaces that are fluid, densely used, and intensely contested? What are the methodologies available to "read" these street scenes? And how might the way hawkers inhabit these spaces offer an alternative to these methodologies?

Aamir's place on the street can be read in multiple ways. From the window of a passing taxi or the view of the casual observer, he might present a paradigmatic image of the city in the developing world: a jumble of crumbling infrastructure, trash, and underemployed men loitering on the street. He sits on the ground amid the detritus of the apartments surrounding him. At his feet is the debris of road construction, concrete rubble, and dirt. Cement planks unevenly cover a drain. A thick tangle of cables erupts from the asphalt. A waist-high brick wall with chipped plaster veneer flanks his back.

A viewer with an eye for architecture might see something else: a forgotten patch of sidewalk transformed into a work space; a single node in a vast, decentralized recycling system; or a reappropriation of a poorly planned sidewalk by a marginal citizen in search of livelihood. If that viewer looked closer, she might see the shifting tableaux of items that adorn Aamir's space on the side of the road. A discarded picture frame, a broken clock, and an electrician's light switch display are hanging on the wall behind him. A plastic bag is casually placed on a hook. Another small clock sits on top of a broken shelf behind his weighing scale. On some days, Bollywood gossip magazines decorate the tree. That observer might notice that Aamir does not only work in this space; he dwells there too. This is not just occupied space, but a space that has been domesticated in a very particular way.

A viewer alert to power inequalities might interpret this scene in yet another way. She might respond to the last viewer by saying that although Aamir may domesticate his space, it is not really his in the first place. His spatial claims are tenuous, and he constantly faces the threat of eviction. Indeed, he lacks a hawker's license, and police and municipal workers demand money from him regularly. Trucks from the BMC antiencroachment department descend on the street nearly every week. His unauthorized presence on the street makes him an outlaw. As Aamir himself says, "I work all day collecting paper from people in this neighborhood. But because I sit on the road, I am treated like a criminal." Aamir must also deal with a residents' association that is famously hostile to hawkers. Being treated "like a criminal" has financial ramifications too. Aamir wastes many hours looking out for the gray BMC trucks that carry out raids on hawkers. He keeps his work space small out of fear of attracting too much attention. Lack of storage space greatly reduces his profit potential. Not only must he limit how much he can collect each day, but when paper prices are low, he cannot wait for a more profitable time to sell.

And finally, a viewer interested in Aamir's agency within this unequal power dynamic might see something else: Aamir is marginalized but not abject. He does not inhabit a condition of "advanced marginality" (Wacquant 2008). Despite lacking a license, he has successfully resisted a residents' association's attempt to evict him. Aamir establishes de facto rights to his spot on the road by cultivating relationships with state functionaries, shopkeepers, and nearby residents. To them, his family's four-decade presence on this same street legitimates his personal claims to the space. He also serves as the informal leader of hawkers in the area, negotiating with municipal workers in the aftermath of a raid and helping others get their confiscated goods back. State functionaries who walk the streets in that neighborhood respect him. Some might even fear his potential political power. He alluded to this on the day when we chatted about his work space. A hawker union certificate hung on the wall behind him. I asked about it, and he said with a smile, "That's my hawk-ers' license." This joke played off his contradictory presence on the road: simultaneously outside the law and enmeshed with the state, simultane-ously part of the neighborhood and an outsider to it.

ANTINOMIES OF THE URBAN

I present these four interpretations of Aamir's scene in order to highlight a problem in interpretations of streetscapes and the worlds of informal practice that produce them. Should we focus on sensory experience, af-fect, and architectural form? Or, alternatively, should we highlight power imbalances, structural inequality, and the way transnational and global processes shape urban environments? Ethnography of unlicensed street vending seems to call for all of these perspectives. And yet in scholarly conversations on the city, we are often called on to take sides. You are either in one camp, or the other; we either read Aamir's street scene as an instance of reimagined and reappropriated urban space, or an example of marginalization; we either read Aamir's presence on the side of the road as constituting a set of unique spatial practices, or as a sign of a broader socioeconomic condition.

Where one stands depends on what "informal urbanism" is taken to mean. Broadly, the term refers to the implicit, casual, make-do, and some-times illicit worlds that swirl around the taken-for-granted, institutional-ized, and legal city.[2] This is the understanding of informality that is found in writings by architects and designers, as well as in journalistic and blog-gers' accounts of cities in the Global South. This marks a significant shift from earlier interpretations of fluid streets. Writings on informal urban-ism since the late 1990s are significant because they have expanded the category of "informality" beyond its former focus on nonwage labor of the urban poor (Hart 1973) to encompass its unrecognized spatial and architectural practices. However, these writings also raise new questions. When the term *informality* is used, does it index a particular relationship to the built environment, an aesthetic sensibility, a legal condition, a sign of urban governance priorities, or an effect of structural inequality?

The confusion over informality reflects an unspoken tension between two ways of seeing the city. The first sees the city as a site of affective experience. This perspective emphasizes form and visuality: the realm of small minutiae, experience, and "tactics" (de Certeau 1984)—that is, the feeling and experience of being there. It is a perspective founded in Baudelaire's representations of Paris in the nineteenth century and informs contemporary literary writings such as Teju Cole's *Open City* (2012) and Aman Sethi's *A Free Man* (2013), as well as scholarly writings such as AbdouMaliq Simone's *For the City Yet to Come* (2004) and Ato Quayson's *Oxford St., Accra* (2014). Its goal is not to explain but to conjure a world through an invocation of the senses. Thus, it can produce depictions of urban dystopia or its opposite. Consider these two accounts:

> Just stepping out on the streets can be a difficult ordeal. The air smells like twice-baked urine, marinated in more urine. The sidewalks are a slalom of legless beggars and feral dogs. Hundreds of times each day you walk right past something so unfathomably sad, so incomprehensibly surreal, so horribly unfair. (Stevenson 2004)

> I began to look beyond the immensity of the slum societies, and to see the people who lived within them. A woman . . . bathed her children with water from a copper dish. . . . Men made repairs to one of the huts. And everywhere I looked, people smiled and laughed. . . . I looked at the people, then, and I saw how *busy* they were—how much industry and energy described their lives. (Roberts 2004, 7–8)

Both writings emphasize the affective life of city streets and public spaces, as well as its imaginaries. They attempt to explore the urban underbelly as well as the more privileged social worlds that intersect it. They produce a range of sensations, from disgust to sympathy and understanding.

By contrast, the second perspective on informality sees urban spaces as manifestations of political economic processes. It emphasizes the embeddedness of power in urban space. Its focus is often on new forms of social segregation and policing, especially as they are manifest in commercial spaces such as shopping malls and luxury complexes. For instance, a waterfront redevelopment project is framed as the "hallmark of the postindustrial city" that "signal[s] a new type of consumer culture"

(Anwar and Viqar 2014, 329). These developments are said to exhibit a "spatial logic that governs the meaning and organization of urban space" and "endeavours to produce a 'sanitized' and 'secure' cosmopolitan city" (328). This is the realm of explicit analysis of underlying trends and abstractions, such as "city of walls" (Caldeira 2000) and "military urbanism" (Graham 2010), which highlight underlying power inequalities and connections with regional and global processes.

My point is not to say that these ways of seeing the city produce inaccuracies but that they highlight certain experiences over others. Most important, both ways of seeing the city produce their own urban mythologies. When applied to Mumbai, they produce images of urban dystopia, neoliberal exclusion, or, alternatively, the enterprising poor. Aamir, from these perspectives, represents Third World squalor or Third World ingenuity—a marginalized underclass or a politically savvy subaltern. Even when these perspectives do not exist in such stark binary terms, their traces can be found in a range of scholarship and literature on the city. I suggest that rather than choose one over the other, we should highlight the unresolved tension between these two interpretive paradigms. I emphasize their differences in order to explore a potential alternative.

This then becomes a question of how to read the city. How do we interpret what people say and make meaning from what people do? What can we infer from changes in physical landscapes? Does attention to affective experience preclude an understanding of power, inequalities, and transnational processes?[3] Since these questions ultimately hinge on form and genre, it is helpful to see how literary critics address them. Frederic Jameson's writing on literary realism addresses a similar tension between an affective and explanatory mode of analysis. He argues that realist literature contains two drives, or "impulse[s]" (Jameson 2013, 10): the need to tell the story—the "tale"—and the need to describe the scene—the "representation of affect." These two impulses "are never reconciled, never fold back into one another in some ultimate reconciliation" (11). Instead, the conflict constitutes the genre itself: "What we call realism will thus come into being in the symbiosis of this pure form of storytelling with impulses of scenic elaboration, description and above all affective investment" (11). Jameson emphasizes the productive tension between these two opposed perspectives; difference is not a problem but is generative.

Could we say something similar about ethnographies of the city? While irreducible to the novel form, they do contain a realist impulse. Realism is not verisimilitude but writing that enacts the real. The past three decades of experimentation in writerly style within anthropology have shown the possibilities for this enactment beyond a naive, unmediated empiricism, even while retaining the goal of capturing experience.[4] We might thus see ethnographies as similarly constituted by two impulses that exist in tension: the need to describe the sensory experience of a place—Jameson's "scene"—and explain their underlying meaning—Jameson's "storytelling." In some instances, these two impulses coexist. But more often, they exist in conflict. The assumption is that the ethnographer must choose one side: describe the affect or feel of a place or how that place is being shaped by national and global political economic phenomena; describe what it is like to be in a city, or the structures of power that underlies these experiences; describe the kinds of reinterpretations of space hawkers and squatters enact, or the injustices that require these practices in the first place.

The multiple interpretations of Aamir represent these different perspectives. They show how the tension between affect and analysis—between the "scene" of the urban landscape and its imaginaries, the "tale" of the urban theory and its politics—is a tension between the feeling of being there and the interpretation of what is really going on. Jameson's work suggests that we do not need to choose one side of this binary or search for a middle ground in describing the reality of the city. Instead, the binary itself is productive. Rather than two opposing camps, these perspectives themselves constitute a world-making dialectic; they are the antinomies that make the urban.

This chapter is about how hawkers occupy the street and how to interpret this occupation, arguing that the story of informal urbanism lies at the crux of this urban antinomy. This perspective provides a way of understanding the affective experience of informality without ignoring the inequalities and power imbalances that underlie it. Moreover, focusing on the antinomies of the urban allows the reader to maintain a critical eye on urban processes without losing the feel of the place.

It was, after all, the feel of the place that drew me to the street. Stories of corruption, citizenship, political subjectivity, and "world-class city" formation came later.

PUBLIC SERVICE

Mumbai's street-side vegetable markets present a scene of sensory juxtapositions. Consider Neeraj's spot on a street in northwest Mumbai: a sea of fresh green leaves against a decaying industrial gray backdrop, rich earthy fragrances mingling with dense plumes of exhaust smoke, the calm of vendors carefully arranging vegetables in neat patterns amid the frenetic rush of pedestrians and the blare of horns from cars, buses, and trucks.

When I first met Neeraj, I remember being enticed by the dense fragrance of herbs emanating from his spot on the side of the road. He sat behind massive heaps of luscious green coriander, mint, and spring onions. A dense thicket of curry leaf branches lay scattered to his side. As the bustle of street life swirled around him, he calmly picked through coriander, searching for rotten leaves before artfully arranging the stems in concentric circles. I was attracted to the rich brown glint of moist earth clinging to the roots—a sign of their recent arrival from nearby farms, a marker of difference from the sterilized aesthetic of the newly opened supermarket down the street called Big Bazaar.

The contrast between the street and the odorless, plastic-wrapped vegetables in the brightly lit, air-conditioned "showroom," as Neeraj called Big Bazaar, was striking. Earlier, a local hawker leader took me on a tour of Big Bazaar to show me the difference between produce sold on the street and produce sold in the supermarket. Indeed, enclosed in plastic wrap and under fluorescent lights, the vegetables looked lifeless. He picked up a cucumber: "Look at this; it has become completely dry." Yellowish cucumbers and wrinkled tomatoes were the price to pay for air-conditioning and checkout lines, it seemed. Outside, he stopped by a hawker stall, grabbed a long green squash, sliced it open, and smiled as small beads of water glistened on its surface.

And yet aestheticizing street scenes has its limitations. It can lead one to overlook the labor required to produce and maintain the sense of lushness. The rich sensory experience of the earthy smell of herbs, the neatly piled mounds of vegetables, the freshness, the visual appeal, and the long-term presence on the side of the road are all forms of unrelenting, and often unpleasant, work.

"Our work is difficult and it is dirty," says Neeraj's neighbor, Anuj, a tomato vendor, as we sit on the road drinking tea. "Look at this shirt; see all the dirt on it. This comes from lifting the crates, moving the tomatoes, washing them, sitting all day outside in the sunshine, sweating. It is dangerous work too. We sit next to this busy road. If a car goes out of control and swerves off the road, who does it hit? It hits us." Our conversation gets cut short when a small truck arrives. Tomatoes from Nasik, he tells me. As a small-scale distributor and hawker, he deals in huge quantities. He gulps his tea and checks on the delivery. A half a dozen 50 kilogram crates are swiftly unloaded to the side of the road before the truck trundles off.

Neeraj's daily schedule is grueling. He regularly wakes at 2:00 a.m. in order to get to the wholesale market in Vashi, New Mumbai, in time for the presunrise trading session.[5] Sleep is irregular for him. Three hours in the dusty cargo bay of a truck often follow twelve on the street. Refrigeration—on the street, among semidistributors such as Neeraj, or at the Vashi market—is not common, so whatever is left unsold at the end of the day gets passed on to a secondary market, often dominated by near-destitute elderly people who sell it at sharply reduced prices. Neeraj credits his customers' discerning taste and his personal sense of ethics for this difficult daily routine. To maintain a steady supply of fresh vegetables, Neeraj and most of his colleagues go to Vashi for produce almost every night, while others travel to farms in places like Palghar, on the city's outskirts, for slightly better deals.

"When do you sleep?" I ask. "I never do," he replies.

His tomato delivery done, Anuj rejoins the conversation. We're standing on the side of the road next to Neeraj's bushels of coriander. I'm attracted to the smell and the image of thousands of hawkers weaving through the city as it sleeps. I announce that I'd like to go visit the wholesale market in Vashi. Neeraj is used to my presence and unlikely questions, but this one worries him. I shouldn't go, he says; the journey is long and difficult. Anuj cuts in, and the two argue over the risks and benefits of my going. Anuj explains to his friend that I am like a journalist, "so he

FIGURE 3.1 *Vegetable vendors waiting for customers in the late afternoon*

should see, and share with others, how difficult hawkers' work is, how difficult their lives are." But Neeraj has other concerns. He is worried about my safety. Strange things happen on these journeys through the city in the middle of the night. Drivers fall asleep behind the wheel. If there is an accident and something happens to me, hawkers will be held responsible, he says. He urges me to take a bus and arrive at a decent time later in the day.

A week later, I find myself sitting in the muddy cargo bay of a vegetable truck bouncing through the deserted city. Anuj won the argument and made arrangements for me to catch a truck heading to Vashi. It is 3:00 a.m. Nine men and women are scattered around me, unmoved by my presence. Some sit against the empty crates. I caught up with these hawkers from the side of a highway in the city's far northwest suburbs. I join those trying to sleep on the floor, but it is wet and the metal ridges unyielding. I try softening it with a patch of plastic, but there is no overcoming the fact that this space is meant to carry goods, not people. When the truck trundles over potholes, we are shaken violently awake with a thunderous noise. Frequent sudden stops have us tossing into each other like loose onions. An hour into the trip, an autorickshaw cuts us off. The truck driver slams on the brakes, causing us to swerve for thirty feet, makes a U-turn in wild pursuit, catches up to the driver, yells at him for a minute, and abruptly returns to the highway. Twenty minutes later, we join the mini-convoy of trucks crossing the bridge over Thane Creek leading to New Mumbai and the Vashi market.

We pass neighborhoods lined with shuttered shops, dark apartment buildings, and rows of parked cars. Even the dogs that own the night are curled up asleep on the curb. But at the market, time seems to be inverted. It buzzes like a mini-city amid a bleak moonscape. Trucks ring the outer edges, their noses pointing out, as if eager to disgorge their innards before starting their long journey home—to Maharashtra's hinterland, as well as more distant towns and villages in Karnataka and Madhya Pradesh. Dozens of small tea, vada pao, and breakfast shops do brisk business. Inside, skinny porters (*mathadi* workers, as they are called) run from trucks carrying 50 kilogram sacks of vegetables on their shoulders like little missiles darting between the tiny aisles. Sturdy, well-to-do traders preside over small stalls (*galas*) stacked high with canvas bags of produce. A small cut is made in one bag, a handful of vegetables—baby eggplant, cucumbers, bitter gourd, and okra—presented as samples on small piles on top. Hawkers such as Neeraj, distributors, hotel commissaries, and caterers form small circles around the traders. Bids are made with silent hand signals. A clap, a quick handshake, and in a flash, the canvas sacks are hauled to the small trucks heading back to the city and its thousands of street markets, restaurants, and hotels.

Neeraj starts the day with three hundred bunches of coriander, a massive thicket of curry leaf branches, and dozens of bundles of mint and green onions. When we last spoke, he sold coriander for Rs 15 a bundle. Few customers haggle. Fixed price, he tells me. His customers are savvy businesswomen—often part-time vendors themselves or owners of small shops in the jhopadpattis nearby. Sometimes they are women from neighboring middle-class housing blocks who closely follow the fluctuating prices of vegetables in the newspaper. Like other vegetable hawkers in the city, he gives away Rs 200 worth of curry *pata*, or curry leaves, for free each day. Like many of his colleagues, he calls this "public *seva*," or public service—the same language he uses to describe his regular trips to Vashi in the middle of the night. The "public" won't go to Vashi, he says, so he goes there for them.

Like most publics, Neeraj's is delimited. Roughly a third of his customers are middle-class men and women walking home from the nearby commuter station. The other two-thirds are women traders who resell his produce in the nearby jhopadpattis. Neeraj and the small-scale traders who buy from him represent the city's socioeconomic margins. However, there are other populations who live at the margins of these margins: the men and women who sell the day-old vegetables that Neeraj and his customers reject, as well as the communities living on the edges of more established jhopadpattis, on forest land—people who inhabit the extreme end of Mumbai's spectrum of graduated illegalities. These are people who live beyond the bustling station road, the new supermarket, the new high-rise complex, beyond the huts constructed of concrete and iron sheets, with pipes and electricity service, up the hills and beyond a creek. They are the ones living on the end of the city's edge, in small clusters of tents made of black plastic, without access to water or electricity. There, one finds the people outside Neeraj's "public." These are people like Yadav, a vendor of fruits that look older, bruised, and are covered in flies—characteristics unheard of in most of the city. Yadav is among the lucky few with access to a man who rents handcarts for Rs 20 a day. A broken fence marks the end of municipal authority. This is the domain of the *forestwale* (officials from the forestry department), he says. The people are poorer here, he continues, and "so I buy less."

There is a bit of an irony in that the freshness that Neeraj's customers expect (and to what Neeraj attributes his taxing work schedule) is precisely the quality that has only recently been discovered by alternative food buyers in North America. Neeraj is part of a vast, decentralized food distribution system; he sells vegetables that are rarely more than a day old and often purchased from traders who work directly with farm cooperatives. His stall offers a rich sensory experience—deep green color and rich fragrance—personal contact with customers, and the quirky "irregulari-

FIGURE 3.2 *Selling onions and potatoes to commuters in the early evening*

ties," such as clumps of dirt clinging to roots, that discerning urban professionals in North America have valued as signs of quality and authentic connections with the land (Paxson 2013). The street-side vegetable market represents an aesthetic valorized among critics of industrial agriculture in the West—such as by "slow food," "locavore," "farm-to-table dining," and even farmers' market advocates—even though, by squatting illegally on the street, he does not quite conform to it.

While the farmers' market phenomenon has appeared in Mumbai, there is a sense among street vendors that their work still represents underdevelopment. When his friends joined me, they would pepper me with questions about markets in the United States. They asked where vegetables were sold, but they knew the answer: not on the streets but in places like Big Bazaar. They had not been inside the supermarket, but their union leader had and told them about it. This was a "showroom," like a showroom for cars, with vegetables for sale in a brightly lit, air-conditioned environment. To Neeraj and his friends, the showroom style represented a possible future. He tells me that we should go back to the United States together and open a vegetable showroom there.

MUSIC LESSONS

My cell phone rings as I am being swept along with a flood of commuters outside one of Mumbai's busiest commuter stations. I am on my way home after spending the afternoon with Neeraj and his friends. The streets pulsate. People crowd around small stalls selling fresh juice, vada pao, and samosas. A man rapidly dips little puris into a big metal pot of spiced water and hands them to customers. As the sun sets, small light bulbs strung up on trees, road signs, and shop awnings light the side of the road, shining down on small pyramids of papayas, pears, apples, and sweet lime. A gray BMC antiencroachment truck is parked on a corner, its cargo bay open, empty, and ready. Young couples spill out of McDonald's licking ice cream cones. Dozens of autorickshaws jostle for space. Double-decker buses tower over the crowd, their drivers desperately trying to honk their way through the crush of humanity. Bells attached to a sugarcane crushing machine chime *tring tring tring*, keeping the beat above the din.

I extract myself from the crowd, catch my breath, and answer the phone. It is Ali, asking to have tea. Ali is a hawker, an entrepreneur, a sharp political critic, a conspiracy theorist, and, as I was soon to find out, an amateur musician. Unlike his colleagues on the street, he doesn't stick to one trade, sometimes selling old newspapers, at other times *idli* and *medhu vada*, popular South Indian breakfast snacks. As usual, I find him near Aamir's spot by the side of the road, standing next to the low wall separating the road from a small hardware store, a small *kinara*, or general store, and a doctor's office. He looks anxious, brooding, and burdened. We forget about the tea—I am jittery from the many cups Neeraj's friends plied me with all afternoon anyway—and walk through the neighborhood until we find a quiet place to sit. We squeeze together on a moss-covered bench and he leans over to confide that playing the piano is his true passion. For years he took lessons as a hobby, but now business is slow and he can no longer afford such luxuries, he tells me. Pausing, he nervously looks around and abruptly changes the subject. There is more to daily skirmishes between hawkers and the BMC, he whispers. "The biggest fight is with the Shiv Sena. Now it has simmered down [*thanda ho gaya*] [but before] . . . it was even bigger than the hawkers' issue. They are against all outsiders—people from Bihar, UP, Chennai . . . you." As a Jewish American, I was not quite a target of Shiv Sena's vitriol against Muslims and non-Maharashtrians. He knew that, so I listened on without correcting him, appreciating his generous attempt to bring me into his world.

We get up from the moss-covered bench, walk past crumbling gray walls encircling housing compounds, a dusty old playground brought to life by the exuberance of a dozen children, and a market abutting a fetid canal. As we walk, he offers a meandering commentary on how the city is and should be. The objects we pass on the side of the road—a plastic blue awning, a chair, a sign board, a crate of bananas, and a fresh juice kiosk—elicit stories of encroachment, occupancy, illegalities, and propriety. He points to a shop whose awning illegally stretches out over the sidewalk, a sweets maker who scatters plastic chairs on the road in front, phone operator booths that block the sidewalk, and semipermanent milk stalls jutting into the road that are protected by a local politician. "This is wrong, they shouldn't be here, but over there," showing spots that might not block pedestrian movement. A middle-aged man sits inconspicuously against a wall, hunched over a small outcropping and picking through little jars. He once had a large and thriving paan stall, Ali says as we walk by, but his business was crushed by repeated demolitions. His back was irreparably damaged from the many swift escapes he had to make ahead of BMC raids. What remains of his stall—a small briefcase—is a compromise worked out with local BMC workers.

Next to him, a women with a gaunt, weathered face weaves elaborate garlands. Her husband passed away recently, and this small business is all she has to support herself, Ali says. A blue awning provides some shade. When it rains, she offers space under the awning to the *paanwala*, as vendors of paan and cigarettes are called. The demolition workers seem to recognize her precarity and keep away, offering both of them respite. We cross the street and pass by a wooden crate where a once thriving fruit stall was replaced by a pot of tea on a small camping burner. The proprietor, an elderly woman with a perpetual smile, is a favorite among autorickshaw drivers and, for that reason, is also a frequent target of the residents' association. She does not have a license, Ali says, but her brother has ration and election cards with their address written on it. "Why can't she sell bananas? She is a resident too."

We turn a corner. The crowd grows thicker as we near the local train station. We are forced into traffic because the side of the road is blocked by a tangled mess of broken wood, signs, beams, and overturned handcarts. "Look at this mess," he says. "The BMC tells us to keep our area clean. 'Don't have any garbage around.' [But] they are the ones making the most garbage. . . . Take a picture and put it in your book and show who makes the most garbage in this city!" Wary of the attention my camera invariably causes, I take a blurry photo and quickly tuck my camera into my backpack. We are standing in the road, and in front us is the local godown, or warehouse for the BMC's antiencroachment department. Big open doors provide a view of the confiscated goods and a window into the inner workings of the local government. We peek inside and see a large pile of wood, twisted bits of metal, and handcarts. "Chinese Kitchen" is painted in red on a small broken sign.

The rubble from past demolitions spills out onto the street, and a narrow path leading to the godown entrance is carved through it: anti-encroachment officials encroaching on the road. To Ali, this is a delicious irony that he was eager to show me. But as we walk around the neighborhood, I hear echoes of the slippage between physical and moral disorder that often makes hawkers into an urban menace. We walk past a day care center with large windows facing the street. During the day, the space is used for children, Ali says. But in the evening, theater actors—men and women alike—use this space to practice. And then he adds something unsettling: "They kiss and act in ways that are not good for the neighborhood." The language of disorder abounds.

Over the following days, we take more walks through the neighborhood. As we wander, he tells tales of corruption, conspiracies, and the lingering echo of incomplete state projects, plans, and promises. These stories were often interrupted. Sometimes they ended without conclusions. They often extended over several days and wove together different narrative threads. Sometimes, days later, he picked up earlier themes, making his account a challenge to record.

On one day, he describes urban space as a tangled web of relationships, forces, and scandal, some of which works for marginal populations like hawkers, while others do not. Where a hotel now stands, there was once a private hospital, he tells me:

> Its owner was accused of illicit organ trafficking so he converted it into a hotel. He paid the BMC five lakhs [Rs 500,000] to evict hawkers from a nearby street so guests could have more parking. The local residents' welfare association, in cahoots with the hotel owner, used membership fees to bribe the BMC too. When people found out that their membership fees were being used to evict hawkers, they confronted the association president. "We didn't give you money to kick out hawkers," they said. You see, people in this area are mostly vegetarian, so they don't go to the old municipal market, which sells meat, chicken, and fish. We only sell vegetables, so there shouldn't be a problem. But the president didn't take responsibility. He blamed the BMC and Supreme Court.
>
> After the demolitions, the police came on patrol five times a day. We met with the inspector, who assured us things would be fine. But the association

offered him a one lakh [Rs 100,000] bribe, and he took it [*usne paise khaya*]. The BMC does not kick the hawkers off sidewalks all in one go. They do it a little at a time. They kick some of us off of one road and at the same time tell others they are okay, they can stay. That way all the hawkers are not united. [We pass a half-built municipal market in the shadow of a busy overpass. Families camp out in the space. A woman boils rice over a small fire. Clothes, a plastic tarp, and a small hammock for a sleeping baby hang from metal frames.]

Hawkers were supposed to be shifted here from congested streets near a train station. Before it got completed, residents from the adjacent housing society learned about the plan and pressured the BMC to get it stopped. They were worried that the whole area would become a hawking zone. The government gave a family living like this a decent place in Vasai. The night they moved, someone else came. Now the BMC dumps wood here after trimming trees. The government doesn't have strength [*himmat*]. . . . Hawking is difficult. The government tried it [running hawkers' stalls] once but failed. Businessmen also tried to sell vegetables in showrooms, but that failed as well. You can't sell things while sitting in front of a computer.

We are born poor, is that a crime? We too are human, right? Can't the United States government do something for us after reading your book? Write a letter in support of the hawkers on your university stationary. Write to Manmohan Singh [the prime minister at the time]. Can you do it?

No, I say, trying to explain my limited power as a researcher. He politely said he understood, but I could see his patience running thin.

Six years later, I am standing with Ali on the side of the road. We had seen each other off and on since those neighborhood walks, but had not had a significant conversation since then. As usual, we sip tea as the early evening traffic flows by. I note the changing streetscape. A man in a greasy white T-shirt deep-fries pakodas, a mix of onions and chickpea flour in a big black *kadai* perched on the curb. Much to the delight of the vegetable vendors, a poorly designed fence installed to keep pedestrians out of traffic (but inadvertently rendering the road edge off-limits to pedestrians and hawkers alike) had been removed. I also note new symbioses: in a metal stall once used to sell shoes, an elderly tailor sits beside a sewing machine, taking advantage of the legal leeway the BMC allows shoe repairmen. A man prepares a sandwich—slicing cucumbers, tomatoes, and onions—on a wooden board propped on stacks of old tires. The tire repairman sits by his side, reading a newspaper.

Ali asks about my book. "How many pages is it?" "Two hundred and fifty," I say, taking what was, at the time, a wild guess. "My story can take up fifty pages. All of it true," he says. He then proceeds to share some of that story with me, talking about growing up in the neighborhood. He was born near the temple across the street, he says, and now lives in a *chawl*. Not a slum, he clarifies: "A chawl is ordered, but a jhopadpatti has little lanes that go here and there." Six years earlier, he left himself out of his neighborhood narratives. I took it as a sign that he did not want to discuss his personal life then, and so I did not pursue it. Now he weaves his personal biography into the neighborhood's complex web of occupancy and relationships—a web that, he explained to me earlier, subtly produces the neighborhood.

His father figures prominently in the account. "He ran vegetable business in this area fifty years ago. Everyone in the area knew him. People would call him over to their house to bring vegetables. He also hawked on the road. It was a nice business." Ali points to a small patch of concrete down the road where a middle-aged woman sold an assortment of leafy greens. "For fifty years, he worked here. He was eighty when he died. That woman works there now." He suggested that this legitimized his presence on the side of the road, allowing him to claim these spaces in the absence of official recognition.

But what potential do these claims have? Who recognizes them, and what power do they have? At the narrative's end, Ali asks, as he often had before, "What can be done?" I understand what he is saying but am reluctant to respond, hoping he might answer the question himself. I ask him to repeat the question. Again he says, "What should be done? What can you do [to solve the *pareshani*, that is, the harassment the hawkers experience]?" Despite stalling, I know I have to give an answer. I say, "For ten years, the residents' association has been trying to get rid of you, but you are still here. That is a kind of victory, no?" As I speak, I can see Ali's displeasure. His dreams are bigger than small concessions acquired through slow encroachment and negotiations with state functionaries. He wants an end to the long-running simmering tension found on the street. Instead of informal rights, he talks in institutional terms, such as about the responsibilities of those in power toward people such as himself who are struggling to survive on the margins. "I want to say to the chief minister, what is your responsibility? What are we supposed to do? Should we take up crime? Should we kill ourselves? What is your responsibility as a politician?" Again, I tell him that I see things differently. People in power talk about clean cities and sidewalks without hawkers. *And yet, you are still here.* There is something unsatisfying about that. Instead of slow accumulation of small spatial rights, he sees a slow bloodletting.

PUBLIC LIFE

"Take a picture!" Syed tells me. I oblige. I point into the jewelry store in front of us. Syed wants me to photograph the shopkeeper inside—a quiet, middle-aged man widely known as a friend of hawkers. We catch him off-guard in a moment of reverie. He is leaning back with his foot perched on the counter, his hands casually placed behind his head. I take a photo and note how different the man's quiet confidence is from the anxious condition of hawkers out front. But Syed's friend offers another interpretation. He tells me their worlds are intertwined: "The shopkeepers worry. If we move from the front of their shops, then who will stop the thieves? If there is a hawker on the footpath, the thief will think, 'How will I manage to escape?' We are a kind of protection for them. If there is a robbery, we will yell out, create a scene, and catch the thief. But if we are not sitting in front [of their store], then it will be easier for them to rob the store and run away."

We are standing on the sidewalk facing this small jewelry store. Syed's brother, Ali, is with us, along with two of his friends, Ubaid and Salim, both full-time street vendors. Ubaid sells used cassette tapes. During Ramzan (Ramadan) he sells kebabs along with the dozens of other food vendors who set up during the holiday. Syed sells sandals and women's accessories. On other days, Syed sells belts and small household items— whatever seems most profitable at the time. His display shows hair clips of multiple designs and colors he buys for Rs 4 and sells for Rs 5. In a week, he can sell a few thousand: "Look at these pieces, how can they make them so cheaply? Made of so many different parts and materials." Recently, he has switched entirely to selling cheap goods imported from China. Impossibly cheap. Holding up a Rs 5 cigarette lighter, Syed tells me, "Even the fuel inside should cost more than that."

The goods are cheap luxuries, affordable to the largely working-class customers who pass through the area. Syed knows his customers well, remembering what they bought in the past and what they want in the future. He is attractive, smiles brightly, and doesn't push the sale. Many customers seem to seek him out. The well-off ones buy dozens of items at a time. A woman stops by once a week and, with a cell phone in her ear, buys hundreds of rupees worth of goods. He overhears her talking about his merchandise on the phone and speculates that she is taking orders from relatives abroad. These purchases are "gifts from god."

I spent time with Syed and his friends in order to understand how they inhabit a condition of legitimized illegality—criminalized but central to the ordinary life of the city. Hawkers like Syed spoke about this condition indirectly. They spoke in terms of enmeshment, history, and entitlement. They spoke as well in terms of imaginative kinship—that jewelry store owner, "he's my uncle!"—of unlikely alliances with small shopkeepers who find their presence comforting, of passing autorickshaw drivers who gesticulate wildly when an antiencroachment truck is on its way to evict hawkers, and of well-connected shopkeepers who mediate conflicts with the BMC: "The shopkeepers come to us if they want help. They ask us to do small work for them. [In return] they take our side when the BMC comes. They tell the BMC, 'If you don't trouble the big shops, why do you trouble these small time hawkers?' Sometimes . . . [as a result of these interventions] the BMC gets ashamed and stops troubling us for some time."

Syed and his friends also live in a condition one might call "legitimately illegal." They lack formal claims to their spot on the road, but their presence on the road is widely recognized. "Either we are here or no one is here. If we are moved from this spot, no one else can come," says Syed. Ironically, BMC hawker eradication drives, or "actions," as they are called, validate his claim. Every few weeks, with terrifying swiftness, the BMC clears hawkers off this street. But rather than create a clean slate, invisible lines delineating ownership remain. Even if it takes days of waiting, hawkers return to the same place as before.

Rather than a space of competition and conflict among hawkers and shopkeepers, the street is shaped by dense webs of relationships. Syed's father worked at the same spot for thirty years. Syed grew up on this street, and shopkeepers and residents know him well. The low-level state functionaries who work in the area are familiar with him. I saw this one afternoon when three men, whom I later learned worked for the state electricity firm, stopped by Syed's stall. They had come to chat about the small switch boxes he and his colleagues cluster around. However, sensing the opportunity for a good joke, Syed gently nudged them behind his table and asked me to take a photo. Syed's friends gathered around to see this unlikely sight of men with coveted *sarkari*, or government, work standing on the street like a hawker. Syed prides himself on the extensive network of state functionaries he has cultivated over the years. "I know all of them, every government official," he says as the men walk away.

But most important, Syed reads the street and the web of sociality, work, and state practices that produce it, knowing when to assert himself and when to subtly disappear. During quiet afternoons, he blends into the backdrop of the street. At other moments, he is the center of attention. This is especially the case during the month of Ramzan, when Syed and his colleagues become the focal point of evening festivities. As in most of Mumbai's Muslim-majority neighborhoods, men and women of all ages and backgrounds crowd the street in the early evenings of Ramzan. Some come out for a casual stroll, others in search of a snack. Catering to this crowd, food vendors multiply during this time of year. Displays of steaming plates of keema samosas, kebabs of all kinds, and naan line the street alongside overflowing trays of popular sweets such as kheer, jalebi, and kulfi—all succulent and rich foods best enjoyed after a day of fasting.

On one night, while Syed and his friend Farooq, a shirt vendor, shared his sidewalk space with dozens of temporary food vendors, we had a wide-ranging conversation triggered by the carnival-like street scene and diversity of people passing by. At one point, after refusing the persistent demands of a musician beggar, Farooq tells me how during Ramzan the street is filled with legitimate, and quite a few illegitimate, beggars. Referring to the few people passing by asking for money, Farooq says, "They are young and healthy but put on a big show; they're not real beggars. We know who are the real [beggars] . . . those who need money but genuinely cannot work." Across the street we see a newly set up row of clothes' hawkers, and the conversation returns to the familiar theme of hawkers' battles with the municipality. "After a big fight with the BMC, they're back," Farooq says. "The BMC knows they cannot harass people and cause trouble while they are fasting; people's nerves are on edge."

As sunset nears, the two men pack away their merchandise and lay out pieces of fruit and pakodas on the table, and the neighboring kebab vendors gather around. An elderly man passing by is invited to join. Waiting for the moment to break the fast, the small group stands around the table of fruit. In contrast to the frenetic pedestrian activity and the noise and movements of a thoroughfare dense with car, bus, and autorickshaw traffic located a few feet to their rear, the group stands in quiet, thoughtful anticipation. Not having fasted myself, and thus lacking the others' sense of expectancy, I still appreciate this small moment of peace; the people standing around the table create a comforting island of tranquility amid the frenetic activity of the street. Finally, we hear the muezzin's call from the adjacent mosque sounding above the din of traffic and bus horns honking, and we all take a bite of fruit.

After this moment of relief passed, I took out my camera to photograph the event. It was an exceptional moment, and so I thought a picture was in order, but I did not get my camera out in time. Friends posed for a picture by each lifting a piece of fruit, reenacting in front of the camera the fast breaking of a few minutes earlier. After I took the photograph, Farooq reflected on the significance of holding festivals on the street. "It is nice to have iftar out in public, on the street, out in the open among people. Everyone is welcome to come and eat." It was the publicness of the celebration that made it notable. "In India, all people can partake in Ramzan, even Hindus. It is good that it is celebrated in public. In Pakistan, where it is all Muslim, religious holidays are celebrated in private, only with one's own." This was a comment driven not by nationalism but by an emphasis on locality; there is something unique about this place; sociality is embedded in street practice. Generalizations about Pakistan aside, of greater importance was Farooq's insight into the potential of public space. To him, it holds the possibility for healthy religious coexistence.

Farooq's comments also echoed the famous writings of Jane Jacobs (1961) and other critics of modernist urban planning, who argued that the health of public space is measured in the possibilities it offers for unexpected encounters and interactions among strangers. Yet at the same time, public space does not offer limitless possibility to Farooq and others like him. It has a moral quality as well that restricts behavior as much as it facilitates sociality. Thus there are "illegitimate" ways of being on the street, as revealed in his earlier comment on the beggars. Farooq's public is thus not infinitely expansive but is shaped by expression of religious identity. The dense mix of activities, moments of stoppages, dwelling in space, eating in public, to him signal the potential for cultural plurality.

On quieter evenings, when Syed's work slowed down before the evening rush, we would chat over tea provided by a friend who runs a tea stall nearby. Sitting in a small lane tucked off the main road, we could see the street coming to life as dusk settled into darkness. Buses packed with commuters make their dull honk—*buhn buhn buhn*—as they try to push through the standstill. Students and office workers make their way to the nearby train station, walking past brightly lit jewelry and clothing shops. A mother holds onto her small child while picking through leafy green vegetables with her free hand. Hawkers sit on the ground next to her, spreading their merchandise—cut watermelon, plastic household goods, bananas—on blue plastic tarp. Another vendor ties bags of oranges to an abandoned metal post. Another sells fried snacks. Young men stealthily sell pirated DVDs displayed on small metal tables. A paanwala works from a small nook in the wall. A single light bulb, its wire hastily connected to the adjacent shop, provides a dull yellow glow.

When we are done with our tea, we return to Syed's stall: a small metal table precariously wedged between the crumbling edge of a sidewalk and a well-trafficked arterial road. I ask about the condition of hawkers in the city. I use the Hindi word *sthiti*, to ask about the hawkers' condition (to which they would often respond, "Condition, what condition!"). Syed and his friends would frequently tell me that they yearn for something simple: "We just want to work in peace." They recount the daily harassment they face from the police and BMC. The more we talk, the more Syed speaks of other, more subtle forms of insecurity. He worries about rumors of road widening and the demolitions that will ensue. He speaks of the indirect ways he is denied full urban citizenship, the small indignities of working on the road, the constant threat of eviction, and the effect of religious and ethnic marginalization.

Syed turns to me. "They said they will make Shanghai; instead they made *kabristan* [a cemetery]," he says as we both stand on a sidewalk's edge, looking down the road where a BMC truck loomed in the distance. It was the third time the municipality had come for a demolition that week, and so it was with good reason that the mere sight of the gray truck filled Syed with apprehension. "The police blame us whenever something goes wrong. This city is full of criminals, but the government targets us. . . . The state treats us as if we are the biggest criminals . . . even though we are businessmen too."

Because traffic moves slowly on this narrow road, Syed and the other hawkers working nearby have enough time to pack up their goods at the sight of the municipal van. It takes thirty seconds to take down their displays. With the help of men loitering nearby—the young assistants, friends who had stopped by for a chat, and clerks from adjacent shops— a dozen tables and their goods are swiftly carried into one of the many small, partially hidden lanes off the main road and inaccessible to the large BMC trucks. With their tables safely stashed out of view, Syed and his friends stand and wait as the truck inches its way toward them. "The government's slogan used to be *Garibi Hatao* [Get rid of poverty]! But now it's become *garibon ko hatao* [Get rid of the poor]!" Syed adds with wit, inverting the well-known 1970s-era slogan associated with Prime Minister Indira Gandhi. At this point, the municipality truck arrives at the spot in front of us, only to continue down the road without incident. Syed tells me that it is probably headed for a demolition raid in a nearby neighborhood. A few moments later, the street is once again brimming with displays of household items for sale. Resuming his business, Syed tells me, "If not today, then tomorrow. They will come back." His friend turns to me and says, "They don't want us here, but where are we supposed to go? We are all from here; there is no other job. . . . They are against hawkers and against slums. . . . [But] we have rights to live as well."

He describes life as a perpetual series of stresses. Each time I see him, the tension on his face seems to have grown. He worries about demolitions and bribe demands. "The BMC and police are constantly bothering us, applying pressure, demanding money, threatening future evictions," he says. Adding to the stress are stories that circle back to him of hawker demolitions in neighborhoods elsewhere and rumors of big infrastructure projects that threaten to upend him, along with his hawker friends from the nearby streets. He tells me that his health is declining; breathing exhaust fumes is killing him. He has chest problems from spending twelve hours a day at the edge of a road clogged with traffic. Doctors' visits and medicines are costly. He needs a CT scan, he says, but that costs thousands of rupees, far beyond his budget. He has little faith in doctors anyway. "Nowadays no one studies for knowledge, but just to get ahead. They don't read books for learning but to get a degree and get a job. With his degree, the doctor can charge five hundred but the people without those degrees only two hundred."

As we spoke, a man dressed in the tattered clothes of an ascetic walks by. "Look at him," says Syed. "He has nothing, but he is happier. He is more at peace than I. He doesn't work. He just goes from here to there and begs. Sleeps at night wherever he happens to be. He is happy. He has no possessions, but he is happy." Syed plans to go visit the *dargah* (Sufi shrine) at Ajmer the following week. He hasn't been in over a dozen years, so he hopes this will help. Ajmer is special, he says; it is open to people of all religions and it makes no difference if you are high or low. When a minister comes, he must keep his bodyguards, armed with machine guns, outside. That is how special a place it is.

"We are not new to this road. We have been [hawking] here for fifteen years," says Farooq, who works near Syed. Pointing to another group of hawkers a few feet away, he explains, "Those hawkers' father worked here thirty years ago; I was brought up here, raised here, and now work here. That is how it is for most people. We have nowhere to go. We are not from

England or Pakistan; we have rights here in Bombay." I ask him what he thinks about work in the Gulf, since other hawkers mentioned experience working in construction. Some described uncles and brothers working there or trying to go to places like Dubai or Saudi Arabia. "Life is lonely there," Farooq tells me. Going abroad is not an option for him. "This is our country." Farooq's words are aimed at potential critics who see him and his colleagues through a cocktail of urban bias and ethnic-religious chauvinism; hawkers' outsider status is established through stereotypes of the country bumpkin and the unruly Muslim (Hansen 2001).[6] Claims reasserting their multigenerational presence help combat the myth of the migrant hawker who brings uncouth practices into the modern city.

Yet despite their marginal position in the city, it would be a mistake to attribute an oppositional stance to Syed and his colleagues—a stance that rejects, for instance, binaries of order and disorder as vehicles of their oppression. Instead, they often speak of morality and property—of the "right" way to inhabit the city. Others who contradict their views on how to hawk, to carry oneself, to use the street, and even to beg are called out for these transgressions. Ubaid reprimands pedestrians for littering. Farooq shoos away young men trying to beg. Syed heaps scorn on the vendors of pirated (and, it is rumored, semipornographic) video CDs (VCDs). They just want quick profits, he says; they block the sidewalks, inconvenience the "public," and sell dirty films.

Syed's dismissal of immoral VCD vendors reflects an ethics of space. The street he sees himself inhabiting is a space of community and propriety. He often tells me that he must treat customers with respect because he is enmeshed in the neighborhood, along with other users of the street, the residents of the adjacent buildings, commuters, and pedestrians. Like many others, he counters the stereotype of the aggressive hawker who calls out to passersby with offers of cheap deals. Syed claims his colleagues show respect in other ways as well: by not occupying too much space, not selling what they consider "immoral" things like illegal VCDs, keeping their stalls in an orderly line, and limiting permanent structures. "We don't make a roof above us or . . . [construct] anything in front of the shops. When it rains, we move our things to the side. Even in the summer, when it is extremely hot, we do not tie [a plastic tarp to protect our heads from the sun]." His efforts are reciprocated, he claims. "The customers behave well with us. . . . They also speak in our favor and say that it is not good that they [the BMC] come and harass you all the time. . . . The public are with us. They are not the ones who file complaints against us. Maybe only some old man [might] make a complaint against us. No one else does. They all help us. Here [in this neighborhood] are all middle-class people, [most of whom] are with us."

Moreover, Syed reads his own presence on the road as a sign of urban disorder—not the kind of disorder conjured by images of the "hawker nuisance," but the disorder of a government that neglects its citizens, a disorder of unactualized dreams. Around the corner from his spot on the road is an abandoned, half-built market under an overpass. This is Syed's example of a disordered urban space: a constant reminder of unkept promises and incompetent governance. To him it is a sign of a state that produces illegality. From the first day we met, he repeatedly told me, "If the BMC gives us another place to work, then we will move. They tell us to move but never give us another place to go." The unfinished market was planned as a compromise: move hawkers from the busy road and give them an ordered, covered market space to sell their goods nearby. In the middle of the construction, however, residents of the nearby apartment buildings objected. The residents "are objecting to us being there. They are saying that they don't need any markets. They do not want any noise or commotion. But we said, if you object to everything, then where will we go?" For years, the half-built market languished as a sign of unactualized possibility. Squatters sleeping by the underpass used the metal beams to dry clothes. Four years after this conversation, the unfinished market was demolished along with the overpass above it in order to make way for a new overpass.

Syed told other stories of more personal unactualized dreams. His father came to Mumbai from their ancestral village in Gujarat to make a better life for his children. He comes from a family where education is everything, he said. "My grandfather said that if you have a choice between eating three meals a day or eating two and going to school, then you should eat only two meals a day and go to school." Once in Mumbai, his father worked as a street vendor to raise money for his children's education so they could get a government job. When Syed was in the tenth grade, his father got sick, so he had to leave school and work on the street. He kept his father's dream alive by passing the bus conductor's exam and getting a license. For fifteen years he waited, but nothing transpired. He got an employment card and searched for other forms of government work. "The government said that there is no job. 'You please do your own business.' Now we are doing our business on the footpath because we don't have that much money to buy our own stall or a shop. My father is not from a rich family."

We chatted while standing on the side of the road. Heavy traffic belched exhaust fumes behind us. It was early afternoon so business was slow. A red double-decker bus caught Syed's attention. He cocked his head toward the driver. "As a Muslim," he said, "there is no chance of getting a government job like that." According to him, the problem is not only prejudice, but the reservation system, which does not recognize Muslims as a historically disadvantaged minority in the way it does Dalits (formerly called Untouchables) and *adivasis* (indigenous people).

Syed's story of joblessness is a story of pride and resignation. His family is worthy of respect, he says. His father encouraged all their children to be educated, and his mother taught him Arabic—their lineage is *ashraf*, or one of the original Muslims in the village, he claims—and yet they all work on the street, unable to acquire a proper job, forced to endure the daily indignities of running from demolition trucks or dealing with the police's extortion demands:

> We don't want to fight with anybody and cause a commotion. We want to earn our daily bread. . . . We don't have anything against the BMC or the police. If they are not giving us any place, then give us some other service job. They say that it is not good that educated people stand on the road and work. So give us work elsewhere. Give us a space and we will go there and work.

When does the street go from a space of possibility to a space of danger? When does it go from a place of exclusion to a place of inclusion? To Syed and his colleagues, the street at different moments represents a space of promise, possibility, anxiety, and danger. The street also raises questions about the possibilities of the "public" and its multiple meanings:

What kinds of ethical responsibility are contained in the idea of the "public"? How is publicness produced through ordinary practice? The street, it seems, is not just a space where public and private life mingle but a space for the forging of the content of the public and private itself.

NEIGHBORS

Kids seem to love Anuj. Perhaps it is his perpetual smile. Perhaps it is his quiet demeanor. Perhaps it is the delicious vegetable sandwiches he makes—spiced mashed potato, green chutney, sliced beets, cucumber, tomato, and onion layered between grilled bread slathered with butter. Or maybe it is the bit of excitement he adds to an otherwise sleepy neighborhood. Throughout the day his street-side sandwich stall is a hub of activity. Toddler girls run back and forth between his stall and their neighboring house. They call him Anuj-chacha (uncle). A boy tentatively cycles out of his apartment compound to snatch a free piece of cucumber. Students at the nearby high school crowd around his stall in eager anticipation of their afternoon snack.

Each year I visit Anuj, his stall is slightly bigger, his utensils of a higher quality, the amenities he provides his customers more sophisticated, and his menu a bit more complex. When I first met him in 2004, he was a skinny young man who worked from a flimsy metal table and sold one item: vegetable sandwiches, plain or grilled. There were no chairs, and only a small umbrella provided shade while he and his father worked. In 2013, Anuj was himself a proud father with the hint of a paunch. His stall was made of sturdy plywood, and there was enough space for him to work comfortably with an assistant from his village in UP. Large bags of puffed rice and puris were displayed behind a new glass shield. His popularity—he claimed to sell seventy or more sandwiches a day—enabled Anuj to branch out to other popular street snacks like bhel puri (a mixture of puffed rice, finely chopped onions, and sweet chutney). His aunt's son was brought from their village in Uttar Pradesh to help meet expanding demand. Anuj and his father managed to save the Rs 500,000 needed to secure a two-room, multistoried home in a jhopadpatti five minutes from his centrally located workplace, a vast improvement from their first home in a distant suburb far from high-quality schools and hospitals. Back at the stall, Anuj put up a new sign, a rarity among food vendors: Anuj's Sandwiches and Bhel Puri. A loyal customer printed business cards for him, which he proudly showed me. Another customer, a journalist, quoted him in a newspaper article: "I came to Mumbai from UP [Uttar Pradesh] fifteen years ago with no money. Now I have a house for my family. I try to work hard, but my only hope is that I can work harder for my family." Anuj keeps a laminated copy in his wallet. He showed it to me one day after I updated him on the status of my book project.

Anuj's quiet entrepreneurship is made possible by a complex series of entanglements with nearby residents. When we first met, Anuj worked in front of an old bungalow, his stall strategically perched in front of a cement gate at the boundary of the property. Anuj's father had secured this spot in the late 1990s by developing a relationship with its elderly owners. Anuj and his father helped them with small chores, carried heavy groceries, and opened and shut the gates when cars came. They also acted in part as informal security guards, monitoring the periphery of the house. The owners reciprocated by allowing Anuj to store his pots inside their compound wall at night. A similar arrangement with residents of the neighboring building provided him with water. Over time, Anuj and his father slowly enmeshed themselves in the neighborhood; rights to this space were acquired not so much through outright land seizure but through the slow accretion of dense webs of relationships (Bayat 2000).

Despite these alliances, eviction always remained a possibility. Insecurities came from many sources. The local police periodically demanded bribes. The BMC periodically cracked down on street food preparation (court-ordered bans on street-side cooking were enforced at random). Neighbors circulated rumors that drunk, lecherous men were frequenting Anuj's stall late at night, ruining the peaceful character of the neighborhood. For Anuj, however, the real crisis came when the elderly bungalow owners passed away. Within a year, the property was sold to a wealthy developer, the home demolished, and construction of an office building commenced. The delicate alliance on which Anuj's spatial claim rested was severed.

For two years, Anuj existed in an uncertain precarity on the side of the road. I asked what he foresaw in the future and he told me, "After the new building gets built, they will kick me out. But I will find something else." His stall still remained at the same spot by the old gate, but kids no longer stopped by to play. The once quiet street corner now bustled with laborers, contractors, developers' assistants, drivers, and potential tenants. The security guards watching over the site became his new friends and provided him with a steady stream of information. He acquired a large new group of regular customers. Despite this, Anuj feared being associated with this transient population. He was once, after all, a neighborhood fixture, deeply enmeshed in the personal lives of its residents, not part of a mobile group of workers.

I visited Anuj again in 2009. It had been a year since we last spoke. The plot on which the old bungalow stood is now a hive of activity. A new tea vendor serves customers through a cut-out in the metal wall encircling the site. Dozens of laborers work amid the skeleton of a new commercial building. A concrete mixer churns without pause. Huge piles of gravel, dirt, and rebar lie on the old driveway. The scene in front of us is a construction site as well. The entire road is being dug up in preparation for resurfacing. Across the street, a half-built luxury apartment building rises on land that was once a gas station. Anuj and I take in this microcosm of a rapidly changing Mumbai, quietly acknowledging the dramatic changes we had witnessed over the years. But he breaks our silence with a surprise. He tells me he is delighted by the new commercial building; residential property owners complain about hawkers more than office workers do, who don't seem to mind his presence. No longer fearing eviction, the despondency of our last encounter is replaced by the self-assured confidence of an entrepreneur.

As Anuj packs up the stall at the end of the busy evening, he recounts the wealth of gossipy detail he has gleaned from guards and laborers over the past year. His favorite bit of news: the property had been flipped three times by speculators and developers, each of whom earned millions of rupees. He knows all this, he tells me, because everyone involved in the deal eats his sandwiches.

With his stall closed for the night, we enter the construction site, now walled off from the road by metal sheets. He continues talking about the ballooning sale price of the property as it changed hands—"first 5 crore, then 12, and then 17."[7] The security guards nodded to him in assent. It was not quite the accuracy of the numbers they confirmed but the reality of the "spectral" (Appadurai 2000) presence of wealth accumulation signified by the space. The guards didn't flinch when Anuj placed his pots in the corner, as he had four years earlier when the elderly owners were alive. Even they implicitly acknowledged his historical claims to this plot. To Anuj, the changing city was not something to mourn.

ACTIVISM

When Farhana gave her first public speech at fifteen, an older hawker activist recognized her skills and made her a leader. At hawker rallies, she stands in front, directing the chants, her fist raised and puncturing the air with each shout. I once saw her at a protest leading a group of men into a waiting police van. She then spent two weeks in jail. When not at her parents' vegetable stall, she travels the city with other hawker activists negotiating with the police and settling disputes with the BMC. At only twenty years old, her activism has brought her some fame. She was invited to an international conference on informal labor. Upon her return home, she was met at the airport by five hundred banner-waving hawkers, news crews, and journalists demanding interviews ("It was 2:00 a.m.!" she told me). She said she felt like a celebrity.

Farhana's family runs a relatively large vegetable stall in one of Mumbai's up-and-coming northern suburbs. Her father arrived in Mumbai, in an area then far from the city center, from a village near Hyderabad fifty years ago when he was just twelve years old. He found work assisting a vegetable hawker. "He did little jobs," she said, pointing to a boy sweeping the ground in front of us, "like him." She continued, "He learned the business fast. He was smart. He remembered the prices well. After two years of selling vegetables from a handcart, he started selling vegetables in a small fixed space. He worked there for years and then moved to this place. That was twenty years ago." They still own some land near the village and go back on occasion, but "there is no profit from farming. Other people now work the land, and they keep everything."

Farhana told me this story while taking a break from working at her family's vegetable stall—four tables stretched along the road displaying an impressive array of produce. When I visit her, she insists I sit on the steps of an adjacent shuttered shop and plies me with tea and orange soda. Her father silently arranges vegetables while we speak. Crates of tomatoes, green peppers, and cucumbers lie at our feet, produce her mother and brother had brought from the wholesale market in Vashi the night before. The family is fortunate to be able to divide the work this way, she said. Well-dressed professionals browse the display as they walk by on their way home from work. Women drive by, roll down the backseat window of their cars, and call out their orders.

When she was growing up, Farhana said, "Things were fine. No one bothered us. No BMC or police came." Then a local politically connected landlord started a campaign to evict hawkers. The area was rapidly changing. The sleepy community that her father had settled in was rapidly transforming into a sought-after enclave for upper-middle-class professionals. Despite its distance from the city's historic center, young professionals were flocking here for the relatively affordable real estate. Glittering new malls opened, and then international chain restaurants opened outposts one by one. Sensing opportunity, the local landlord pressured (and, says Farhana, bribed) the BMC to evict hawkers in the area. Even those working on streets declared hawking zones were not safe: "He threatened us and said we must go. Most hawkers got scared and left. We stayed on and fought for five years. The BMC would come often. Sometimes [they would come] just as we returned from Vashi and take our vegetables, and we would suffer huge losses." Then:

> One day the BMC took all our goods and smashed our stall. I was not there at the time, but my mother and father were. When I arrived, the BMC truck, loading inspector, and a police van were standing in the road. I approached the loading inspector and showed him a "stay order" from the Supreme Court. I told him this street has been declared a hawking zone. He refused, instead pointing to the landlord.
>
> We tried to stop the van. My family sat in front of the van and started a protest [right there]. We were ready to sleep on the road. The police backed off after seeing the Supreme Court order, but the loading inspector continued to fight us. So we said we will stay here and wait until more police come. The ACP came and ordered a *lathi* charge [an attack with long thin rods] on us.

At that time [the hawker union leader] was not there, so things got really bad. Most hawkers panicked and ran to save themselves. My father, brother, brother-in-law, and myself were jailed for causing a nuisance. We spent fifteen days in jail.

People told my mother, "How can you let your daughter fight like this? She'll die." But my mother said, "God is bigger than this man. If he allows it, then we will survive." And so we continued our fight. The BMC and police would come often and the landlord would threaten us. But [ultimately] he lost and we won.

Now he doesn't bother us. He even drives by and says "Namaskar."

Farhana told me this story on multiple occasions, her way of showing me the importance of organizing and activism. Witnessing police brutality compelled Farhana to take a leadership role among hawkers across the city. She thanks her parents for allowing her to thrive in this environment dominated by men; she is grateful that they recognize her leadership skills and do not restrict her constant travels through the city.

Farhana describes this mobility as a privilege. She says that she has it relatively easy compared to most other female street vendors:

For them, it is very painful. They have to get up at 4:00 a.m. every day and leave their children. When they come back [from Vashi] they have to clean the vegetables and then sit at their stall. Only by 2:00 p.m. can they return home, cook, and feed their children. After that, they go back to their stall and work through the evening. Often they work late into the night.

This is not a problem that only hawkers face. Even service class [secretaries and domestic workers] faces similar problems. They too have to get up at 5:00 a.m., cook for their children, and then go their office.

Due to this gendering of space in Mumbai, according to Farhana:

A woman sits on the footpath only when all her other sources for jobs are cut off. It is a painful job, but a helpless person has no other option. When a woman sits on the footpath for the first time, men bother them. Rude men harass them and make comments. But as she gets more experience on the road, she figures out how to handle the situation.

I was surprised to hear Farhana talk of hawking as a last resort. Stark economism never quite captured her relationship to the practice. Until then, it was always more than just a livelihood. It was an identity, the source of her activism. Likewise, when Farhana speaks of "women," she both is and is not including herself. She does not work on the street because "all her other sources for jobs are cut off"; her family, while humble, is not destitute. At the same time, she inhabits a gendered public sphere; she too must deal with a male sense of entitlement over public space; she too must inhabit the double sense of being "out of place" as a woman and hawker (Phadke, Ranade, and Khan 2009). Activism, like hawking itself, is a way of inhabiting the world as much as it seems to be a necessity. Affective connections to the street are inseparable from more explicitly politicized spatial claims.

DREAMS OF THE FUTURE

In a brief lull between customers, Ramesh told me his story of the changing city: "Before the 1960s, India was a poor country. It had to import food. But after the 1960s, things improved. People now may be poor, but at least they are not hungry." He motioned to the scene around us—heavy traffic, trucks rumbling down to a nearby factory, a steady flow of pedestrians, bustling shops, massive buildings under construction, and a new shopping mall with an air-conditioned supermarket. It wasn't always like this, he said. It was all wild. "*Jungal* [a forest]."

This was hard to imagine. The only hint of the area's bucolic past was an overgrown lot behind us that had escaped development because it was managed by a temple trust. A small structure was vaguely visible through the thick foliage. This undeveloped land gave Ramesh some security; down the road, ten hawkers had recently been evicted. For years they had worked in front of a factory. It closed, and a Big Bazaar supermarket and luxury multiplex theater opened on the site. Uniformed guards and large cement planters now occupied the space in front. So Ramesh was lucky; eviction wasn't a constant threat. He had enough space to clean vegetables and display them on the street. Leafy trees provided protection from the sun. A neglected drain served as a convenient spot to hide his goods when the BMC trucks came.

Ramesh is a keen observer of city life and had an unceasing patience for my questions. After being introduced by Amar, a local hawker leader, Ramesh graciously allowed me to sit with him on the side of the road. I visited in the afternoons when business was slow. Seeing me walking from the nearby train station, he would quickly drape an old canvas sack over an empty wooden crate and beckon me to sit. We chat about his work, his experience on the street, and life in the city. When customers come, I use the break to jot down quick notes—fragments of conversation, words, and impressions that I hope to reconstruct that evening—first on the train platform, then on the train, and finally at home in front of my computer. Vendors of okra, tomatoes, chilies, and bitter gourd, or *karela*, flank him on either side. Traders trickle by, offering their services to his friends. A knife sharpener cycles by, lowers his kickstand, adjusts the chain to the sharpener, starts peddling, and unleashes a shower of sparks. A middle-aged woman lugs jugs of kerosene from stall to stall to light up hawkers' lamps; a skinny boy carries a tray with a dozen little cups of tea, handing them out to hawkers, one by one. Friends stop by to tell me stories of dislocation, persistence, and struggle, such as Dharmenda who, at sixteen, came from a village in Bihar, called to the city by a distant relative in the wholesale vegetable trade. Ten years later, he lives with four other hawkers in a small room in a nearby jhopadpatti. Every six months he visits his wife and daughter who live in the village because their family income isn't large enough to survive in Mumbai. And besides, he says, "There is no space for them here." Or Yadav, who sells baby eggplants that he purchases from farms in Gujarat. Nearly every evening, he takes the last train out of the city and returns to the spot next to Ramesh by sunrise. On his rare days off, he takes me to his favorite spot—a quiet corner on the first floor of a half-built apartment building, where a man boils up rich dark tea with heaps of grated ginger for construction workers. His brother recently passed away, so he is busy helping his family. Soon, he tells me, he will fly to Dubai or Oman, where he once worked as a carpenter.

I admire Ramesh's ability with a knife. In minutes, he can clean a large sack of overgrown heads of cauliflower. Four motions—a swift chop at the stem and three quick hacks at the greenery—transform a profuse mess of greenery into artfully prepared bulbs. Preparations are over by sunset, in time for the rush of customers. Commuters walking home from the station stop by Ramesh's stall to make small purchases. Men and women come out to buy food for their evening meal. Mobile vendors who resell vegetables in the jhopadpatti up the hill fill big bags with produce. Passersby ask for the price of spring onions and move on without making a purchase. The price of nearly all vegetables fluctuates daily, sometimes wildly, so these passersby are checking to see what is affordable. Bargaining is common, but few are successful. Ramesh makes meager profits—a few rupees per bunch of spring onions, for instance—so he offers discounts only to the women vendors who buy in bulk. Haggling attempts by men who look as if they just stepped out of an air-conditioned office are ignored.

One evening, customers' attempts to bargain were particularly intense. It was the day after Ganesh Chaturthi, an important holiday in Mumbai. The wholesale market had been closed for the holiday so Ramesh could offer only day-old green onions. He offered them at Rs 8 a bunch; his customers demanded Rs 5. Young women dressed in expensive *salwar kameez* picked at the wilted greens while vigorously demanding a discount. He offered Rs 6, but they refused. "Go to Big Bazaar; you'll get it cheaper there," he muttered under his breath as they walked away. While Ramesh was still snickering, a regular customer, a man who cooks Chinese-inspired noodle dishes from a roadside stall, walked by. He carried huge bags emblazoned with the Big Bazaar logo. Ramesh heckled—"What, you went to Big Bazaar?"—knowing that the man was merely using a recycled bag.

At times I was also the subject of his mockery. One afternoon, he asked about my family. I told him I was married. "Do you have children?" I said no, I didn't. "How long have you been married?" "Four years," I replied. "Family planning *ho rahi hai*?" he said, without skipping a beat.

"You're doing family planning?" I was pleasantly startled by this unexpected turn to intimacy and use of the term *family planning* to describe birth control. I tried formulating a reply about "careers" and "waiting." The right words wouldn't come. There *was* no right response. He provincialized my universalizing assumptions about sexuality. What I saw as a decision made by an autonomous couple he considered to be childlike naiveté. "Family planning" is what the state says you should do. I thought I was exercising free will; he thought I was being duped by the authorities.

Ramesh interpreted development projects in whatever form—family planning interventions, food production, wide roads, and air-conditioned supermarkets like Big Bazaar—not as threats but as forces to maneuver within. Family planning discourses are backed by the power of the state, but that doesn't mean anyone's sexual life should be subsumed to it; Big Bazaar represents the future, but that doesn't mean hawkers are the past. Ramesh interpreted the globalized aesthetic of the new Mumbai in similar terms. The brightly lit air-conditioned "showrooms," as Ramesh and his friends liked to call supermarkets, were not signs of changing consumer preferences (as if one day people would prefer stale shrink-wrapped vegetables to his fresh produce sold on the street) but a shift in government attitudes toward the poor. Urban transformation and development, in whatever form, were not the problem, but their exclusions from it were. Anuj, hanging out with us one evening, makes a similar point while talking about open space—to many, a marker of a developed city *without* hawkers. But rather than reject this dream, he tries to find a place within it. "There should be free space to walk on the sidewalk," he tells me as I frantically dig out my pen and notepad from my backpack, sensing a conversation I needed to record on the spot; he had stopped by after work because he wanted to tell me something. We are sitting on crates still wet from a sudden downpour, tucked under a plastic tarp on the side of the road, bunches of greens scattered around us. I look for a place to rest my small notebook. "Just like you need a space to write, we also need a space to work, other people need a space to walk, others to drive. But look out there," and he points to the road we are facing with its constant stream of cars, trucks, buses, and pedestrians. "There is space for all of that. If they don't want us there, then fine; build us a market, provide us with another space to work. Everyone wants nice things. We all want a nice table, a nice place to drink tea with a clean floor, a nice city, nice roads, and nice sidewalks. So give us a nice space to work also. Give us a nice market, and we will go there. Everyone wants nice things . . . but the government doesn't [help]."

Ramesh and his friends mingle references to "showrooms" and politicians' fantasies of "global Mumbai" with their own accounts of developing space. Hawkers would often describe themselves as entrepreneurs opening frontiers. Ramesh proudly referred to his arrival in the city's frontier—when it was a jungal. Farhana told a similar story of her father settling on the city's sparsely populated outskirts. Others spoke of the authorities' vision of "turning Mumbai into Shanghai" and then saying, "Before everyone else came, hawkers made all this. We made the shopping malls. Actually, we developed this area."[8] Narration of presence in Mumbai's past is an assertion of one's legitimacy in the present. Sometimes development doesn't come from above, but means inserting oneself into a transnational conversation (Tsing 2005).

But sometimes development means being done unto. In 2008, I visited Ramesh after a two-year absence. He was still there, but his colleagues, including Neeraj and Anuj, were gone. The market had vanished. I asked how this happened. Demolitions occurred regularly during my fieldwork two years earlier, but the hawkers were able to return after each one. This time, he speculated, it was because of the coordinated effort by the various branches of the state and political parties. "It is 50 percent the problem of the police, 25 percent the BMC and 25 percent the MNS," referring to the Maharashtra Navnirman Sena, a political party that periodically riles up anti–North Indian sentiment on the basis of a virulently pro-Maharashtrian, "sons of the soil" rhetoric. But it also seemed that road widening and sidewalk construction had done what regular raids could not. What was meant to be a temporary eviction became permanent; construction went on for so long that most vendors left to work elsewhere. Some returned to their villages. Ramesh was one of the few who stayed on. He could only afford annual visits to his family in UP. He worked in the same place but could no longer display his vegetables, so he hid them under a canvas bag tucked next to the fence and sold them furtively to occasional passersby, small shop owners in the jhopadpattis, and small food stall operators.

With his profits a quarter of what they used to be, he described his condition as a slow suffocation—"like fish taken out of the water—still alive, kicking around, but unable to do anything. . . . We are living, but barely. I get enough [to] eat, but that's it. We aren't able to work and live as we should." Part of his frustration owed to his being squeezed out of a spot he felt deeply connected to. As we stood on the new sidewalk, where he once had a vegetable stall, he pointed to a heavily trafficked spot and read its overlapping layers of meaning like a palimpsest: "Twenty years ago we sat there"—directing my gaze a few yards closer to us, "and then there"—and finally, pointing to the dirt space beneath the fence— "and now we are here." The street's varying textures—the smooth asphalt center, the cement brick edge, and the new sidewalk—represent his past spaces of dwelling. He told me this with his back against a fence: the city, at least for now, did not have space for him.

A year after this conversation, a group of machine-gun-wielding men rampaged through downtown Mumbai. In the aftermath of this horrific attack, authorities called for the removal of street markets near high-profile buildings. Trying to prevent their imminent eviction, hawkers "plead[ed] with the military that this is our second home" (Koppikar 2009). Invoking "home" as a strategy for staking a claim to space might come as a surprise. Writings on the politics of the urban poor often focus on rights, citizenship, and social justice. Yet these vendors, faced with the destruction of their livelihood, invoke a language of connection, sentimentality, and intimacy.

Perhaps we might take this as a cue. The "politics of the urban poor" is less about rebellion than about accommodation. It is about squatting, occupation, and protest, but also about cultivating relationships, "quiet encroachment" (Bayat 2000, 545), and, most important, dwelling—infusing a space with meaning so that it conjures "the notion of home" (Bachelard 1964, 5). The hawker and the squatter inhabit spaces "inscribed" with "relations of power and discipline" (Soja 1989, 6), as studies of spatial conflict around the world have shown, but they also inhabit densely affective spaces, made meaningful through entangled histories, relationships, and mundane practices. Like the alternating conditions of hope and despair that Ramesh and others navigate, these binaries do not exist in opposition to each other but in a productive tension. The "scene" that hawkers (and anthropologists) experience and the "narrative" (Jameson 2013) that explains it simultaneously produce the city.

CHAPTER 4

MANAGING ILLEGALITY

ONE AFTERNOON, a conversation in a tea shop with Prasad, a hawker turned full-time activist, was interrupted by an incoming call. Prasad put his phone down and told me he had to go urgently to the nearby BMC godown. We quickly walked to the main road and hailed an autorickshaw. When we arrived at the godown five minutes later, we were greeted by a small crowd of men—hawkers whose property had been confiscated by the BMC, I later learned. Prasad pushed through the crowd and hurriedly went inside. The godown office was in fact just a small space, large enough for a desk and a few chairs, that looked as if it had been carved out of a sea of material collected in recent demolition raids, or "actions," as they are called. Prasad took a chair for himself and motioned for me to sit next to the clerk's desk. We were surrounded by handcarts, tables, sign boards, broken bits of metal and wood, bundles of coconuts, and baskets of fruits and vegetables. A display of potato chips was precariously perched at my side. The room was dusty and dark. The door leading out to the street provided the only sliver of light.

As a prominent hawker union leader, Prasad has many roles. He is a political organizer, an activist, and a skilled negotiator.[1] He represented hawkers' interests in the Supreme Court litigation discussed in Chapter 1 and coordinated an effort to increase the number of hawking zones in the city. I also saw him lead protests and enforce unwritten rules that

107

hawkers should keep streets clean and unobstructed. Most important, I witnessed him negotiating with the BMC and police. After an action, he meets with BMC officials to get hawkers' goods returned. If the police in a particular neighborhood are too extortionate, he meets with officers to negotiate a compromise. Many vie for his time, so I was delighted by this rare opportunity for a private conversation. I prepared questions about his role in the Supreme Court case, his negotiations with the BMC, and the content of his many negotiations with officials. I wanted to know how he managed advocating for people—unlicensed hawkers—whose livelihoods were premised on illegality. Before the conversation could go into much depth, however, the call came and our meeting came to an abrupt end.

I trailed behind Prasad as he pushed his way through a crowd of men lingering in front of the godown. Although they knew who I was—my field research had begun a month earlier—I was treated as part of his entourage and ushered inside. I expected a round of polite introductions with the clerk and other BMC workers, but Prasad had other plans. Instead of making pleasantries with the clerk, he turned to me and continued the conversation we had been having in the tea shop moments earlier: "You see, during the day the BMC takes the handcarts, tables, and goods from the hawkers and brings them to this place. And in the night . . ."—at which point, Prasad looked over to the godown clerk and gave him a knowing smile and a raised eyebrow—"that's when they make their profits." He explained that with the help of middlemen, this godown served as the center of a brisk business renting previously confiscated handcarts back to hawkers. As the BMC workers looked on speechlessly, Prasad explained the illicit arrangements among municipal workers, local "businessmen," and hawkers that constitute, to him, the real work of this anti-encroachment office. Following an action, BMC trucks bring confiscated goods back to this godown. The staff are permitted to sell the goods at a public auction if they are not retrieved within thirty days. As a result, confiscated goods, and especially handcarts, are often left unclaimed. Since so few hawkers are able to retrieve their possessions, local businessmen have accumulated a small fleet of handcarts, all of them stored in the godown when not being rented out.[2] I wanted to learn about how the city's streetscapes are managed, and here was the beginning of an answer.

Prasad and his union objected to this arrangement for multiple reasons. Handcarts owned by businessmen and rented out via BMC godown staff—the so-called *markedwali* handcarts—were allowed to work freely on the streets, while independently operating hawkers, such as those in his union, were frequently targeted for demolition and confiscation. Prasad showed photographs to prove his point. In the images, markedwali handcarts stood conspicuously unscathed amid the shattered remains of a small vegetable market. Side markings of multicolored stripes and symbols indicating ownership were the telltale signs that the untouched handcarts were the ones rented from the godown. The presence of these handcarts on the city's streets challenged the union's ability to create a sense of ordered public space. A few weeks later, the union circulated a letter saying these BMC-protected hawkers give *all* hawkers a bad name. It said that those hawkers disregard the unwritten rules to treat customers respectfully, not to litter, and not to block pedestrian traffic.

What can be made of encounters like the one in the godown office? On the surface, Prasad was protesting corruption. However, something more was going on. This was also an effort to manage the balance of power and operations of the state. Prasad's performative explanation of the illicit markedwali handcart dealings—an act of public shaming—was a tactic to achieve this aim. When Prasad began telling me about the real "profits" being made in this office, the clerk was stunned into silence. The clerk listened respectfully to Prasad's accusations and laughed nervously at his jokes, some of them at his expense. The encounter was also an attempt to manage the relationship between the letter of the law and its manifestation on the street. In his defense, the clerk explained that handcarts are confiscated if found within 100 meters of train stations and schools; hawkers can pay a fine of Rs 1,200 to get their goods back, but those that are unclaimed after thirty days are sold at a public auction. But were these regulations grounded in law—the Supreme Court had yet to decide on the 100-meter rule (or maybe 150 meters; that too was up for debate)—or simply a localized state practice? And besides, nearly all hawkers were unlicensed anyway, so why should distance from a train station or school matter?

The irony was that markedwali hawkers protected by the BMC were just as illegal as the non-markedwali hawkers Prasad represented. So "corruption" does not seem to be the best lens through which to make sense of this encounter. The difference between hawkers from markedwali and regular handcarts was that one group had a different embeddedness with the state than the other. What mattered was not simply the regulation's application but the process through which regulations were negotiated, as well as how these negotiations manage a kind of equilibrium on the street. To the union, the problem was not so much the "corruption" per se but the effects it was having on the balance of power on the street. The goal for both parties, union and BMC workers alike, was not the eradication of illegality but the better management of it.

This chapter is about the thick embeddedness of the routine practices of hawkers with the state. Although hawkers experience persistent harassment by the authorities, their relationships are not only exploitative. As I describe in this chapter, despite being criminalized, relationships between hawkers and state functionaries are not only combative but also collaborative, in Sherry Ortner's sense of the word: "more than opposition[al]" but potentially "creative and transformative" (1995, 191) as well.

Illicit arrangements that characterize hawkers' encounters with state functionaries are typically considered a failure of governance. But I argue that these failures are productive—not in the utopic sense of producing a perfectly equitable society but in the sense that they produce practices of citizenship, contested meanings of rights, and new forms of politics. What is often vaguely glossed over as corruption can also be an ordinary space of negotiation within which fundamental rights to space are worked out and the condition of illegality is recalibrated. The result is that the state is experienced less as an extension of disciplinary power than as a locus for the negotiation and legitimation of spatial claims— claims that, ironically, are often ignored in formal institutional contexts in the city. Thus, by describing the experience of illegality in Mumbai from the perspective of unlicensed hawkers who have extensive unofficial encounters with state functionaries, I show how criminalization does not produce abjection, but that power is dynamically inhabited by those commonly thought to be objectified by it.

But first, I offer a qualification. A goal of this chapter is to describe the ordinary operations of power in Mumbai through an account of people's experience of illegality. I approach corruption nonnormatively. However, the people about whom I write often approach corruption from an explicitly evaluative stance, and rightly so. My hawker friends and informants would often tell me that they are forced into illegal arrangements; that illogical regulations make working within the law impossible; that "senseless" laws and regulations make life incredibly difficult; that the real corruption is the state's criminalization of a practice essential to the city; that in a city full of illegalities, the obsession with hawkers seems oddly misplaced. As Syed said, "This city is full of criminals, but the government targets us."

On numerous occasions when I introduced myself and my research goals to hawkers, they would sum up their experiences with a simple phrase: "We just want to work in peace." The threat of municipal actions and bribe-seeking police and municipal officials would dominate our subsequent conversations. Making sense of the ordinary experiences of illegal livelihoods thus runs the risk of trivializing these experiences, as well as of romanticizing the condition of being outside the law. Simply put, whereas this writing emphasizes the spatial claims that proximity to the state makes possible, Syed and others, such as Ali discussed above, are more likely to emphasize how repeated contact with state functionaries makes life miserable.

I contend that there is something more to the persistent harassment by the authorities than straight-forward exploitation. Hawkers are effectively criminalized, and yet they remain a vital presence on the city's landscape and its political sphere. The language of extreme marginality is inadequate here because the streets do not contain a world of sharply delineated legalities and illegalities. Rather than navigate a political sphere consisting of legitimate, rights-bearing, privileged citizens and abject, "abandoned" subalterns, hawkers navigate a tense spectrum of greater or lesser illegalities.

THE INTIMATE STATE

When I first visited the BMC godown with Prasad, I was still unaware of how hawkers navigated a state that seemed so hostile to their presence. Stepping out of the autorickshaw with Prasad on that day, I could make little sense of the group of men lingering in front of that dreary gray building. I wondered, Were they BMC workers? Were these the men who jump down from vans to tear down hawkers' stalls during an action? After our meeting with the clerk, Prasad introduced me to the men outside and explained that they were in fact hawkers waiting to retrieve confiscated equipment. But what struck me about this scene was that the men lingering outside were familiar with the space. They seemed to *own* it. Belying the violence that brought them there, their interactions with BMC workers who came and went were casual, even friendly. The scene did not present a picture of a state dichotomous with its citizens—that powerful image of state "verticality" critiqued by Ferguson and Gupta (2002). Instead, this was a space of intimacy. One hawker described his experience at the godown. His regular encounters with the BMC were a kind of slow, grinding process that, he said, gets into your very being. "We are married to the BMC," he said. Whether you like it or not, it is a relationship that shapes who you are. As his friends gave a laugh of approval, he added: "It's like a marriage, the good and the bad."[3]

Often tucked beneath overpasses, BMC godowns are easy to overlook. To most people, they are a forgotten site of officialdom, and yet to hawkers they loom large. This is where hawkers go to retrieve property confiscated during actions. When they are unable to pay the official Rs 1,200 fine, a lengthy negotiation ensues.[4] The BMC staff have little desire to keep hold of the iron griddles, weighing scales, and display tables, so after a few days, they release the hawkers' property for a lesser, unofficial, and unrecorded amount. At times, this negotiation is verbal, but at other times, it is conveyed through the hawkers' act of standing in front of the warehouse office, leveraging the nuisance their presence creates for a lower payment. At times they are successful; at other times, they are not. A dosa vendor who worked near Aamir came here almost every month to retrieve his iron griddle. For a few years, his stall was successful enough to cover the expense of the repeated raids. Eventually the raids became too frequent, and his large griddle, often piping hot when the gray antiencroachment trucks arrived, proved too difficult to stash ahead of an action. Two years after we met, he gave up and returned to his village in Karnataka. A tea vendor with an easily portable kettle now works in his spot.

The past two decades of research on the "everyday state" helps elucidate these experiences. From Timothy Mitchell's critique of the idea of the state as "an autonomous entity whose actions are not reducible to or determined by forces in society" (1991, 82), itself indebted to Michel Foucault's emphasis on the micropractices of power, anthropologists have emphasized the cultural production of the state. Refutations of the myth of the state as a "monolithic entity 'acting' impersonally above or outside society" (Fuller and Harriss 2000, 15; see also Ferguson and Gupta 2002) have been aided by studies of the state at its margins (Das and Poole 2004). As the authors of these studies have shown, the state is, ironically, often most tangible, and its meanings most worked out, at the places "where state authority is most unreliable, where the gap between the state's goals and their local realization is largest, and where reinterpretation of state policies is most extreme" (Tsing 1993, 27). Thus, in a larger sense, the project of an anthropology of the state is to develop an analytical perspective that always questions the boundedness of the state without denying its effects in the world—to empirically explore how the state operates in the everyday without forgetting that its objective quality is an "effect" (Mitchell 1991, 90).

In this way, my focus on the condition of illegality, and on how power is inhabited, is different from most writings on urban marginality that seem to question the conceptual autonomy of the state while still implicitly ascribing to it a coherent internal logic or ideological project (Ferguson 2007). Ethnographies of governmentality have provided refutations of technocratic perspectives that divorce institutions from history, context, and power. For instance, there have been a number of studies of how states act—such as explorations of how the state "sees" populations (Scott 1998) and how "the aura of sovereign ultimacy is sustained and internalized" (Chalfin 2008, 520)—all of which provide important analyses of governmental tactics and the way populations are managed that reveal the implicit rationalities of rule. Less well studied is how people make meaning of these practices and what forms of citizenship or political imaginaries might emerge through—although not solely as a product of, or in resistance to, but simultaneously with—these tactics. Taking the lived experience of the state as a starting point thus complements and elaborates on these studies by showing that power often works through moments of negotiated contingency. Furthermore, looking at how hawkers navigate state practices reveals an implicit understanding of power that challenges some scholarly assumptions that categorize states according to their underlying rationality of rule (e.g., liberal or neoliberal).

To illustrate this point, I discuss two examples of state documentary practices that have had some unexpected consequences. The first is the BMC's *pauti* system (Bunsha 2002), which ran from 1988 to 1998. During this period, the BMC collected small daily fees from unlicensed hawkers under an arrangement officially described as "unauthorized occupation cum refuse removal charges."[5] This was colloquially named after the pauti, or receipt, that was given to hawkers following payment of these fees. Despite what seemed like a system of surveillance and an exercise in disciplinary power, hawkers saw the pauti system as a tool through which they could strengthen their claims to urban space. For instance, in 2005, hawkers told me that until 1998, they would show old pautis to hostile municipal workers and the police as proof of their rightful claims to particular spots on the side of the road, preventing some of the worst extortion demands. The pauti's legitimizing effect was further demonstrated by the remnants, now crumpled and frayed, that hawkers continued to carry in their wallets seven years after the last one was officially issued. Within the juridical world as well, the pauti was understood to confer legitimacy to hawkers' illegal presence on the city's landscape. Bombay High Court ended the pauti system, "cit[ing] it as a major hurdle [to eradicating hawkers] since hawkers claim the receipt is a sign that they pay the BMC to allow them to hawk . . . [and receipts] are also used to secure injunctions from the lower courts to restrain the BMC from taking action against unlicensed hawkers" ("BMC to Create" 1999). In this way, drawing from a broader logic of occupancy, citizenship, and materiality,[6] in which the possession of paper proving continuous physical presence, even if illegal, confers considerable legal and symbolic power, hawkers understood the pautis to be an official recognition of their illegal use of the street—a view that, remarkably, the courts affirmed, if not considered valid, in the decision itself. Finally, recognizing that this specific evidence of the law's transgression conferred legitimacy to hawkers' claims over public space, Bombay High Court declared in 1998, at the urging of civic activists, that for the municipality to effectively regulate hawkers, ironically, it must stop fining them.

The second example is a survey of hawkers that took place in the late 1990s. Following the 1998 ruling in which the Bombay High Court instructed the BMC to replace the pauti system with licenses, the municipality decided to conduct a survey of the city's hawkers. A team of researchers from Tata Institute of Social Sciences (TISS) and Youth for Unity and Voluntary Action (YUVA) collected information on the income, work practices, and family arrangements of over 100,000 unlicensed and licensed hawkers. The findings provided an unprecedented picture of the conditions of this vast population, but even more significant were the controversies and interest produced by the act of survey taking itself. For instance, members of the research team reported that most hawkers demonstrated a surprising interest in the survey. Rather than being suspicious of this official act of information gathering, they "were generally quite cooperative and were keen to fill up the forms as they felt it might give them some legitimacy for carrying on their activity" (TISS–YUVA 1998, 6). Ironically, although the survey was sponsored by the BMC, it was the lower-level BMC officials and their staff, as well as the police, who were most suspicious of it and who appeared to undermine it, fearing the diminishing of their hold over the hawkers in their jurisdictions (R. N. Sharma 2000). The survey organizers wrote, "In contrast to the cooperative attitude of the hawkers and their unions, the BMC Recovery Staff by and large was indifferent or even against the present survey" (TISS–YUVA 1998, 6). Moreover, they found that

> many [hawkers] were under fear/instructions not to even identify themselves [to survey takers] as "hawkers" as they were . . . recent arrivals under "protection" of police or other officials. In fact, there was at times stiff opposition during the survey, so much so, that in one ward the police personnel threatened the survey staff not to talk to "their" hawkers without their permission. (TISS–YUVA 1998, 5)

After publication of the findings, the career of the survey took a further twist: civic activists campaigning for more open space and good governance recognized the survey's potential to enable unlicensed hawkers' claims to the street and argued in the courts and in BMC offices that the municipality did not have the authority to carry out such a survey. Affirming these civic activists' fears, during the 2003 Supreme Court case on the regulation of hawking in Mumbai, unions cited enumeration in the survey as a reason specific locations should be declared hawking zones. Indeed, as hawkers, police, and municipal officials predicted in 1998, the effect of this governmental survey was not to cement state control over people who work on the street but to subvert it.

Although these examples are certainly part of the large repertoire of tactics by which the poor combat their "invisibility in urban life" (Appadurai 2001, 28), I bring them up for what they say about the possible kinds of engagements with state institutions that, on the surface, might be seen to deploy straightforwardly disciplinary forms of governance. In these instances, power works in such a way that it matters less that the state objectifies a population by creating knowledge of it than it does how this population uses its objectified status. For instance, just as inclusion in the TISS–YUVA survey enabled hawkers' claims on the state without conferring legality, the pauti conferred substantive rights that were, in the end, recognized within the formal juridical discussion. In other words, even though possessing pautis and being included in the survey never established hawkers' legality, they nevertheless produced extralegal recognition of hawkers' claims in an official sphere. The legitimizing power of the pauti and the survey suggests the gradual usurpation of the legal by the ethical so that, for instance, hawkers' ability to remain on the street was worked out not in a proceduralist realm of rights but in a "material" (Hetherington 2009, 232) realm grounded in everyday practice.

THE WORK OF CORRUPTION

Most unlicensed hawkers secure access to space on the side of the road through unofficial payments called *hafta*. Literally translated as a weekly payment, hafta more accurately refers to any kind of regular monetary transaction with state functionaries. Hafta can be given, taken, or asked for; it can increase or decrease; and, at least implicitly, it can be excessive or appropriate. It is notable that unlike *bhrastachar* (a Hindi word for corruption that connotes moral decline), hafta lacks normative content.

Translating the word into English is tricky. Is it an extortion payment? Or is it a bribe? One's definition of the word depends on where agency is assumed. Each translation conjures an imaginative world of interaction with state functionaries. The first suggests state officials preying on powerless subalterns; the second suggests wily traders tempting greedy officials. In common use, the meaning of *hafta* falls in the middle, indexing an exchange, arrangement, and negotiation. Indeed, hafta is structured and, very often, public.[7] Hawkers know how much they will have to pay depending on what they sell and their location; produce hawkers pay the least and (relatively high-profit and higher-volume) hawkers of cooked food, such as Anuj, discussed in Chapter 3, pay the most. Likewise, hawkers working on well-trafficked streets in upmarket neighborhoods pay more than those working in poorer parts of the city.

The connection between hawking and corruption in Mumbai (and certainly elsewhere) is expansive. A journalist estimated that the BMC alone collects Rs 11 crore, or $2.5 million (R. N. Sharma 2000) from hawkers a year, whereas others estimate that hawkers pay the BMC and police combined Rs 45 crore, or roughly $10 million a year (Bunsha 2007).[8] But what conclusions should be drawn from this connection? The various participants in the hawker controversy—civic activists, journalists, hawker union activists, and hawkers themselves—often frame corruption in moral terms. Civic activists read hawker-lined streets as evidence of a state unwilling to wean itself from the easy money of bribe givers. They also argue that the pervasive networks of bribe giving constitute a nexus of BMC officials, hawker union leaders, and the police that keeps in place a status quo that renders hawkers' and pedestrians' livelihoods difficult. There is some truth to this. Hawker union leaders, for their part, frame the conversation in terms of power inequalities and social justice. They argue that the corruption to which civic activists refer is in fact extortion: state functionaries demand money from hawkers as a price for being left alone. They also argue that what is "corrupt" is the criminalization of an essential service. There is some truth to this as well.

The link between hawking and corruption can also be drawn in metaphoric terms. The classic definition of corruption within the sphere of governance is remarkably similar to the way civic activists describe the city's hawker problem: "behaviour which deviates from the formal duties of a *public* role because of *private*-regarding ... pecuniary or status gains" (Nye, quoted in Olivier de Sardan 1999, 27, emphasis added). Like the politician who corrupts the state by using public power for private gain, the hawker is said to corrupt the city by using the public realm (the thoroughfare) for private gain. In this sense, the immorality of hawking, like corruption, owes to the "blurred boundaries" (Gupta 1995) it produces. The figurative connections between hawking and corruption can be extended further. Because hawkers make a living on the street—traditionally a morally compromised space in India (Chakrabarty 2002)—they are understood to defy categorical distinctions (Herzfeld 2006), which animates hostility toward their occupation regardless of its formal legal status. By sitting on the side of the road, hawkers often symbolize the failure of modernist urbanism to take root in Mumbai. To civic activists, the ubiquitous hawker seems to signal the city's rejection of the ideal of the street being solely a space of movement. Indeed, both the modernist architectural vision of the street promoted by civic activists and normative understandings of corruption are premised on a sharp distinction between the public and private spheres, which the hawker contravenes as a matter of fact.

However the connection between hawking and corruption should go even further. The point is not that hawking is inherently corrupt, but that its very condition is shaped in negotiations over, and threats of, unofficial payments to the authorities. The word *corruption* signals a deviation. However for hawkers, hafta payments are less deviations from a norm than the very basis on which the state is experienced. Hawkers have some sort of unofficial encounter with representatives of the state almost every day. The word *encounter* here encompasses a wide range of scenes that include demolitions and tense verbal exchanges, friendly chats, surreptitious exchange of glances, and bribe demands—from the most obvious to subtle requests for goods in kind.

The interwoven nature of daily life and extralegal state encounters is reflected in the literature that argues for a view of corruption as signifying something more than merely the breakdown of urban governance. For instance, Akhil Gupta (1995, 2005) and Jonathan Parry (2000) show that in India, narratives of corruption in fact produce the state, even indexing the new strength of the modern state concept. These studies, rather than "treating corruption as a dysfunctional aspect of state organizations" (Gupta 1995, 376; see also Eckert 2004), have attempted "to anchor corruption in ordinary everyday practice" (Olivier de Sardan 1999, 26), which entails an eschewal of moralism (Leys 1965) in favor of a close ethnographic view that focuses on "its banalisation" (Olivier de Sardan 1999, 26), routineness (Oldenburg 1987), and even its "bodily" connotations (Robertson 2006, 10).

The broad literature on corruption shows that the complicity of the state in illegal practices is not restricted to India. Accounts of the state's role in facilitating illegal street vending in New York City (Austin 1994; Moskin 2009a, 2009b), as well as Michael Herzfeld's (2009) ethnography of the meaning of corruption in Rome, show similar processes. Moreover, Herzfeld's (2005, 375) analysis of the ways seemingly monolithic bureaucracies are fragmented through compromises such as "muddling through," as well as the way "common economic interests and areas of social interaction" (372) produce official complicity in illegal activities, reveal the broader implications of an ethnography of corruption.

These studies aside, owing to a well-justified skepticism of received categories of social analysis, especially one so deeply associated with the good governance rhetoric of transnational lending institutions, critical studies of corruption have tended to emphasize the "*idea* of corruption as a category of thought and organizing principles" (Haller and Shore 2005, 2) through critiques of the cultural specificity of the public–private divide on which it rests (Olivier de Sardan 1999) as well explorations of the stories, scandals, debates, and ordinary talk around and about it. For this reason, much of the literature has approached the topic primarily through a focus on the discourses surrounding corruption rather than on the practices that are considered corrupt and the worlds they might produce.[9]

HAFTA IN PRACTICE

Jawahar, a sandal seller, described his daily encounters with state functionaries: "[Throughout the day] they all come. Every one of them. They take Rs 10 or 20 or sometimes more, clasp their hands in thanks. Smile. Nod their head. And walk away." Although a local union organizer had recently urged him not make any payments to officials, he feels compelled to do so. He understands these difficult payments to be a necessary part of daily work: "We know what we have to do, we have been here for twenty years. We say, 'When the dog barks, you must give it a bone.' If the dog barks and barks without getting a bone, he will bite."

To people like Jawahar, the state is experienced simultaneously as a spectral entity and an insatiable force. At times dangerous and fickle like an aggressive dog, it can also be placated. Many officials abide by hafta agreements, but some see vendors as potential sources of quick cash. A casual chat with Aamir, the raddiwala introduced in Chapter 2, is interrupted by a man roaring up to us on his bike. A police constable in civilian clothes arrives, having just finished his shift. "Hafta do!" [Give me the hafta!] he declares. Seeing me at Aamir's side, he abruptly cuts off the encounter and drives off. He'll return tomorrow, Aamir explains. He wanted his usual Rs 200 from each of the hawkers on the street. As the de facto leader of the street, Aamir is tasked with collecting the money from everyone to make it look more subtle.

Regular hafta arrangements may be the norm, but they are also interspersed with random demands for bribes, a situation that creates a palpable sense of tension. The bribe-seeking state functionary exists as a simultaneously material and ghostly presence, explains Ramesh:

> We worry about them [the BMC and the police] all the time. Even when they do not come, they cause us great problems. I constantly think about them: "Will they come today? Will they come tomorrow? Will they ask for fines?" They cause so much stress. That is how they cause us such great problems even when they are not here.

Farhana echoes this sense of the persistent state:

> Some police have fixed payments. Some ask for money for drinking from time to time, and others ask for vegetables. On one street, hawkers have to pay 100 kilograms of vegetables to the police each week. . . . If we try to hide our goods when the police come, they take away our [weighing] scale and then demand Rs 200 to Rs 400 for its return. Sometimes they demand Rs 1,250 instead of the [official] Rs 1,200 fine. . . . Other times they say, "If you deal

with us we'll return Rs 600. But if you appear in front of a judge you will have to pay Rs 1,200."

What does power look like in this context? It is not so much a disciplinary regime—of governance through regulating, ordering, and knowing—but a regime of ambiguities, a state whose power "is harnessed not so much from the rationality of ordering practices as from the passions of transgression, in which the line between the legal and illegal is constantly blurred" (Aretxaga 2003, 402). Indeed, it is the legal flux that produces hawkers' anxiety. Power is not experienced in instances of regulating and disciplining, but in the perpetuation of legal ambiguities. One of Aamir's friends tells me that there is a deliberate strategy to keep hawker regulation ambiguous. "The BMC and the police want to keep things on a boil," he told me as we chatted at the side of the road. "They don't want a solution to the hawker issue. Because if there is an end to the issue, then they won't get their hafta." Indeed, it seems that in this context, the power of the state comes from keeping hawkers in a perpetual state of uncertainty—illegal but also recognized. So at times, it seems, the subversive act of the hawker is not to circumvent the state's surveilling eye but to find the most productive place within it.

If the BMC and police deliberately keep the hawkers' precarious condition unresolved in a kind of "boil," as Aamir's friend put it, or simmering tension, then the hawkers' goal is to manage that "boil" successfully. As hawkers who have been able to subvert residents' association's cleanup drives, they know that there are possibilities here as well; regulatory ambiguity and contradiction constitute a form of power with indeterminate effects. In some instances, they open space for greater extortion. This was the case on the street where Ramesh and his colleague, Anuj, worked. One day BMC workers installed a no-hawking zone sign on their road. Anuj pointed it out to me as we walked down the road a few weeks later. "Pheriwale Ke Dande Pratibandhi" [street vending is prohibited], it said. The sign was in the shape of an arrow pointing left. Vegetable hawkers lined the road in both directions, forming a busy market. "Why put up a nonhawking zone in the middle of the street? . . . What is the point of half a road being a nonhawking zone?" Anuj asks rhetorically. Installing nonhawking zone signs to increase hafta payments was, of course, a practice that I had seen and heard about elsewhere. At that time, in the mid-2000s, the Bombay High Court had established three-member committees to survey the city and decide on hawking and nonhawking zones. However, the list was tentative (and hotly debated). No street had yet to be officially declared a nonhawking zone, yet signs were installed anyway. To add to the confusion, the status of spaces adjacent to nonhawking zones was unclear. If hawking is banned on your neighbor's street, does that make hawking legal on yours? To the hawkers who worked beneath these signs, however, the logic was clear. While lacking legal validity, they enhanced state functionaries' ability to extract more hafta.

In other instances, legal and regulatory ambiguity produced spaces of possibility. Anuj, along with his father, had been working at the same spot for decades, selling vegetable sandwiches from a 1 square meter booth. As he explained to me, every two weeks an off-duty police constable or BMC worker comes by and collects money (Rs 1,200–1,600 at a time) for his superiors. This arrangement allows Anuj to stay, but at the cost of over a third of his monthly income. These arrangements have multiple effects. For instance, following the calamitous Mumbai flood in 2005, the BMC declared a ban on street food as a public health precaution. Anuj explained that this ban (on a practice that is already illegal) had specific, and not necessarily disastrous, effects. Following the announcement, he was instructed to close his stall for a few days. After paying the authorities some extra hafta, he was allowed to reopen. Anuj put it succinctly: "Because of the floods, they asked for double hafta this month." To him, the street food ban, like all other regulations, was less an instance of the brute force of the state than a flexible practice to be negotiated. Since the ban was initiated at the upper level of the bureaucracy, Anuj knew that rather than lead to his eviction, it would simply be a tool for lower-level officials to extract more money.

The effects of laws regarding street vending thus often far exceed, and at times invert, their intent, which suggests the need to focus on the life of laws rather than on the question of whether they are successfully implemented. In Anuj's case, the effect of the law's malleability was profound: by banning cooking food for a finite period of time, the state legitimized the practice at other times. Ironically, it is this double illegality—the fact that hawkers are unlicensed *and* momentarily subject to regulations—that contributes to hawkers' continued presence on the streets. The constant adjudication of some groups of hawkers has the effect of legitimizing others, as well as of legitimizing those same vendors at a different time. In this way, the convoluted and often conflicting laws and regulations inconsistently result in hawker eradication. There are possibilities, it seems, in the "boil" as well.

While I was sitting one afternoon with Dubey, a tomato hawker, a young uniformed police constable interrupted our conversation, asking for the local hawker union leader. Dubey explained that he was at home and, motioning to me, said, "He too is waiting for him," implying that the leader was genuinely busy and not trying to avoid the police. As I looked on, Dubey and the constable exchanged small pleasantries, reflecting a casual relationship that had been formed over many previous encounters. The constable then handed Dubey a crumpled piece of paper, chatted a bit more, and walked off. The hawker leader was quickly summoned by cell phone from the nearby slum settlement. As Dubey bagged tomatoes, he explained to me that this young constable had come to collect vegetables on behalf of his superiors, who had written their shopping requirements for the week on the slip of paper. The leader arrived and collected bags of vegetables from hawkers on the street, checking items off the small list he held in his hand. A half-hour later, the constable returned dressed in civilian clothes, collected a dozen or so bags laden with produce, and then walked away without paying, looking like any other shopper on this busy commercial street. The chitchat between the police and the hawker that comes from their regular contact creates a casual scene. Few passersby would know that a hafta exchange was taking place.

Despite this naked display of power, Dubey maintains a friendly relationship with the constable. After he walks away, he expresses a bit of sympathy for the man. "Poor guy, he's sick," Dubey tells me as he restacks tomatoes. "His brain is a bit messed up."

Later that day in a tea shop, Dubey helped explain the encounter I witnessed earlier: "Every part of the government wants money, and within each branch are other branches. You must pay the municipality, the police, traffic police. The morning and afternoon shifts. You must pay everyone." Dubey and his father had been working in the same spot since 1972, and, Dubey claims, the behavior of state officials had not changed since then. However, he says, the situation is worse for the newer, less organized hawkers working farther away from the center of this busy commercial area. Thus, despite the precariousness of his claim to the street and the regular loss of produce to bribe-seeking officials, Dubey viewed his situation with surprising stoicism. "Because of the union," Dubey said with a smile, "the police and the BMC are a bit scared of the hawkers here, and so we are harassed a bit less."

Whereas the vast amount of money and goods that changes hands suggests large-scale exploitation, arrangements such as these point to the momentary, if unequal, partnerships between hawkers and state functionaries. For instance, before municipal actions, Dubey often receives a phone call warning him of the impending demolition. Other times, the BMC van parks around the corner from the street market, giving him and his colleagues enough time to pack up their goods and flee before a raid. It is also common for the state functionaries who actually do the work of hawker eradication—who walk on the street, tear down the stalls, confiscate the goods, and drive the municipal vans—to disobey their superiors' orders to demolish street markets because of the income that they would inevitably lose. Reflecting the extent to which lower-level authorities are potentially aligned with hawkers, BMC officials periodically confiscate the cell phones of the men who carry out the antiencroachment work to prevent them from informing hawkers and wait until the last minute to disclose a raid's location (Lewis 2005).[10] In this context, "corruption" is more than mere bribery or extortion; it is a field of negotiation that enables unlicensed hawkers at least momentary claims to the street.

These arrangements reflect low-level municipal workers' and police constables' dependence on income from the hafta system, and they are also partly a product of a shared social world. Despite the clear differences in their respective relationships to structures of power in the city, lower-ranking police constables and their male hawker counterparts at times inhabit intersecting worlds: they consume the same goods, spend time at the same street-corner spots (the ubiquitous paan and cigarette stalls), and experience the same sense of alienation from the city's new sites of consumer spectacle, such as cafés and shopping malls. Moreover, with many police constables living in jhopadpattis, they too are familiar with what it means to illegally live in the city.[11] Says Aamir of a police constable who frequents his street, "He is a poor man too, and so he understands us." The persistent threats of demolition, he speculates, are a result of the constable's superiors having taken substantial bribes from the local residents' association. "He's on our side," Aamir continues, but the "higher officials don't listen to him. To those big men, he is small."

Demolitions and hafta demands suggest a predatory state, but at the same time, relationships that emerge from routine encounters such as I describe here reveal a formal incoherency that opens up possibility. Rather than make claims on an abstract state, envisioned as an entity distinct from society, Aamir and Dubey navigate a force inextricable from the vagaries of daily life with as much potential for expanding rights as it has for foreclosing them.

COLLABORATIONS

Life with the state is a life of contradictions. Although they lack licenses themselves, hawkers often speak of the state's responsibility to abide by the law. Although they regularly experience persistent extortion demands as well as overt violence at the hands of the police and municipality, they also see the state as a locus of hope and potential source of justice. In spite of the fact that their claims to city space are legitimized through daily, if unofficial, negotiations with state functionaries, hawkers and their representatives simultaneously make political claims in formal juridical realms as well.

These seeming incongruities are made visible by means of an open-ended approach to power; the tussles involving hawkers, municipal workers, and the police are about recalibrating power rather than challenging it. This is not a straightforward resistance to structures of domination. Instead, it is most often a contestation over the condition of illegality (hawkers certainly express the desire to work legally, although this a future goal rather than an immediate political reality). And in these tussles, challenges are made on both ethical and practical grounds: hawkers claim an abstract right to space while simultaneously paying hafta; their representatives speak in terms of principles of universal citizenship while also agreeing to municipal workers' bribe demands.

These heterogeneous engagements with the state were vividly demonstrated in two protests against excessive hafta demands. The first was organized by Prasad's union. The impetus for the protest was, he said, harsh police extortion from hawkers in the area—a neighborhood surrounding a busy train station. His claim resonated with what hawkers had told me earlier. Following the end of the pauti system, police in that neighborhood had been making unreasonable hafta demands. While the BMC carried out sporadic raids, the police seemed to have a persistent presence.

On the day of the protest, the streets and sidewalks were unusually clear. Most hawkers in the area stopped work in order to participate in the event. Throughout the afternoon, except for the flower hawkers and shoe repairmen, who are treated less harshly by the authorities, the area's hawkers stood by the side of the road and milled about with growing impatience, waiting for Prasad's signal to start.

As the crowd grew restless, Prasad proudly emerged from a tea shop and walked over to the group of police who had come for the occasion. Notified of the protest ahead of time, they had brought plastic chairs with them, which they casually placed amid the bustle of commuters flowing in and out of the station. I awkwardly stood at Prasad's side as he spoke with the policemen in charge. He listed the hawkers' complaints, explained the purpose of the protest, and concluded with a declaration that hawkers have a right to work on the streets. The group of police looked on with a disinterested expression. Patiently waiting for Prasad to conclude, the official in charge coolly responded: his job is simply to "keep the area clear of hawkers" after "the BMC calls us following an 'action.'" Negotiation is futile, the police implied, since, after all, evictions are initiated by the BMC.

As the conversation ensued, it became apparent that the police were more concerned about the logistics of the protest than about the content of Prasad and the hawkers' demands. This was no dramatic challenge to authority but a cordial encounter. Despite the high stakes (Prasad, in fact, spent the following two weeks in jail) and its very public spectacle, the encounter was casual—informal at times, even friendly. It was also carefully crafted. The more Prasad spoke, the larger the crowd grew around us. The police issued quiet requests to disperse. No one paid attention. Prasad then turned around and shouted at his supporters to move aside. With looks of embarrassment, the group scattered, signaling the first performance of Prasad's authority for the benefit of the police in a longer, carefully choreographed protest that also required the willing participation of its target.

After another half-hour of discussion, Prasad informed the police official in charge that the protest would begin in another thirty minutes, when the municipality trucks (parked, as ever, to ward off hawkers) had left the area. The municipality trucks departed on time and were replaced by two police trucks of similar size. At the other end of the lane, a small crowd gathered, consisting of a few dozen hawkers, shopkeepers' assistants, passersby, and a dozen police constables. A few women emerged from the crowd and handed Prasad baskets of vegetables and dry goods, and Prasad sat on the ground between two cement planters as if to hawk goods. Surrounded by the crowd and on cue, a police constable walked up to Prasad and instructed him (all the while knowing that he was the union leader) that hawking was not allowed on that spot. After Prasad's response of feigned innocence ("I am just a hawker trying to sell vegetables," he said), the police picked him up from the ground and arrested him. As he was marched into a waiting police van, chanting ensued, led by Farhana: "Prasad zindabad!" (Long live Prasad!), "Hum sub ek hain!" (We are united!), "Inquilab Zindabad" (Long live the revolution!)—slogans commonly heard at Mumbai street protests. Farhana's enthusiastic chants had an electrifying effect on the hawkers who had been standing around earlier and caused even the jaded passing commuters to stop and look. An act of *jail-bharo* [fill the jail] ensued. Over seventy women and men hawkers, including Farhana and Prasad, climbed into the police vans to have themselves arrested.

Despite the chants, this protest was less an act of resistance to power than a moment of collaboration in which both sides saw value in creating a very public street spectacle. As Prasad performed the role of the hawker by squatting on the ground, the constable arresting him performed the

role of the impartial law enforcer: the hawkers demonstrated their political efficacy, and the police used the event as a chance to demonstrate
their law-enforcing power and ability to control what is widely considered an unruly streetscape. And yet this was not just a performance for
mutually beneficial ends but also a performed negotiation of hawkers'
place in the urban landscape, as well as over how the law was to work in
practice. As Farhana later told me with much pride, "We all went to jail,
over seventy of us. I was there for three days. Prasad *sahib* was there for
twelve. Now they are afraid of us. They think of us before harassing the
hawkers. Of course there are still problems, but hafta demands are less."
The police's fear of further nuisance caused by the protest trumped their
loyalty to their institutional role as keepers of public order on the streets,
as well as their desire to collect greater hafta. This was, in other words,
a protest worked out beyond a formal world of rights and citizenship.
Although the idea of a protest suggests confrontation with power, its
content conveyed something else. A maneuvering within structures of
power rather than an overcoming of them, this protest signaled the wide
spectrum of possibility for inhabiting a realm of illegality.

SURVEILLING THE STATE

A few months later, hawkers working near the BMC godown were subject to an increase in the rate and severity of municipal demolitions.
To address this problem, Prasad and his colleagues decided on a new
form of protest. After issuing a formal letter listing their concerns—
high hafta demands, illegal demolitions, and leniency toward hawkers
operating from the so-called markedwali handcarts rented from local
businessmen—Prasad, Farhana, and a small group of other hawkers
marched over to the godown office and sat in a small space on the side
of the road adjacent to the entrance, beginning an indefinite *dharna*, or
sit-in, against the BMC. Eschewing the sign boards and public speeches
typical of a street protest, the strategy here was to maintain a continuous
presence at the godown, much as the hawkers described earlier do who
stand in front of the office to retrieve their confiscated goods. However,
the goal of this act of squatting was expressed differently in this case. It
was simple, explained Ramesh, a clothes hawker and regular participant

in the dharna: "We just want the BMC to follow the law, and to stop their corruption."

But this was not a conventional anti-corruption protest. While dharna implies an act of public shaming, or "moral pressure" (Hardiman 2004, 45), this protest was also mixed with surveillance. The act of continuously monitoring the activities of this BMC office was also meant to bring about the possibility for negotiation with it. Yadav, a snack vendor who regularly took days off from work to participate in the protest, told me, "We sit here from the moment they unlock the office doors in the morning, to the moment they are locked again in the evening." This was not just a moral assertion but an act of surveillance. It was also an ironic effort to co-opt the Indian government's decades-old anticorruption method to "maintain 'proper surveillance on officers of doubtful integrity'" (Corbridge et al. 2005, 157). Plastic chairs were brought for the event, newspapers were passed around, and the tea vendor around the corner opened accounts for his new customers. From this space at the side of the road, the union organizers held their usual meetings, received visitors, and attended to their everyday affairs, so after the first few days, the union office effectively relocated to this spot.

For eight weeks, working in four- to six-hour shifts, hawkers maintained a continuous presence at the godown. With conspicuously held cameras, the corruption-monitoring hawkers witnessed the twice-daily arrival of municipality trucks loaded with handcarts, boxes, and stalls collected from demolitions. I joined them for much of this protest. Casually chatting with vendors as they sat at the side of the road, I took notes and sometimes photographs, along with everyone else. Throughout the day, trucks would arrive burdened with fresh produce, handcarts, baskets, and pieces of broken stalls. BMC workers, unnerved by the audience, would unload the trucks in haste, spilling fruits and vegetables on the road.

After weeks of sitting and watching trucks come in from around the city, the protesters had honed their skill in identifying the incoming vehicles, whose visual cues, contents, and workers could be read for what they revealed about the nature and location of that day's demolitions. The protesters, sipping tea and offering a running commentary, made a habit of giving the trucks names as they rumbled in from different neighborhoods in the city. "Goregaonwali," announced Rajesh, a man with whom I sat most days, describing how the vehicle in question is well known for its actions around the city's northwest suburbs. At another time, Farhana called out "Mumbai Special," identifying a truck that attempted to circumvent hawker spy networks by conducting surprise raids all over the city. A few hours later, another truck came in: "Saat Bungalow returning from action," said a few people sitting nearby. The pleasure of monitoring the BMC office was enhanced by the casual exchanges between the dharna participants and the municipal workers, who had quickly gotten used to the protesters' presence. With little to do themselves, some workers, even those associated with hawker demolitions, at times sat outside in the plastic chairs brought for the protest. And in a characteristic performance of power reversal, when Prasad visited the protest site, he would always be sure to send an extra three cups of tea for his BMC "guests" sitting inside the warehouse.

What can we learn from the fact that the municipality did not exercise its legal authority to forcibly remove these protesting, and obviously encroaching, hawkers? What is to be made of the seeming contradiction in the BMC's continued demolition of hawkers' stalls elsewhere in the city while implicitly allowing hawkers to remain in front of its office, watching, photographing, and documenting municipal workers unloading confiscated goods? Perhaps this situation suggests that alongside the violence it exacts on the city's hawkers, the state acts as a differentiated site of exchange as well. Although certainly it could be said that allowing a spectacle like the dharna is itself an act of power, the effects of this spectacularization nevertheless opened a space of negotiation, enabling the possibility of recalibrating the basis on which claims are made, as well as the very form of those claims.

In a formal sense, both hawkers' claims on the municipality and the municipality's activities fall outside the realm of legality; none of the protesting hawkers had a license to sell food on the street, and BMC officials never refuted the existence of the illicit handcart rental arrangement. The next month, Farhana, the hawker and activist who helped coordinate the dharna, told me that the protest ended with an implicit understanding between the parties, after which the municipality conducted fewer raids and released confiscated goods more promptly than before. Thus, despite the protesters' claims that they merely wanted the municipality to follow the law (although surely this was not desirable because its strict application would have denied the means of livelihood to all participants of this protest), this conflict exceeded the binary of legality–illegality. As in the encounter between Prasad and the BMC staff already described, this was more a negotiation over what the rule of law meant than a protest over the state's failure to live by it, as well as over the particular configuration of hawkers' illegality rather than their illegal status itself. For Farhana and the other participants, the success of the protest was not judged by victories in a normative political sphere (such as the acquisition of formal rights, which did not happen) but in the better management of what is formally an extralegal arrangement, as well as in the recognition that hawking, although criminalized, is not necessarily illegitimate.

Prasad's confrontation with the BMC godown staff represents a charismatically based "urban infra-power" (Hansen and Verkaaik 2009) that is necessary for navigating the city's densely interwoven official and unofficial realms. More than an index of an individual's idiosyncrasy, this kind of maneuvering indexes a larger world of political practice that constitutes an innovation on political form within what is formally a liberal state structure. To Partha Chatterjee, negotiations of this sort represent a "constantly shifting compromise" (2004, 41) between the conflicting ideals of political modernity and universal democracy. The postcolonial state's (at least nominal) commitment to social welfare obligates it to recognize morally derived claims so that, for instance, populations such as hawkers and squatters—whose "very livelihood or habitation involve violation of the law" (Chatterjee 2004, 40) and therefore are no longer citizens that share in "the sovereignty of the state" (34)—can nevertheless make successful claims on the state. Although Chatterjee might overstate the case for the demographic uniqueness of this political practice (see Baviskar and Sundar 2008), what matters more than the existence of a demographically distinct domain of politics is how these practices shape the form of democratic practice more broadly.

"Success [in this hybrid political sphere] is necessarily temporary and contextual" (Chatterjee 2004, 60). This is not a utopic politics. The contingencies of power I have described prevent demolitions of hawkers' stalls in some instances just as they enable them in others. The arrangements one group of hawkers negotiates with state officials could also potentially exclude others. Moreover, compromises on the rule of law do not necessarily lead to a more equitable society. As Hansen (2001) points out, in Mumbai the Hindu nationalist Shiv Sena party also combines electoral politics with extralegal maneuvering to promote its influence. Indeed, "nuisance-value" political practices, a label Hansen uses to describe Shiv Sena tactics such as loud street festivals, is also applicable to hawkers' practices such as the dharna at the BMC godown. Surely uncivil behavior is not restricted to a specific political perspective. I argue that what is significant about these methods of political claim making is thus not only their content but their work, which suggests a heterogeneously operating political landscape that, as in all forms of messy democratic environments, has the potential to enhance substantive citizenship as well as the capacity for its suppression.

Perhaps assertion of political claims based on premises other than universal citizenship—even those based on moral assertions or nuisance—reflects possibilities for new kinds of citizenship arrangements that exceed those delimited by a formal civil society framework. Conversely, as I show in the following chapter, calls for equal citizenship and the rule of law can sometimes be tools to restrict democratic participation. In this context, one might understand the informal arrangements negotiated by the protesters and the BMC staff as a way to legitimize hawkers' extralegal claims to livelihood, just as, in a separate instance, Prasad's charismatic power enabled him to secure hawkers' claims to urban space.

In this chapter, I have described a space of negotiation between state functionaries and hawkers whose livelihood is based on an illegal practice. On one hand, the violence of the state indicates a kind of abstract sovereign power; on the other hand, there are moments of compromise that enable people to make morally infused demands on the state that exceed a proceduralist regime. An ethnographic exploration of what practices of corruption produce has the possibility to expand how scholars think about the state and political claim making in liberal democratic societies at large. Owing either to the assumption that the "informalization" of the state necessarily leads to the diminishing of citizenship rights (even though bureaucratic efficiency rarely leads to a more humane society; Sundar 2004) or, more speculatively, to a long-standing social scientific tradition that sees corruption as a "subversion of rationality" (Robertson 2006, 8), corruption is widely understood to be inherently antidemocratic and antipolitical. And yet here, illicit, "unofficial" transactions with the state—not just the acts themselves but also the world of discussion, protest, and negotiation they inhabit—constitute the terrain on which new forms of democratic politics may be worked out.[12]

Critiques of "corruption," as well as the realm of unofficial engagements with the state that it glosses, have recently become a central theme in Mumbai's public debates. Indeed, Mumbai's citizens' group movement emerged in the 1990s precisely to combat the kind of extralegal negotiation among hawkers and state functionaries that I have described here. How civic activists understand these negotiations and their implications for democracy, citizenship, civil society, and the status of the middle class in the city's political sphere is the focus of Chapter 5.

CHAPTER 5

ESTRANGED CITIZENS

A 1968 CARTOON BY RD LAXMAN shows what Mumbai's informal urbanism looks like from the outside looking in. The image depicts a government official telling a family of squatters to make way for an infrastructure improvement project. The state functionary holds a file in one hand and points across the street with the other. A laborer stands at his side holding an axe. "You have been allotted alternative accommodation on *that* pavement," reads the caption. At the center of the cartoon is an elderly man dressed for a casual walk. He is shown midstride, his walk having been interrupted by this unexpected spectacle. In the mid-2000s, a cartoon with a similar theme hung prominently on the wall of a Mumbai civic group office. It also showed an elderly man attempting to walk through a messy sidewalk scene. Vegetable vendors were shown squatting on the ground next to haphazardly scattered goods. Frustrated by the interruption, the old man says, "You got your hawkers' zone, where is the walkers' zone? There is no space to walk!"

Much like the 1930s letters to the *Bombay Chronicle* complaining of congested streets that I discussed in Chapter 2, these cartoons emphasize three elements: an unruly streetscape, a complicit state, and a middle-class witness. They show sidewalks blocked by the encroachments of hawkers and squatters. They depict a state that rather than working to eliminate the chaos, seems content to shuffle it around, doling out half-baked social

135

welfare measures rather than upholding the rule of law. They also show a professional-looking man observing the scene. He is depicted as a figure outside the spectacle, looking on in wonderment as the principles of modernist urbanism and rational governance are flouted around him; he is represented as someone in the street but not quite of it.

I begin with these two artifacts because they depict a sensibility of urban estrangement that powerfully shapes the Mumbai hawker controversy. I use the term *sensibility* in order to emphasize the subjectivities that emerge through engagements with the city's streetscape. Appraisals of one's place in the city, imaginations of its past, and visions for its future emerge from these sensibilities. They are not mere reflections of class positions but affective responses to the city and its public spaces.

The sensibility of the "estranged citizen," as I call it, emerges from a feeling of being an outsider to the traditional circuits of power in the city. The source of estrangement is something more than the state's corruption—which is certainly a persistent theme, as I will show—but comes from the sense that the state operates with a different set of values from their own—that legality and illegality exist on a spectrum rather than in absolutes; that laws are malleable, rights not universal but granted through an opaque, ad hoc logic; and that citizenship is not an abstract legal category but a negotiated process. Estranged citizens imagine themselves to be excluded from the politics of both the elite and the poor. They lack the wealth necessary to influence politics; more important, they lack an understanding of the tactics through which people such as hawkers make spatial claims—the embodied practices, cultivation of personal relationships, and appeals to morality and social welfare.

This political subjectivity is connected to a longer history of middle-class alienation from politics. As Leela Fernandes (2006) writes, "By the mid-1980s, the political identity inherent in organized middle class activity was shaped by a sense of state failure in delivering on its promises of the benefits of modernity to the middle class" (27).[1] This subjectivity also parallels contemporary political discourses, such as invocations of the *aam aadmi*, or "ordinary man," that have been especially prevalent since the early 2010s. Social activist Anna Hazare's 2011 anticorruption protests and social-activist-turned-politician Arvind Kejriwal's 2013 campaign both mobilized the idea of the "ordinary" outsider to traditional politics, with Kejriwal's party calling itself the Aam Aadmi Party, or the Party of the Ordinary Man.[2] And yet the sense of alienation depicted in the cartoons, and that dominates debates over public space and informality in Mumbai, is irreducible to these political campaigns. As I will show in this chapter, they represent a sensibility that exceeds stable political positions.

This estrangement emerges in part from witnessing the matrix of infrastructural improvisation, flexible governance, and negotiated rights on the street. The estranged citizen feels marginalized because the political system seems to privilege populist politics and context-specific citizenship over liberal ideas of rights, the rule of law, and technocratic forms of governance. Estrangement thus emerges from a putative disjuncture between how citizenship and governance ought to be and how they exist in practice. In this way, it is a sensibility that is a response to and product of witnessing the informality of the street.

THE *CHALTA HAI* ATTITUDE

Some people feel they inhabit a lost city, while others feel they bear the responsibility to do something about it. Speaking to a reporter for a Mumbai newspaper, an experienced civic activist said that what "puts [her] off" is the "'chalta hai' attitude of people here" (Punj 2007). In Hindi, *chalta hai* means "anything goes." Less literally, it implies "live and let live." In the context of this interview, it implies a toleration for informality, flexibility, and make-do solutions to urban problems.[3] She argues that the city's quality-of-life issues such as encroachments and poor infrastructure are the result of this attitude. To her, it explains both state incompetence and middle-class apathy. Moreover, she refers to the "attitude of people *here*" (emphasis added) to stress the comparison with presumed civic sense elsewhere. Living abroad showed her possible alternatives. In contrast to cities in Southeast Asia and the Middle East, where "political will shape[d] the city," "Mumbai is apathetic" (Punj 2007). Her goal has been to eradicate this apathy, take the initiative, and address local urban problems. Speaking of citizens' groups such as her own that have fought against encroachment, she says, "People are coming forward to take care of their own areas. The changes one sees in the city are only due to its citizens. . . . People are asking questions and do not allow authorities to get away with anything."[4]

The people this civic activist refers to, sometimes called citizen activists by the Mumbai press, are those who campaign on behalf of quality-of-life issues in the city. Since the 1990s, organizations of civic activists—such as residents' welfare associations and advanced locality management organizations (Baud and Nainan 2008)—in cities around India have been increasingly vocal on issues such as hawkers' encroachment, air and sound pollution, and transparency in municipal governance (Zérah 2007). A number of researchers have explored this new form of activism, raising some important questions regarding their relationship to the changing tenor of urban politics more broadly. These scholars suggest that these groups represent the decline of working-class politics, the dominance of a "managerial and technocratic elite" (Chatterjee 2004, 185), and an "assertive new middle class identity" (Fernandes 2006, xvii) that accompanies neoliberal urban transformations.

In light of these writings, one might suggest that the sensibility of estrangement I describe is in fact a justification for taking back the city from the poor—in other words, that it is simply a politics of maintaining class privilege. In a way, it is. Certainly civic groups motivated by a feeling of estrangement "elevate the rituals and comforts of a middle-class domesticity to city-wide priority" (Nair 2005, 345), in which specific class-based concerns are "normalized and universalized as those of the 'public'" (Baviskar 2007b, 11).[5] Moreover, the new legitimacy of quality-of-life issues such as urban beautification can be linked to broader political economic changes. Liberalization of the Indian economy in the early 1990s led to new wealth and the valorization of a consumer-oriented lifestyle throughout urban India. Seen in this light, middle-class alienation from the city might be understood as a product of the disjuncture between the promise of consumerism and global belonging (Mazzarella 2003), on one hand, and the gritty local reality—the informal urbanism of the street that one must continue to contend with—on the other.

Furthermore, scholars have argued that the transformations in the physical appearance of the city accompanying liberalization are correlated with a transformation in politics. For instance, John Harriss (2007) argues that "citizen" activists represent "entrepreneurial consumer-citizens" (2717), distinct from the subjects of traditional urban politics not just in content but also in form. This politics, he continues, rests on a "dualism that distinguishes 'citizens' from 'denizens' (inhabitants, who may be 'done unto')" (2719); whereas "citizens" invoke abstract rights in order to make quality-of-life interventions, "denizens" invoke citizenship-based entitlements and ethical pleas for basic amenities. Attempts to "reclaim public space" (Fernandes 2006, xxiii) are thus considered partly a "corollary to new regimes of accumulation" (Rajagopal 2001, 109) and partly an affective response to the dream of global belonging these "regimes" offer.

And yet while this sensibility of estrangement emerges from the middle class—a term loosely defined here to encompass the city's apartment-living, private-school-educated, English-speaking population—I argue that it is not reducible to a politics of a class-based takeover of space. There are two reasons for this. First, civic activism mobilized on the basis of "taking back" the city targets not only the poor. People who care about the "hawker problem" also object to developers building over open spaces and heritage structures, corporations maintaining parks, and municipal services being privatized. Second, those who act on the sensibility of estrangement inhabit a political subjectivity that shows elements of the neoliberal entrepreneurial citizen but is not identical to it. The estranged citizen blames both populist politics *and* the new culture of consumerism for the city's problems. Indeed, what is so striking about the chalta hai attitude, as the civic activist put it, is that it is used to explain both municipal workers turning a blind eye to unlicensed hawkers *and* the lack of civic responsibility among the middle class. Thus I argue that conflicts over public space involving civic activists should be seen as encounters among urban sensibilities. How people inhabit the city is shaped by these sensibilities, but they do not determine political outcomes.

ENTERPRISING CITIZENS

"Most people in the city don't care . . . it is only the 5 percent who are like us that keep this city from total disaster," says Alex, the president of a residents' welfare association, as we sit in his small office, an aluminum-clad shed tucked between high rises in a leafy Mumbai neighborhood. He had been telling me about his association's work on the hawker problem. He had recently been successful—two dozen vegetable vendors had been evicted from a nearby street in recent months—and yet Alex was not hopeful. He explained that the hawker problem was connected to a much larger "disaster" going on in the city. The little open space that remains in this densely populated city is being illegally taken over with the help of politicians. It is not only hawkers and slum dwellers who are doing this, he said, but also "the builders [who] are the culprits [in] Bombay's disaster. They build over any open space. Politicians are in office for only a few years, so they give the builders rights to build for a few lakhs and then move on to someplace else, not caring about the locality." Despite this widespread theft, few people seem to care. Encroachment, it seems, does not inspire passion.

Alex was inspired to act because he saw the battle against illegal encroachment as a natural outgrowth of his church charity work. "There is just no space. There is now a free-for-all of hawkers," he said. "[Hawkers say,] 'I can put up a stall anywhere,'" but children need a place to play and the elderly need a place to walk. With recent accidents in the area, encroachment has come to represent a matter of life and death; at a recent meeting "we told them [hawkers] that you are a threat to our lives." The BMC would not listen to residents' complaints, and so the association started a public campaign. Their protests against hawkers brought them notoriety. Articles described residents' association *morchas* [marches] against hawking and other encroachments in the neighborhood. Stories of middle-class professionals protesting in the streets made good copy. In the media coverage of these groups, they were framed as a new political entity that promised to transform the city's political culture. Bold headlines declared them "citizen warriors," and articles celebrated their individual initiative and the break from the preliberalization populism and complacency they seemed to portend.[6] They heralded, it seemed, a new era of entrepreneurially minded citizenship in which people are "construed as subjects of choices and aspirations to self-actualization and self-fulfillment" (Rose 1996, 41).[7]

Enterprising citizens work from small offices tucked away in quiet neighborhoods. They also work from home, in borrowed spaces in corporate offices, and in apartment complexes. They meet in places such as the common room of an apartment building in fashionable south Mumbai neighborhoods. To get there, sometimes they travel on a street lined with stylish gyms, yoga studios, and juice bars. They pass through a gate manned by uniformed security guards and wind their way through a thicket of freshly washed cars and SUVs to arrive at the meeting room. Inside are two dozen men and women, some middle aged, others elderly, most dressed in crisp salwar kameez or dress shirts and pants, and engaging in a lively debate.

I arrived at one of these meetings when civic groups were in the midst of the court battle over the creation of new hawking zones in Mumbai, discussed in Chapter 1. An organization working for good governance in India put out a call for a citizens' response to an impending ruling by the Supreme Court. The court was about to decide on a plan to create hawking and nonhawking zones in the city. The plan was developed by the BMC in order to put in place a formalized hawker regulation system in the city, the first since new licenses stopped being issued in the late 1970s. Nevertheless, the attendees were not hopeful. A rumor circulated that one of the judges privately called civic activists such as themselves "nuisance makers." To many, this did not bode well.

As participants trickled in, they sat at a large table and swapped war stories. They spoke of encounters with hawkers openly violating municipal codes, stubborn union leaders, unsympathetic judges, and corrupt police. A man turned to his friend and said with frustration: "A hawker can ask for space legitimately, . . . but it must be within the guidelines!" He said that one such guideline that described what can be sold, where, and at what time was posted to a tree. It was surreptitiously removed, and the BMC had not bothered to replace it. This was evidence, it seemed to him, of a conspiracy between hawker unions and the BMC to keep the laws fuzzy.

Photographs and letters to officials circulated around the room. An elderly man, his hair wrapped in a turban, sat quietly on the side. A bloated manila folder lay on his lap. He briefly opened it, flipping through newspaper clippings, legal documents, letters to municipal officials, and photographs of messy street scenes—photographs of men selling goods under clearly visible "nonhawking" signs, of pot-bellied men in greasy shirts frying pakodas in vats of oil precariously perched on the corner of a busy road. These were photographs that circulated around the city as well.

I would later see the same pictures on the desks of civic organizations and in the offices of the BMC department that deals with encroachment. On that day, the photos were meant as proof of the state's lenient approach to practices such as cooking on the street, which had been banned by the Supreme Court in 2003. As a result, these documents of hawker illegalities were also meant to inspire action.

While the men and women in the room held corrupt municipal officials and the police responsible for enabling illegal vending, they identified a deeper root cause of the problem. To them, the presence of encroachment also represented the absence of a civic consciousness. The need to instill a sense of responsibility among ordinary citizens animated the discussion. Participants remarked that friends, family, and neighbors insist on buying fruits and vegetables from popular hawkers. This elicited a cacophony of response from around the room: "We must educate the public not to buy from hawkers," declared an audience member. "The big problem are housewives. They must be educated because they use hawkers the most." Participants in a march against hawkers around that time said something similar: "The only way to get rid of these encroachments is for people to stop buying from these hawkers. . . . People need to show some responsibility and not patronise [them]" (Verma 2005).

Echoing this view, another participant spoke up: "Many . . . say that the best fruit to be found in Bombay can be purchased from the hawkers in front of Breach Candy Hospital." Her affect and mannerisms, crisp clothing, and eloquent, unaccented English suggested that she occupied a space of cultural privilege. However, rather than entitlement, her voice was tinged with frustration. Her neighbors, it seemed, had as little concern for public spaces as the hawkers with whom they fought over the sidewalk.

Maya, the veteran civic activist in the room, said she knew the spot well: "[Those] hawkers have been cleared away a few times, but they come back." She recalled an interaction she had had with local women: "[I told them], 'Well, if you like the fruit and you like the hawker, then move them into your compound. The footpath is for the public.'"

Another woman finished describing the encounter: "The [housewives] said, 'What? Into *our* compound? That is not possible.'"

"That is a real selfish, NIMBY attitude," said Maya.

Here, the presence of encroachment is interpreted as a lack of civic consciousness. Indifference to encroachment was a view I had heard other activists express on earlier occasions. It was also how civic activists described what being middle class meant: "The poor don't care about open spaces. And the elite, they just fly off to Geneva," Maya told me one day in her office. Roshan, another civic activist, expressed similar frustration at her neighbors' lack of enthusiasm for removing hawkers. Some "residents have complained about the lack of vegetable vendors in the area," she said. Rather than be thankful for her efforts, some even seem hostile. Referring to angry shoppers, she joked, "Maybe I will get shot for what I am doing!" She told another story about a residents' association that organized a boycott against hawkers in a nearby area that failed after two weeks. "[At first] no one bought things from them, but the hawkers still stayed, persisted. Then one resident came, and then another, and the boycott ended. People all went back to shopping from these hawkers."

Civic activists battling against encroachments believe they are uniquely situated in the city. They see themselves as neither poor—a population too deeply embroiled in everyday survival to care—nor elite—a group not connected enough to the daily life of the city. For the middle class, in contrast, estrangement from the informal life of the street inspires action; their goal is not only to "take back" public space from squatters but to usher in a new ethic of civic consciousness. They are not only witnesses to the spectacle of the informal city but, like the man in the cartoon who demands, "Where is the walkers' zone?" attempt to bring about its transformation.

RECLAIMING THE CITY

It was Christmas Day when I arrived at Roshan's house. Her family makes a big deal about the holiday even though it lacks religious significance for them. I sat in a plush living room while she instructed servants in the kitchen in preparing the afternoon meal. Her elderly husband engaged me in conversation about the neighborhood, a mixed residential and commercial area in the northwest Mumbai suburbs. It is only by historical accident that people call this area the "suburbs." Neighborhoods like this were once located on the city's outskirts but now represent its bustling center.

Their bungalow was built in the 1950s. "It was so nice back then—very peaceful and quiet," said her husband. "Now everything has changed, but I have nowhere to go. I guess I should go to a small village and live there." Roshan emerged from the kitchen to join us. I explained that I was writing about the hawker controversy and wanted to talk about the work of her residents' association. It had gained some notoriety in recent months for effectively keeping hawkers at bay. I was curious to hear how they did it. She began with a story:

> In the 1960s, the area was very quiet. There were no vendors sitting on the street. Not even a tea stall. When visitors came from downtown, it was a problem because there was no tea for them (we Parsis don't usually serve tea to guests, just cold drinks). For vegetables, we would go to a small market near the station. But there was not much there. The vegetable vendors in those days would carry the vegetables in a basket on their heads. They weren't lazy in those days! Now the hawkers have become lazy; they don't want to carry their goods, they just want to sit on the footpath!

I could understand her sense of loss; this once sleepy neighborhood dotted with modernist-style bungalows was now a hodgepodge of tall apartment complexes, hotels, offices, banks, and shops. As she told this story, we could hear traffic heading toward the nearby commuter train station. In fact, I had heard similar stories before. Hawkers Farhana and Ramesh similarly spoke of semirural urban peripheries rapidly transforming into urban centers. They also spoke of lost pasts and quieter times. They too described themselves as islands of calm amid the tumult of the rapidly changing urban landscape. For Roshan, however, hawkers *are* the rapidly changing city. They index alienation from a neighborhood she once felt at home in, a street she once felt at ease walking on, and a political system with which she once felt connected.

I heard other stories of quieter urban pasts. Maya, a prominent civic activist, began one of our conversations with a similar story:

> When I was growing up, there used to be a coconut man. He carried a basket of coconuts on his head and walked around. If you wanted one, he would stop and cut it open for you. Same for the peanut vendor; he had a big basket in front of him, which he carried with straps around his back.

Her friend added:

> Even now there are people who move around hawking. Fruit and vegetable vendors come to my house who I've known for generations. I remember when growing up, an old man, an egg and *breadwala* [literally bread-man, or bread vendor], came to our house with his small child. Now the child has grown up, and he comes to our house. We have known the family for so many years.

These are expressions, as William Glover (2007) puts it, of "a nostalgia for a previous era when urban life was imagined to be more decorous, less congested, and more 'civil' than it is today" (221). It all changed in the 1980s, said the civic activist, when "migrants started coming specifically to hawk on the footpaths. They are not the traditional hawkers. They have come to set up a business on the footpath—to occupy a place on the footpath and call it their own." With the rise of populist politics and the increasing political and visual presence of slum residents (Kaviraj 1997), the intimate city of the past gave way to the contested city of the present.

Nostalgia, writes Svetlana Boym (2001), is as much about the future as it is about the past. Indeed, narratives of a "more decorous" (Glover 2007, 221) urban past represent aspiration as much as memory. Maya, Roshan, and Roshan's husband shared these memories of Bombay's past as a way of teaching me a lesson. Their comments on what the city once was were also a commentary on what it should be. Nostalgic stories of Mumbai's past were meant to make sense of the present, but they also contained a message for action.

Roshan's neighborhood association certainly acted. The association was formed in response to a hawking zone proposed by the BMC in their neighborhood. It fought the proposal in the Bombay High Court in the early 2000s and won. Following this victory, the association continued to evict hawkers in the neighborhood. A tea and vada pao stall popular with autorickshaw drivers was dismantled. A few months later, the association pressured the BMC to demolish a popular vegetable market. Thirty hawkers were evicted; only a dozen managed to return. The association's work also expanded beyond the hawker problem. They cleaned clogged drains, removed the so-called community bins that would overflow with garbage, added landscaping along boundary walls, and transformed two overgrown plots into well-loved parks. They organized music events, medical clinics for the elderly that provided cheap checkups, and meetings with the local police in an effort to improve security for homeowners.

Activists in the association understood these activities as expressions of one of its mottos: "Self-help is best help." For Roshan and the other leaders of the neighborhood association, the first steps in reclaiming the lost city and overcoming political estrangement had to come from within. Hawkers and the state might be producing the chaotic streets, but it was up to ordinary residents such as herself to deal with the problem. As Roshan said:

> The association was formed in the late 1990s when the BMC started regularizing hawkers. We residents were outraged. They were going to permit 100 more hawkers where there were already 28! Once the BMC started to draw lines [dividing the plots] and allowing the hawkers to stay legitimately, we residents organized against them. . . .
>
> The hawkers caused such problems. They were so dirty, they would wash themselves on the side of the roads. They would throw trash, sleep, and eat there. It was very dirty. And it was dangerous too. With so many hawkers, there were people behaving badly; many people had their chains [gold necklaces] stolen.
>
> Hawkers would dump garbage in the drains, clogging them and causing a mosquito problem. Even now, the mosquito problem is so bad in the area. This is because back there [pointing behind us toward the east side of the neighborhood] there are jhopadpattis. They link up with the *nalas* [drains] and dump sewage and garbage into them, the water flows into the small drain in front of this bungalow, and that is why there are so many mosquitos. I have to pay the BMC from my own pocket every two weeks to clean out the drains.

Hawkers created a mess—"they would throw trash, sleep and eat there"—and they introduced a literal and symbolic disorder that facilitated a broader immorality. And yet state functionaries did not seem to mind. For years, they ignored hawkers, only to propose a system of regulation that would expand their presence in the neighborhood. Rather than impose order over the street, the state appeared to be the very agent of its disorder. Roshan pointed to an abandoned BMC project to build an organized hawkers' market as evidence of this:

> The metal pipes next to the high school, on the other side of the flyover . . . were built by the BMC to house a hawkers' bazaar. We stopped it. [However] now there are people living there. They have hung up some sheets. They have built a nice house there. The BMC is doing nothing to stop this. Look how dirty that area has become.

The state removes encroachments in one part of the city while facilitating encroachments elsewhere, an echo of the cartoon discussed in the opening pages of this chapter in which municipal workers tell squatters to move to another "allotted" sidewalk. For Roshan, it is inconsistencies like this that compel activists in the residents' association to take matters into their own hands. One story she told me emphasized this need for self-motivation and direct action:

> There used to be a Chinese man cooking food in front of the neighboring building.[8] The residents of the building, who are all vegetarian, said they would get sick from the smell coming from his stall. At night people would come to his stall after drinking beer; it was all very disgusting. We complained many times to the BMC and the police, but he would still not move. The women from the adjacent building planned ahead. They knew of the impending [BMC] demolition, so they bought landscaping materials, tools, and shovels. Immediately after the stall was broken, they rushed out and quickly built a planter and planted plants over the spot where the stall stood, preventing his return.

This is a familiar story: instances of middle- and upper-class residents "cleansing" their neighborhood of the visible presence of the poor has been documented around the world. In this instance, we see also these processes intersecting with a violent politics of ethnic exclusion; perceived ethnic difference becomes racialized, and nonvegetarian food is read as a sign of disorder and immorality. And yet calling this "cleansing" suggests a totalizing and unequivocal vision at work when in reality, these are piecemeal attempts to reclaim a city perceived to be already lost.

They are also a series of attempts, which often fail, to overcome a sense of alienation. While at times violent, in other instances they are characterized by equivocation.

THE AMBIVALENT ACTIVIST

Mumbai's streetscape is rapidly changing, and Paritosh, president of Roshan's neighborhood association, wanted to talk about those changes. However, unlike his colleagues' narratives of urban change, his lacked nostalgia. I met him at his office, a sparsely furnished space adjoining a warehouse tucked in a vast industrial park. The austere surroundings reflected his pragmatic approach to public space. He offered opinions on a wide range of topics: Why was there so much garbage in the neighborhood? Because "at 2:00 a.m. workers from McDonald's would dump the [restaurant's] trash in the community's garbage bin." Why can't the BMC successfully keep hawkers off Mumbai's streets? Because "all the hawkers cannot be removed from the city because of democracy." Why were there hawkers in the first place? Because "India is a Third World country, and hawking is a problem especially in Third World countries." What is the future of consumption in Mumbai? "Housewives . . . will go to the shopping mall."

Paritosh mentioned shopping malls because they indexed the possibilities and problems of the changing city. Stories about the new malls being built in the city dominated the newspapers. In these articles, they represented the city's hopeful future: a cosmopolitan aesthetic and the possibility of eliminating the street as the primary location of consumption. Articles such as one titled "From Mills to Malls, the Sky Is the Limit" (Bharucha 2003) included exuberant quotes from visitors impressed by a new mall's amenities and promise of global belonging it offered.

Paritosh saw things differently. The mall was a sign of the urban future certainly—it meant air-conditioned atria, brightly lit supermarkets, shrink-wrapped vegetables, shopping carts, and checkout lines—but he interpreted the effects of these changes less optimistically. "Housewives will change and go to the shopping mall [instead of street markets]," he told me matter-of-factly. "[But] many people will get unemployed. When that happens, there will be civil riots. There will be a revolution. Young people will be frustrated, and they will start a war."The implications of this prediction were not clear. Was this uprising by the unemployed a sign that shopping malls might not be good for the city? Or was he saying that this violence is the natural outcome of any political-economic transformation? Either way, Paritosh did not celebrate the new globalized architecture of the shopping mall, but he did not condemn it either. He did not see large-scale urban transformations as a loss. To him, they were an inevitability.

Paritosh did not see himself as an agent of globalizing Mumbai, but he did see himself as an agent of change. He told me that because of his neighborhood association, streets are less congested, sidewalks are cleaner, the overflowing trash bins are gone, drains that were once infested with mosquitos now flow freely, and two parks have been cleaned up. The park project was his greatest source of pride:

> Our biggest achievement is cleaning up the gardens. Five to eight years ago, they were dirty, dangerous places. People even urinated and used [them] as a bathroom. The [local] residents would not go inside. Couples—people from outside the neighborhood—would come sit in the park and do inappropriate things. But now look at the park. It looks so nice. People can use it now.

Landscaping has long been a tool for managing unruly populations. We see a similar strategy in Paritosh's account. Parks were cleaned up in order to attract certain city residents who acted a certain way. Cleansing the physical environment accompanied a moral and class-based cleansing. Couples no longer felt free to use the space for romantic rendezvous, and working-class men no longer felt free to use the park to urinate. At the same time, however, these spaces signify something more than just exclusion. As Amita Baviskar (2003, 97) argues, conflicts over public space also signify encounters among "dreams for a better life." These dreams are not class specific. It was, after all, Ali, a hawker (whom I discussed in Chapter 3), who introduced me to Paritosh's park and the quiet pleasures it offered. Paritosh would have been pleased. Was this an example of successfully disciplining marginal populations? Or was it a momentary intersection of diverse urban aspirations?

Yet to Paritosh, the new parks signified the success of the entrepreneurial citizen. He was so proud of them because they represented individual initiative. They are "my dream come true," he said. "I started the park cleanup with my own personal funds. I first started by cleaning and painting an outside wall myself. Then the project grew and the others joined." Like the drains that Roshan arranged to clean with her own money, the parks represented the power of ordinary individuals to make the city more livable. They represented the ability of citizens to transform the city outside traditional political channels.

Yet Paritosh and his association ran into greater difficulties when they tried applying this enterprising ethic to the hawker problem. Despite his association's relative power, he could not quite manage the illegal hawking in the neighborhood. Popular food stalls had been evicted and a thriving street market demolished, as Roshan explained earlier, and yet a small group of hawkers remain: the tea stall popular with autorickshaw drivers was gone, but vendors selling greens and lemons from a handcart now wheel up to the spot every night. Across the street, two men still sell grilled vegetable sandwiches. A man sells roasted corn on the cob. Around the corner, a woman sells bananas. Up the road, men and women sell flowers, cigarettes, fruit, shoes, and magazines. Like everywhere else in Mumbai, these hawkers have gradually developed deep ties to the neighborhood, cultivated relationships with state functionaries through hafta, and express a sense of ownership, even a right, to their spots on the side of the road.

Thinking that because hawkers are unlicensed, they are vulnerable, Paritosh and his colleagues thought they would listen to the civic activists' directives: "We told them, 'Make your size small; we don't mind if you stay. Just reduce your size, don't take up more space, stay clean. You can't have eatables because a school is nearby and students will fall sick.' We even provided them waste baskets out of our own money and told them to keep the street clean."

Paritosh urged the hawkers: "You get organized, and we will help you." But they already were organized, just not in a recognizable way. They too had a loosely associated organization that was negotiating with the authorities. As a result, the hawkers ignored his suggestions. Shortly after, the BMC started drawing red lines on the side of the road delineating where vending would be prohibited. Ironically, Paritosh interpreted this as a sign of the imminent creation of a hawking zone. It was also a sign that the BMC seemed intent on regularizing hawkers' presence in the neighborhood rather than appreciating his association's work in the neighborhood:

> They [the BMC] didn't listen to our complaints about the hawkers to keep them controlled. The hawkers didn't listen to us [either]. They didn't do what we told them to do. We gave them an opportunity to stay, but they didn't listen. That is why we had to fight against them in court. We would have allowed the hawkers to stay if they were [working] in an organized manner. Finally the residents took a *morcha* against the BMC....
>
> We received threats from the hawkers. I received very dangerous threats. They told me that my blood will spill on the ground. But I didn't mind! We told them we will persist. You get organized and we will help you.... We will permit a little bit [of hawking]. They are human too. We understand that they are human and need to live. But when the BMC drew lines [red slashes painted on boundary walls delineating hawking and nonhawking zones] to provide for three hundred hawkers in the area, then the problem worsened.

Paritosh's account of his engagement with hawkers is full of important, and unresolved, ambiguities. Was the association's conflict with hawkers, or with the BMC? Was the problem hawkers' mere presence on the street, or the nature of their activities on the street? Why were the BMC's "lines" more significant than other, similarly arbitrary actions by local BMC workers (such as installing "no-hawking zone" signs that, ironically, implied hawking was acceptable elsewhere)? This last question is especially important because far from being settled, the hawking zone system was still being hotly debated by hawker unions, civic groups, and the BMC when Paritosh told me this story.

I tried to get him to clarify, but my questions missed the point. The more I spoke with Paritosh and his colleagues, the more conflicting accounts of the hawking and nonhawking zone situation I heard. The confusion *was* the reality. It set the terms of the conversation and of the various actors' interventions in the city. Confusion surrounding hawker regulations was particularly pervasive. Was hawking banned 100 meters or 150 meters from train stations? Did "nonhawking zone" signs on one street corner mean hawking was allowed elsewhere? I also heard conflicting accounts of the proposed nonhawking zone: Would the main street or the entire neighborhood (which had the same name) be off-limits to vending? This confusion was partly a product of a lack of clarity governing all regulations in the city resulting from the multiple branches of government, often with overlapping authority, that regulated space. However, it also signified the association members' hazy understanding of their streets, how they were governed, and how successful interventions could be made. Confusion, in other words, was a product of a particular kind of political alienation.

Paritosh described the park cleanup project as a story of ordinary residents coming together for the common good; however, his dealings with illegal street vending had a more ambiguous message. Intervention in the hawker controversy was a work in progress. It was defined by miscommunication, conflict, and equivocation. Paritosh saw himself as an enterprising citizen, but also as a man waging a lonely battle amid the slow boil of the street. Ignored by hawkers and the BMC, he inhabited an urban landscape that was not quite his own.

THE PRAGMATIC ACTIVIST

Elsewhere in the city, enterprising citizens managed the hawker situation more successfully. Leela, the charismatic leader of an ALM (advanced locality management group) in a wealthy Mumbai neighborhood, managed to do what Paritosh could not. ALMs were started in the late 1990s to forge partnerships between residents and the BMC on issues such as drains and trash removal.[9] The idea was that neighborhoods would become cleaner if local residents got directly involved in their maintenance. Leela took this literally. When she wanted to fix the neighborhood's trash problem, she asked a BMC officer if she could accompany garbage workers while they worked:

> I told the BMC I would work on the garbage issue. [I] told them I would walk with the garbage truck. They were shocked. "But madam, you want to walk with the truck?" But to understand what is happening in our area, you must go, am I right? They couldn't believe someone like myself would walk

with the truck. But I went. I went with them to a building of very wealthy residents. I couldn't believe what I saw! The garbage was just dumped in the middle and the BMC staff had to cart it out in buckets. . . .

A Swiss diplomat lived in that building. I told him, is this what you do in Switzerland? . . . I have lived in Switzerland, I know what it is like there. . . . I also organized to clean up the garbage around the post office and sports club. I [also] organized ragpickers to come to the buildings to segregate the garbage.

Leela seemed to enjoy sharing this encounter with me. The incident was meant to be provocative: she wanted the story to be told. The disbelief of a BMC official, hanging out with garbage workers, telling off a Swiss diplomat, exposing the hypocrisy of her wealthy neighbors, and organizing ragpickers were all instances of her audaciousness. Leela was once a well-known actor in Hindi films. She now lives in a spacious apartment in one of the city's most prestigious neighborhoods. She knows that people think that members of the city's glamour set do not walk with garbage trucks.

She described herself as a persistent irritant—"poison ivy," she said—to the city's better-known civic groups. She was an outsider to this group of outsiders because she approached the hawker problem differently. Rather than support massive evictions, Leela encouraged citizens to cultivate relationships with hawkers. Rather than support the proposed plan to issue new licenses through a lottery to people who would then work in designated hawking zones, she advocated the idea of developing an unofficial hawker regulation system. "We know and trust the hawkers in our area," she said, so rather than rely on the BMC, residents should work directly with them. This was because to her, the problem was transience—mobility—not encroachment or squatters. Those hawkers with a long history in the neighborhood could be used to keep out the occasional newcomers. This strategy is uniquely suited to Mumbai's hawkers because "they are very territorial. They are watching very carefully who is coming in. We can work with them to control the space and prevent new hawkers because they are watching."

The idea that hawkers might be an asset to a neighborhood was not well received by her neighbors. At the first ALM meeting dealing with hawking, "the women all said, 'Get rid of hawkers!' [But] I told them: stand outside and watch who uses the hawkers, who drinks their tea and eats their food. . . . I told them: 'The hawkers who have been here for thirty years, we know them and trust them. They have proof they can stay. They collect the pauti receipts they received from the BMC over the past thirty years.'" She argued that old hawkers could keep the streets clean and new hawkers out. She won her neighbors over by showing that working with hawkers was not a question of moral obligation but a strategy to assert control over the neighborhood. Indeed, she bristles at what she sees as the other civic activists' (and hawker union leaders') moralizing. "I am not for or against hawkers," she said. It is "solutions to the city's public space problem" that she desires.

Leela also delighted in showing BMC officials her idiosyncratic perspective. Shortly after a new BMC officer in charge of encroachments started his job, she encouraged him to go for a walk around the neighborhood in disguise. "I encouraged them [the hawkers] to talk [to him]. They went on with their complaints. They were honest and said the truth about the BMC, corruption, and their problems." She saw this encounter as a great success, unlike her previous attempt, in which all the hawkers had vanished before she arrived. "[That officer] only told two people, but somehow word got out . . . that he was coming on an inspection." Leela interpreted this as evidence of hawkers' savvy: "You see, the hawkers have a spy network. Yes, a spy network. Don't be surprised; they find out everything. They could be used in a disaster because they know everything."

I accompanied her on one of these walks through the neighborhood. All work stopped as hawkers recognized us coming from a distance. Vendors of tea, sandwiches, and vegetables stood in polite deference. Their assistants—the young men who clean cups and sweep away vegetable clippings—paused while we walked by. Leela pointed to a barber working next to a small tea stall. "I told him, 'Would you cut hair next to an eatery in your village?' We will have to take care of him." We walk no more than two blocks when a small crowd forms around us. A man emerges from the group to assume the role of the hawker leader. Leela instructs him with a list of demands, speaking in Hindi for the first time that afternoon: "Fix those wastebaskets. What is that attached to the tree? What is that bag of garbage on the ground? Who are these new guys? What about that barber? Why are you not telling him to leave?"

The leader tried to explain that he told the barber to leave, but the barber replied, "Who are you?" as in, "Who are you to tell me what to do?" Leela shrugged: "Be strong. If you gather ten, twelve men, don't you think he will move?" "But … it is difficult." "Don't cry," Leela replied, as if to say, don't be helpless; you can make change happen if you take the initiative.

We continued on down the road. She spotted trash next to a hawker's stall and some poles holding up merchandise attached to a tree. Leela reprimanded them: "Would you act like this in your village? Would you throw trash like this and leave things on trees in your village?" They stood on in silence as we continued down the road.

Leela prides herself in her ability to read the street. She was "poison ivy" to the other civic activists involved in the hawker issue because she tried to distance herself from the subjectivity of the estranged citizen. Unlike them, she claims that she knows how the informal world of the street operates and can work with it. Indeed, she demonstrates a sensitivity to how populations relate to one another, how different practices are connected and the unofficial ways the street is governed. She recognizes the services hawkers provide to the army of drivers, guards, and domestic workers who flow through the neighborhood. She talks fluently of BMC extortion demands and informal strategies hawkers use to assert rights to space, such as the use of pautis as evidence of their long connection to a place. She reads the mixed-use street not as a sign of urban disorder but as potentially containing the tools for order—an entrepreneurial citizenship decoupled from modernist urbanism—and thus, ironically, as a step toward the imaginary of the active citizen. This is not a utopic vision for street-level democracy but a focused attempt to overcome the sensibility of estrangement produced by the informal city.

EXCLUDED CITIZENS

These conversations took place when the BMC was drawing up a list of hawking and nonhawking zones in response to a Supreme Court directive. The plan was never implemented. Hawker unions and civic activists fiercely opposed the proposal, and by 2011, the list was abandoned.

But these unactualized plans had concrete effects. The new wave of civic activism that swept Mumbai in the early 2000s, the subject of this chapter, was one of them. Residents' welfare associations were formed when people learned that streets near their homes might be turned into hawking zones. Older, dormant groups were infused with new life as their members found a cause to rally around. Their activism was wide ranging: they organized street protests, met with members of the "three-member committee" of retired judges tasked with developing the hawking zone list, and attended heated meetings where hawking zones were discussed. Some filed petitions with the various courts to challenge the proposal. The sense of outrage was a by-product of a feeling of disempowerment—the sense that ordinary residents were being left out of the decision-making process. Others, such as Paritosh, were angered at the state's violations of its own laws, pointing out that hawking zones violated regulations laid down by the Bombay High Court.

The effect of the hawking zone plan was that people previously distanced from the everyday operations of the state were thrust into its messy world of governance. Many saw for the first time how the street gets regulated in practice. They saw the extralegal means through which hawkers acquire rights to space. They observed hawkers with no legal title to a spot on the road talk of ownership over it—and they saw state functionaries acknowledging this ownership. They uncovered hawkers' alliances with the same BMC workers responsible for their removal. They saw other things: police hanging out at hawkers' stalls, indifferent to their illegalities, hawkers "giv[ing] BMC official[s] hafta so boldly," as if they had nothing to hide, and BMC antiencroachment department workers surreptitiously renting out handcarts to unlicensed vendors.

Indeed, state indifference to the illegalities that so openly flourished animated civic activists' conversations at the meeting of nongovernmental organizations and citizens' groups discussed at the beginning of this chapter. "The BMC knows the hawkers are selling goods on the street, but they do nothing about it," said one participant. "Hawkers are not using the BMC markets and the hawkers' plaza [built by the BMC in Dadar, central Mumbai] but instead are storing goods there and hawk out on the street illegally. So the BMC *must* know what is going on." Personal encounters with state functionaries were especially disheartening. "The police say their vans are not big enough for confiscating all the hawkers' goods," said a prominent civic activist who, after a pause, mimicked the police officer's words in Hindi: "'Hum kya karein?' [What are we to do?]."

"Then take the hawker away!" shouted a man listening from the side of the room, as if the police officer was present to hear the outrage. Another participant asked rhetorically, "Why is it so easy for hawkers to get their goods back for just Rs 100?" "If someone breaks the law, why should the goods be returned?" "According to the 2003 High Court order, cooking on the street is banned." "But entire streets are full of cooking!" interjected another participant.

Noting how the state fails to uphold its own laws, Maya added, "There is not *one* circular issued by the BMC saying that cooking on the street is banned." She described a recent encounter with the police: "The senior police officials say they do not have the manpower to keep nonhawking areas clear. They said that 'watch and warn' is not the job of the police. Instead, it is their job to catch thieves and murderers."

Other activists such as Alex learned of this parallel world of the law when he tried to get unlicensed hawkers removed in the early 2000s. As he explained on a separate occasion, "They are vending on our footpaths, on spaces meant for the public at large. On spaces meant for specific purpose. They say there are no laws for me. I can put up a stall anywhere." He discovered people who felt a sense of ownership over their illegally occupied plots—hawkers who even felt entitled to those spaces—and, perhaps most troubling, state functionaries who recognized these claims. Here is how he described the problem:

> The hawkers who are there now, although unlicensed, refuse to move. They feel that since they have been at that spot for years, they will lose that right to that space if they move. But they do not own that space.
>
> Also, it is never just one hawker. They are constantly bringing in others from outside Bombay. Others are always coming from the village. Brothers, uncles, are invited to come from the village to work at the same spot. So, they come from the village to Bombay even when they originally had no intention of coming. But there is money to be made. I know it is hard work but . . .

A middle-aged woman who had quietly been reading a newspaper lying on Alex's desk—in fact, a copy of that day's *Midday* that contained an article about their association—interrupted him:

> I don't have any so-called sympathy for these people. They just come whenever they want and set up and make money. I was born and brought up here; I have seen how the area has changed. These people don't care about the neighborhood. They are making lots of money.

"Sympathy" might be understood as code for compromised principles: the antithesis of technical efficiency. However, Alex suggested a less hard-boiled approach. He understood that he does not work in a vacuum: "People say that hawkers have a right to [a] living. . . . Yes, they have a right to [a] living, but not at the cost to our public spaces, our roads."

What at first seems a straightforward problem of an obstructed street becomes a trickier problem of citizenship. Hawkers'—and, it seems, state functionaries'—understanding of rights conflict with Alex's. Like other civic activists, he advocates a society based on the rule of law, governance based on procedure, and citizenship based on abstract universalisms. But through involvement in the hawker controversy, he has learned that power works through a series of compromises. He has discovered a system of spatial claim making that seems to be grounded in material processes (Hetherington 2009). For instance, unlicensed hawkers "refuse to move," Alex says, because they feel their occupation of space has been legitimized by long-term presence—"they feel that since they have been at that spot for years, they will lose that right to that space if they move." On the street, rights do not circulate through a logic of universality but through a logic of contingent practice; rights are tied to place and history rather than abstract persons; the legitimacy of street vending is determined not by its legal basis but by negotiation and compromise with local authorities. Civic activists' biggest realization, it seemed, was that they were participating in a game whose rules they did not quite know.

Partha Chatterjee describes Indian politics since independence as a product of a "constantly shifting compromise between the normative values of modernity and the moral assertion of popular demands" (2004, 41). The "alternative accommodation" on a sidewalk and "hawkers' zones" depicted in the cartoons described at the beginning of this chapter are instances of a similar compromise. Framing these scenes as compromises allows us to think through governance, citizenship, and spatial conflict outside analytics that read them as instantiations of particular ideologies, political economic processes, singular governmental visions, or class interests. In the cartoons, universalizing notions of technocratic governance and abstract rights mingle with the pressures of everyday life in the city. The estranged citizen must similarly contend with the realities of grounded rights and negotiated legalities, even as she aspires for principles such as the rule of law and forms of governance based on strict ideas of rational modernity. Recall Paritosh, who wondered whether removing squatters would provoke a "revolution"; Alex, who spoke of hawkers' "hard work" and their appeals to the Indian Constitution; and Maya, who spoke of the middle class's unwillingness to reclaim the sidewalk. Impulses that appear to be contradictory—and in which one must ultimately win out over the other—might instead exist in a generative relationship which produces the street and its politics.

CHAPTER 6

IMPROVISATIONAL URBANISM

MUMBAI'S LANDSCAPE of squatters, informal settlements, and mixed-use streets was once considered a paradigm for urban dystopia. For instance, in his 1979 ethnography of a potter community in Dharavi, Mumbai, the anthropologist Owen Lynch (1979) wrote that his field site was widely considered "a stinking slum-town . . . bursting at the seams" (*Economic and Political Weekly*, quoted in Lynch 1979, 4) and "a hell hole" (*Free Press Journal*, quoted in Lynch 1979, 4). This settlement, located in central Mumbai and soon to acquire the title of "Asia's largest slum" (Sharma 2000), was similarly said to contain "cesspools of filth and crime" (*Indian Express*, quoted in Rajyashree 1989, 370). However, since the early 2000s, something seems to have changed. Informal settlements and eclectically used public spaces are increasingly interpreted as signs of creativity, resourcefulness, and ad hoc entrepreneurialism. What were once seen as "underdeveloped" cities became "squatter cities—where a billion people now make their homes—[and which contain] . . . thriving centers of ingenuity and innovation" (National Public Radio 2012). Reflecting the wide-ranging appeal of this new perspective, Prince Charles, following a visit to a Mumbai slum in 2003, stated that it demonstrated "an underlying intuitive grammar of design" and that architects and planners in the West should take heed of its "built-in resilience and genuinely durable ways of living" (Booth 2009).

Reflecting architectural trends toward "new urbanism" and sustainability since the early 2000s, designers, curators, journalists, bloggers, and scholars have argued for new attention to the ordinary ways people in megacities of the Global South use and produce city spaces (Koolhaas et al. 2000).[1] This new perspective is evident in a range of fora, from architecturally oriented publications and blogs[2] (e.g., Engqvist and Lantz 2008; Burdett 2012), to museum exhibitions, films, literature, and scholarly writing. Numerous recent architectural exhibitions on Mumbai's spatial form, often in conjunction with cities such as Rio de Janeiro and Lagos, are premised on the idea that informal landscapes are not merely signs of poverty and infrastructural collapse, but also contain characteristics of "sustainable communities" (Burdett 2012, 93). For instance, the Museum of Modern Art's Tactical Urbanism, held in 2014, and *Jugaad* Urbanism: Resourceful Strategies for Indian Cities, held in 2011 (Roy 2011a), were devoted to "explor[ing] how the energy of citizens 'making do' can be an inspiration and a catalyst for the worldwide community of architects, designers, and urban planners" (American Institute of Architects New York 2011).

I call this approach to reading urban landscapes the "improvisational city perspective." This perspective focuses on the everyday spatial practices of the poor with a particular emphasis on their ingenuity and resourcefulness. It focuses on the diverse ways people use mundane city spaces such as walls, bridges, and the side of the road to build homes and establish communities and livelihoods and reads these as a rejoinder to political economic approaches that focus solely on structural inequality and deprivation. It is a way of seeing urban landscapes and the people who inhabit them in terms of everyday spatial practices rather than an underlying socioeconomic condition. As a result, the improvisational city perspective casts a new eye on poverty and infrastructural absence. Density, mixed use, fluid streetscapes, and blurred boundaries are not seen as signs of a city's failure as an earlier generation of urbanists might have considered them, but as possible design successes; landscapes and spatial practices that once signaled a disconnect from global modernity are now offered as a possible model for a global urban future.

Because of its shift away from a critique of social injustice, the improvisational city perspective is more politically ambivalent than urban studies that focus on marginalization and poverty. Some scholars are critical of it for this reason. For instance, Ash Amin (2013) argues that architectural, journalistic, and academic focus on the spatial ingenuity of the poor excuses local states from providing social services or adequate infrastructure. The term he uses to describe this urban studies lens—the "human potential optic" (479)—deliberately echoes the language of neoliberalism in order to highlight its valuing of ideals of self-actualization and individual initiative over social and economic justice. My term, improvisational city perspective, is inspired by Amin's critique and yet is different from it. Rather than show the material realities this perspective overlooks and the elitist political projects it can at times support, I explore the work of this perspective through several important questions it raises: How does infrastructural absence become affective presence? What does it mean to revalue spatial disorder? What unlikely political projects might this perspective enable, as well as foreclose? And, finally, how does this perspective contribute to recalibrating the relationship between the local and the universal outside the older categories of postcolonial theory? While I do not advocate for or against this reading of the city, I do argue that it matters. How and with what consequences is something yet to be determined. With the term *improvisional city perspective*, I deliberately emphasize its open-ended political and conceptual future.

The broad circulation of the improvisational city perspective, and in particular the "international cultural cachet" (Harris 2012, 2956) it has given Mumbai, also offers a new lens on issues raised in the preceding chapters. First, what are the consequences of the new images of Mumbai's informal landscapes as spaces of ingenuity and resourcefulness? How do these images manifest and circulate within the city itself? Second, what are the links between the ethnography of the street I have provided and the new imaginary of the megacity as a space of design innovation? And third, what is the role of ethnography itself in the improvisational city perspective? For instance, Ash Amin (2013, 480) describes writings that employ the "human potential optic" as "complex ethnographies of being and becoming." Indeed, while often lacking the long-term fieldwork required of the anthropological monograph, these works are inspired by ethnography; the quotidian, ephemeral, and spontaneous acts of life are precisely the kinds of affective registers featured in improvisational city exhibits, design writings, and architectural analyses. Turning Amin's formulation around, can the improvisational city perspective be an object of ethnographic inquiry when ethnography itself is implicated in it?

In this book so far, I have shown how streetscapes are produced through hawkers' everyday spatial practices and negotiations with authorities. I have also shown how this world of informal spatial claims animates a middle-class, good-governance-oriented social movement. As I have argued, the stakes of the hawker controversy are not only about who has rights to the street but the content of those rights, as well as the spatial imaginaries that give those rights meaning. The hawker controversy is animated by questions that have long been central to Indian politics: How should rights be expressed, and on what basis does the state recognize them? And how are the city and its future imagined? The new architectural, curatorial, filmic, media, and scholarly attention to cities like Mumbai raises an additional question: How do seemingly local conflicts over public space resonate internationally as well? In this concluding chapter, I discuss a provisional outline for the contemporary transnationalization of the Mumbai street. This is not to suggest that the street is newly transnationalized. As I showed in Chapter 2, spatial imaginaries have been a product of a transnational traffic of ideas since at least the eighteenth century. Rather, the content of this transnationalized imaginary might be new and worth considering for what it says about the future of urban studies.[3]

DESIGN DISCOURSE IN ACTION

On a cool afternoon, a working-class family out for a stroll in a central Mumbai park might have caught sight of a strange spectacle: an eclectic crowd sitting beneath a bamboo enclosure with stylishly designed transparent maps lining one side and elaborate architectural models lining the other. Braving the glares of security guards, the family might have taken furtive peeks through a padlocked metal gate but then, feeling out of place, moved on. If they had lingered longer, they would have learned that the event was officially open to all. They would have seen a three-dimensional modeling of the city's density, innovative mapmaking techniques, and the potential for infrastructure repurposing. They would also have learned that they were not just spectators, but subjects of a new transnational urbanist discourse. The gathering was not just meant to display architectural design ideas, but also to engage Mumbai's residents in a conversation about the future of the city.

The gathering was the BMW Guggenheim Urban Lab, which took place in Byculla, Mumbai, in December 2012. Its website (http://www .bmwguggenheimlab.org) describes the lab as "part urban think tank, part community center and public gathering space." Conceived and directed by a Guggenheim museum curator, the mobile venue arrived in Mumbai after stops in New York City and Berlin. While in Mumbai, the six-week-long event hosted dozens of panel discussions on topics such as housing, transportation, and public space and organized a diverse range of events for a variety of audiences, including puppet shows, screenings, design competitions, and neighborhood food tours.

The exhibit promoted a vision of the improvisational city that was simultaneously universalizing and rooted in place. The lab's focus on design, experimental mapping, and public workshops reflected the shift toward a more eclectic approach to the city among American and European architects since the early 2000s. It also demonstrated attention to local context by creatively incorporating cultural practices. The physical structure that housed the events, a bamboo frame tied with rope and partially covered with canvas, was modeled on the temporary tents Mumbai residents erect for weddings. Artists were brought in to make *rangoli* designs with colored powder. Sachin Tendulkar, a famous cricket player and Mumbai resident, spoke one day about growing up in the city. Local schoolchildren were invited to watch a puppet troupe perform the history of Bombay. Coming from local municipal schools, these children represented the community that the lab aspired to include in its events. During the show, puppeteers told an abbreviated but engaging story of the history of the city, including its many problems, such as lack of running water, hygiene, and infrastructure. After the performance, one of the directors asked the children, many of whom themselves lived in slum settlements, "How is your neighborhood? Are there similar problems where you live?" "Accha hai! [It's great!]," the excited children politely shouted back in unison. The event organizer gave an embarrassed smile, disappointed by this response.

The lab offered a moment in which the improvisational city perspective met the ground, so to speak. However, no easy conclusions can be drawn from this meeting, since it opened up new possibilities as much as it foreclosed them. This was not simply an instance of globe-trotting experts bludgeoning local residents with the aid of universalizing discourses. Instead, the encounter was marked by tense engagements that emerged in the attempt to rethink the relationship of the particular to a new universal story outside the postcolonial narrative, in which the Third World city merely lags behind the West.

Contradictory possibilities characterized the Landlink design proposal produced by members of the lab's team as well. The proposal was to develop a new pathway for autorickshaws, bikes, and pedestrians, along with a series of public spaces above a massive water pipe that runs along the spine of the city. Prominently displayed throughout the event, the miniature architectural model served as a reference point for what a reimagined urban landscape could look like. Echoing New York City's celebrated High Line, the model reflected architectural trends such as sustainability, green design, and the reuse of redundant infrastructure. It reinterpreted a massive piece of water infrastructure—currently used by the poor as a walkway, a shelter, a place to play and to dry clothes—as a stylish, gently undulating walkway. Little figurines indicated people walking or standing in groups. Rectangular shapes representing buildings irregularly punctuated the scene. This was a vision of a vibrant public space on parts of the city that are often literally invisible on its official maps.

The design was provocative as well as unsettling. This was, in part, the intent. According to Neville Mars, its creator, the design was not meant as a final statement but as a device to start a conversation about Mumbai's physical environment (McLaren 2013). The Landlink was premised on the need to embrace the contingent and informal life of the city. In this way, a highway exclusively for autorickshaws, bicyclists, and pedestrians represents a significant departure from previous infrastructural practices such as the recently built $2 billion Bandra-Worli Sea Link, which privileges private car owners. The Landlink also attempts to harness the city's resourceful spirit. Mars notes that traditional infrastructure such as roads, overpasses, bridges, and the land beside train tracks and water pipes are "often just taken over by other activities—whether [they are] commercial, or leisure, or praying, or whatever—and we can really learn from that" (McLaren 2013). Echoing Simone (2004), Mars calls the ordinary practices that envelop and co-produce the concrete infrastructure of the city "infraspace" (McLaren 2013). The Landlink design attempts to use this infraspace by connecting distant slum settlements with one another rather than with wealthy neighborhoods. "We should start linking slums," Mars says, in order to facilitate "connections" (McLaren 2013) across the informal spaces of the city.

As grounded utopias, architectural models are compelling objects from which to imagine city futures. They are found in diverse contexts: not only in design exhibits and architectural firms but in places as varied as corporate complexes and transportation companies. Models fuel dreams of urban futures: fantasy worlds of clean streets, a civil public, and orderly traffic. Models such as the Landlink do even more; they are at once a dreamscape and purportedly a concrete design rooted in the micropractices of the city (McLaren 2013). The Landlink model was meant to capture a dynamic public space as well as intervene in public debates around the future of the city. Yet in doing so, it was simultaneously an object of contradictions. While inspired by the fluid infraspace of the city and intended to democratize urban planning, the materiality of the Landlink model is static, its imagined users exhibiting a restricted range of activities. Towering structures dominate the imagined scene, while the public spaces are segregated and sanitized; the figurines stand or walk rather than sit, squat, or shit. Even this utopic dreamscape of sustainability and inclusivity replicates formal discourses of the unwelcome city; there are no cars, but also no street vendors, stray dogs, or garbage (McLaren 2013). The fluidity that inspires the design is excised from its realization.

Thus, when the improvisational city perspective encounters its purported objects of inquiry, tensions emerge. The lab's organizers hoped to "provide everyday urban citizens with better tools to speak up about their lives in the city" (Brooks 2013) and so ensured that the exhibition was free and open to the public. However, the goal "to involve citizens more actively in complicated planning processes" (Iyer 2012) was upended by the very universalisms on which it rested. Community engagement sounds politically benign, but as Anand and Rademacher (2011) have shown, it has "in some ways supplanted equality as a guiding aspiration for urban development." Furthermore, whereas the curators aimed to get "people to begin thinking about and discussing their urban environment" (Van der Leer, quoted in Iyer 2012), to the audience, passersby, and some of the local activists and academics invited to participate, the lab was a spectacle disconnected from the conversations on the city that were already taking place, ignoring many of the avenues of political engagement that slum residents already deploy to access resources, most of which are not products of "stakeholders [coming] to the table for an informed discussion" (Sunavala 2012) but of stealth, informal negotiation, and direct possession (Björkman 2013; see also Anand and Rademacher 2011).

However, transnationally circulating ideas and discourses can have other effects. As in the preceding chapters, my goal is not merely to expose how concepts that claim universality do violence to local realities, but to explore the life of these concepts as they circulate, acquire new meaning and link up with various "projects" (Tsing 2000, 330) that might produce their own particularities. I examine one such example at the end of this chapter.

DISTINCTION AND UNIVERSALITY

Explaining why he decided to locate the BMW Guggenheim Lab in Mumbai, its curator said that "many urban issues that one can find around the world are more intense in Mumbai and for that reason it really can function as a microcosm of sorts for urbanism" (quoted in Sunavala 2012). Initiatives such as this lab reflect the expanded geographic lens of urban design practitioners, countering Mumbai's prior associations solely with poverty and underdevelopment. In projects such as these, Mumbai serves as an indicator of larger urban trends, as well as the locus of a distinctive practice of space. The juxtapositions to be found in the city—between, for instance, economic vibrancy and transnational connection, on one hand, and poverty and sprawling slum settlements, on the other—are taken as indicators of global processes such as growing inequalities, while the striking qualities of its heterogeneously used streets and dense and economically vibrant slum settlements are understood to make the city a paradigm for a new kind of spatial and architectural ingenuity.

Descriptions of the megacity through the improvisational city per-spective establish urban distinction through affect, intangible practice, and sensibility: their focus is often on what people do in space—how they inhabit the built environment and use infrastructure. Writings and curatorial exhibits often focus on the bodily experience of walk-ing through slum settlements or navigating the streets. For instance, a cycling journalist accustomed to car-centric US cities finds, on Mumbai's streets, a "benevolent democracy at the core of the mayhem" (Roach 2013, 98), consisting of "rubble, open manholes, [and] pedestrians sprinting for buses" (95). A city defined by the sensory is also what the journalist Somini Sengupta observes in her discussion of the production of the film *Slumdog Millionaire*: Mumbai "is not distinguished by its architecture . . . [but] by its atmosphere, its noise . . . [and] the way it smells: part drying fish, part human waste" (Sengupta 2009).

The improvisational city perspective frames public spaces in terms of the aesthetic experience of its jostle of bodies and practices. Streetscapes that were once a sign of cultural difference—as in Sidney Low's account of Mumbai's inverted streetscape, where "people do all sorts of things in public which to our thinking should be transacted in privacy" (Low 1906, 23)—are now reframed as alternative urban configurations; infrastruc-tural absence becomes affective presence. The intangible characteristics of the city, which are often viscerally felt but not immediately observable, now represent the aesthetic of the city as a whole. Dharavi is described as a space of "inventiveness and productivity" (Betsky 2013), where residents exhibit "incredible strength and discipline," doing "all kinds of activity" (Brand 2009) in "a churning hive of workshops" (Yardley 2011). "I must admit," writes another author, "that when I entered Dharavi for the first time, I could immediately feel the verve and energy of the people around, being proud of their homes and self-created livelihoods" (Spies 2012).

The effect of these narratives is a city conjured not in a traditional manner—through landmarks, monuments, and iconic skylines or through economic or demographic indicators—but through sensory experi-ences. Again, this is not entirely new. Nineteenth-century travel writings often commented on the corporeal experience of encountering the city (Chakrabarty 2002); however, whereas colonial-era accounts interpreted

Mumbai residents' public practices as an indicator of their nonmodernity, contemporary invocations of urban difference now signify a new kind of futurity. In this new temporality of the improvisational city perspective, European and North American cities are no longer recognized as the logical end point of development; instead, places like Bogotá, Manila, Mumbai, and Nairobi represent the "cities of the future" (Zeiderman 2008, 24)—the "prototypical urbanism of a new urban age" (Harris 2012, 2956; see also Roy 2011b).[4]

Within the improvisational city perspective, the megacity of the Global South thus simultaneously represents a space of difference, an object of desire, a site for design intervention and experimentation, and a challenge to normative ideas of urban planning. This is the view most famously articulated by Rem Koolhaas, who, after visiting Lagos, Nigeria, noted that "[infrastructural] shortcomings have generated ingenious, critical alternative systems, which demand a redefinition of ideas such as carrying capacity, stability, and even order, canonical concepts in the fields of urban planning and related social sciences" (Koolhaas et al. 2000, 652). In this urban narrative, difference is not a sign of deficiency but promise. At the same time, local practices and sensibilities are potentially assimilable to a universalizing language of architectural urbanism and sustainability.

This tension between the irreducibly particular and a new universalism is also evident in the creation of new urban "brands" that attempt to rethink universalizing categories in urban studies by emphasizing the distinction of local ingenuity. For instance, cities that were once "underdeveloped" are now called "squatter," "makeshift," or "tactical" cities. Likewise, the urbanism these cities exhibit—their ad hoc configuration of built space and practices—are called "flexible" or "hactivism, guerilla, DIY [do-it-yourself] . . . subversive, stealthy or wiki urbanism" (Courage 88, 2013). The anthropology of cities and globalization has grappled with such questions surrounding the branding of cities under globalization; for instance, researchers have studied how cities must carefully navigate the line between universality and locality in their bid to attract foreign investment (Kanna 2010). Cities like Dubai and Shanghai are especially notable in this regard; creating a "business-friendly environment" requires a certain visual aesthetic, standardized airport experience, and labor and development policies—in other words, the careful circumscribing of difference, even while at times the same cities must reinvent a sense of locality through the commodification of cultural heritage (Bagaeen 2007). In these instances, competitive advantage is achieved by navigating the tension between difference and sameness. Spatial transformations such as cleansing downtown areas of "visual signs" of disorder (Chesluk 2004) and the development of "mega-projects" (Yeoh 2005, 947) are central to the transnational "inter-urban competition" that aspires to both "connect to a global imaginary" as well as "appropriat[e] the 'cultural' realm as a means of maintaining a sense of unique identity" (Yeoh 2005, 947).

The new image of the improvisional city is produced by journalists, curators, architects, and academics rather than civic boosters, business groups, planning authorities, and policymakers. Books such as *Shadow Cities* (Neuwirth 2005) and photography exhibits such as Noah Addis's *Future Cities* (Rosenberg 2013) establish cities' international recognition through the intangible practices of informal life. These are transnationally scaled narratives, but they also focus on overlooked, mundane practices: "the restaurants, markets, clinics and effective forms of self-organization" (National Public Radio 2012) found in informal settlements, how people turn water pipes into shelter, build shanties out of found objects, and creatively weave living and work spaces (Neuwirth 2005). Richard Burdett (2012) argues that such attention to detail is necessary for successful design intervention. It is essential, he continues, to "[build] on the spatial and social DNA of their cities from the ground upwards, rather than [import] generic models that cater to the homogenizing forces of globalisation" (2012, 95). What we have, then, is a new transnational engagement with place that is recalibrating the relationship between the universal and the particular. This form of brand making relies not on the denial of place but on its reassertion. Is this simply a reiteration of neoliberal branding processes? Does it represent the subsumption of local practices into a universalizing rhetoric? Or might this "new" universalism offer other possibilities? As I discuss below, even though the "stardom" (Dasgupta 2006) of the megacity of the Global South might emerge from universalizing—and even neoliberal—discourses (Ferguson 2007), its political and economic effects are still open-ended.

ENTREPRENEURIALISM AND ITS CRITICS

The image of Mumbai as the improvisational city par excellence was popularized in 2009 following the worldwide box office success of *Slumdog Millionaire* (2008). While Mumbai books such as *Maximum City* (Mehta 2005) and *Shantaram* (Roberts 2004) were widely read, *Slumdog Millionaire* brought unprecedented media attention to life in the city's underbelly. As the *New York Times* put it, the film provided a glimpse into "Extreme Mumbai, Without Bollywood's Filtered Lens" (Sengupta 2009). The various interpretations of the "slum" in *Slumdog Millionaire*— a sign of cultural otherness, a celebration of the neoliberal entrepreneurial subject, and a representation (and, to some, a misrepresentation) of subaltern ingenuity—also represent the various stakes of the improvisational city perspective that is the focus of this chapter.

At the center of *Slumdog Millionaire's* narrative are the inventive practices of the poor (Anjaria and Anjaria 2013). The film opens with an energetic shot of young boys running away from a police constable. The constable is chasing the boys because they were playing cricket on the runway of a private airport, which, we later learn, is adjacent to the jhoppadpati they call home. The boys quickly escape into the settlement's narrow labyrinth of lanes. The constable lags behind, frustrated by the boys' deft navigating. During their escape, the boys run past rows of kiosks, a barbershop, and a video game parlor. The scene momentarily cuts to a man collecting plastic bags from a canal. The camera then zooms out, showing the vast tangle of lanes that enable the boys to elude the authorities. Viewers are thus shown a world of poverty and violence, but also a world of clever manipulation and skill by the poor themselves.

Slumdog Millionaire produced a range of responses in India and abroad. To some critics in India, the film's representation of Mumbai suggested the return of old stereotypes. Commentators, including Amitabh Bachchan, Bollywood's most famous actor, criticized the film's focus on the city's grimy underside. Some accused the film "of being poverty porn" and that "Danny Boyle [the director], who is British, has created a film about slum life that ignores India's recent economic prosperity" (Divakaruni 2009). Meanwhile, city newspapers reported on a smattering of protests by slum residents protesting the use of the word *dog* in the film's title for its derogatory and dehumanizing connotations ("Slum Dwellers Protest" 2009). Film critics and journalists took a different perspective, arguing that representing the poor as ingenious and wily supports the neoliberal ideal—presenting India as "a land of self-makers, where a scruffy son of the slums can, solely of his own effort, hoist himself up, flout his origins, break with fate" (Giridharadas 2009).

Urbanists Rahul Srivastava and Matias Echanove offered yet another interpretation of the film. In the aftermath of its box office success and worldwide media attention, they observed that reports of the "slumdog" controversy miss an important point: "The Indian media widely reported that the outrage was over the word 'dog.' But what we heard from Manju Keny, a college student living in Dharavi, was something else. She was upset at the word 'slum'" (Echanove and Srivastava 2009). The shift from *dog* to *slum* as the offending citation suggests that at stake is not only the refutation of cultural stereotypes, but the vocabulary used for understanding urban space. The word *slum* has a long history of denigrating not just a neighborhood but the people who live in it as well. Indeed, Srivastava and Echanove go on to argue (2009) that the nineteenth-century stereotype of slum despondency, immorality, and criminality "does little justice to the reality of Dharavi . . . probably the most active and lively part of an incredibly industrious city. [A place where] people have learned to respond in creative ways to the indifference of the state—including having set up a highly functional recycling industry that serves the whole city" (Echanove and Srivastava 2009). While the film is not explicitly about Dharavi, many writers have similarly felt that the ways people live and work in Dharavi challenge old assumptions about spatial disorder. For instance, Lantz (2008, 41) observes that "the people of Dharavi have developed systems of multifunctional surfaces, where private and public share, where work and recreation take place at different times or side by side."

Echoing critiques of *Slumdog Millionaire*, some scholars argue that the improvisational city perspective is also just another instance of the increasing sway of neoliberalism over urban studies discourses. From this perspective, emphasis on the poor's ingenuity is said to excuse elite-oriented urban governance, while overlooking structural violence. For instance, the geographer Ananya Roy cautions against romanticizing "economies of entrepreneurship and dynamic informality" because they are, in fact, "strategies of improvisation devised under conditions of deprivation and vulnerability" (Roy 2011a, 20). Ash Amin (2013, 480) echoes this view: this perspective, which "finds signs of deprivation and misery but also many stories of hope, resilience and human vitality," absolves those in power for not providing adequate infrastructure in the first place.[5] Amin argues that urbanists who privilege the improvisational perspective are complicit in perpetuating serious structural inequalities, if not in the abandonment of the ideal of an equitable city altogether. Again, by calling the emphasis on slum dweller resourcefulness the "'human potential' optic" (480), Amin explicitly highlights how these writings echo the enterprising and self-actualizing subject of neoliberal rationality.

These critiques are important and may very well be true. However, they tend to overlook what the improvisional city perspective does, and what it does may exceed its direct political linkages. Indeed, whereas the improvisional city perspective echoes the neoliberal valorization of the enterprising subject, its political consequences remain open-ended. For instance, if we situate this renewed attention to the quotidian practices of the poor within a longer history of critiques of modernist urbanism, other possible understandings of its stakes emerge.

Indeed, calling attention to the ad hoc practices and spontaneous sociality of everyday city residents was central to critiques of modernist planning in the 1960s. Most famously, Jane Jacobs, in *The Death and Life of Great American Cities* (1992[1961]), showed readers the hidden beauty of the rapidly disappearing American urban core. Her audiences were city planners, politicians, architects, and bankers, such as the man who called Boston's North End (now considered a pedestrian paradise and tourist destination) a hopeless "slum" (10). To Jacobs, the disjuncture between the feel of urban neighborhoods and how those same places were understood by experts represented the larger problem with urban renewal. This man's "instincts told him the North End was a good place ... [b]ut everything he had learned as a physical planner ... told him ... [that it] had to be ... bad" (10–11). Those who read places like Mumbai's slums from the improvisational perspective similarly question the presumed "problem" of disorder. People preparing food on a small lane or making clay pots in a residential courtyard are framed as challenges to modernist orthodoxy. Writes the architectural critic Stanford Kwinter (2010), "Dharavi is also a city in itself, and its streets and alleys know no distinction between work and social space or even domestic or residential functions" (101).

Publications such as *Dharavi: Documenting Informalities* (Engqvist and Lantz 2008) interpret Mumbai's jhopadpattis through an interpretive lens that parallels, and at moments diverges from, Jacobs's perspective. The *Dharavi* project, a collaboration by architectural critics, photographers, and artists, documents how the settlement's flexible design style enables an unmatched sociality. As one of the editors writes, "The informal city is . . . less anonymous and better adapted than the formal city. There is elasticity and a local presence that the formalised city lacks" (Lantz 2008, 38). However, where this perspective on flexible landscapes diverges from Jacobs is its emphasis on enterprising vitality: "Perhaps the most entrepreneurial place I have ever visited is the Dharavi slum in Mumbai. . . . Dharavi reminds us that urban poverty can often be a sign of success, not of failure" (Glaeser 2011). An architectural critic echoes this view of Dharavi: "The novel ways of conducting business there represent an efficiency . . . [that] could be achieved in no other way or place" (Kwinter 2010, 102).

As in Jacobs's work, one can sense in these writings a palpable joy of finding a sense of community that no longer exists at "home" (i.e., in Western Europe and North America). "At the micro scale of the back-streets of Istanbul, São Paulo or Mumbai," writes the director of the London School of Economics' Urban Age Project, "there is evidence of creative ingenuity that both fosters identity and promotes a form of inclusion among the most excluded" (Burdett 2012, 93). Describing her experience of a slum tour on an urbanist blog, another author says, "In this *real, not manufactured*, street, community people interact; they talk, they laugh, they shake hands, they share, they drink Chai with friends. . . . Children walk to school hand in hand, bicycles carrying cargo weave around the groups of chatting people" (Smith 2013, emphasis added). In these accounts, slums represent a sensibility of enterprise, ad hoc innovation and sociality. They contain an "inspired, duct-taped ingenuity" (Kanu Agrawal, quoted in Roy 2011a, 19); they are places "more dense, more interactive," and where "social capital . . . is at its most urban" (Brand 2009). Despite dilapidated infrastructure and "the large-scale crime of social inequity" it reflects, Dharavi is thus "also a place of visible and palpable civic pride" (Kwinter 2010, 102). A writer in an architecture journal echoes this optimism of the mundane: "Dharavi made me believe again in the ability of humans to remake even this former swamp with almost no infrastructure—and to build a community in the process," even while "the horrors of life there are very real and very evident" (Betsky 2013).

Writers who criticize this optimistic interpretation of informality agree that places like Dharavi exhibit a compelling dynamism and vitality, just as the authors of books like *Dharavi* would not deny the material hardships its residents face. But the impetus among many scholars and academics to dismiss this optimism as neoliberal means that they are unable to explain this impasse—or, more important, examine the work that the improvisational city perspective does, focusing instead on its exclusions. For instance, the emphasis on spontaneous sociality and enterprise might better be understood as an allegory than as an assertion of a particular political agenda or empirically based project. Allegories are not simply falsehoods or static observations of reality, but stories of something else, at times "used for didactic purposes" (Caton 1999, 143) and at times providing commentary on contemporary conditions. Perhaps descriptions of the ground-up acts of city-making and small-scale entrepreneurialism in places like Mumbai, Rio, and Lagos are attempts to locate the spontaneous community that is absent in the (supposedly) concretized and insensuous cities of the West. Stephen Greenblatt's observation that "allegory arises in periods of loss" (quoted in Caton 1999, 142) is especially apt; narratives of the dynamic megacity of the Global South offer readers the possibility of retrieving the lost urbanity of the postindustrial metropolis.

This recovery narrative informs many accounts of the enterprising spirit of Mumbai's street and squatter landscapes. Does this perspective merely support the ideology of individualism, while letting the state off the hook for its failure to provide social services? Or perhaps might something else be going on? A richly allegorical tale that appeared in the

Economist ("A Flourishing Slum" 2007) challenges the supposed direct link between an emphasis on entrepreneurialism and elite-oriented governance agendas:

> If poverty can seem dehumanising from afar—especially in much reporting on it—up close Dharavi, which is allegedly Asia's biggest slum, is vibrantly and triumphantly alive. . . .
>
> An evening stroll through Dharavi with Mr. Korde, a well-liked local, is inspiring. Think 19th-century boom-time Brooklyn. In fluorescent-strip-lit shops, in snatched exchanges in the pedestrian crush, as a hookah is passed around a tea-stall, again and again, the stories are the same. Everyone is working hard and everyone is moving up. All Mr. Korde's friends—or their fathers—arrived in Dharavi much poorer than they are now. Most own at least one business. Some of these slum-dwellers employ several hundred people.

Comparing Dharavi to "19th-century boom-time Brooklyn" suggests what a city like Mumbai can mean in a transnational context: developmentalist teleology mixed with nostalgia and paternalistic envy. It also reflects the multiple meanings of the improvisational city narrative. On one hand, the celebration of the enterprising individual echoes the neoliberal risk-taking subject. Dharavi is a space of buzzing entrepreneurialism "vibrantly and triumphantly alive" with the energy of the free market where, without the help of government, "everyone is working hard and everyone is moving up" ("A Flourishing Slum" 2007). This view overlooks structural inequalities and seems to excuse the government from providing essential infrastructure (Amin 2013). On the other hand, observing that "poverty can seem dehumanising from afar—especially in much reporting on it" ("A Flourishing Slum" 2007) suggests an author grappling with the legacy of slum stereotypes and reformist, pitying narratives.

Certainly the description of slum residents as business-savvy wheeler-dealers subsumes complex processes within a narrow framework of the market economy. And yet it also allows for an expanded notion of who counts as "city makers" in the first place. Slum residents produce the city as much as they benefit from living in it. Framing the slum as a bastion of entrepreneurialism mystifies socioeconomic inequalities, but it also has the potential to challenge dominant concepts of what a global city looks like. In this free-market vision, the slum, ironically, is not framed as an impediment to global capital but as its realization.

These possibilities are only visible if we trouble the assumption that power works unidimensionally. As Ferguson (2009) has argued, the assumption that manifestations of neoliberal ideas are necessarily linked with actual political economic transformations conflates two distinct processes. Drawing on his fieldwork in South Africa around the Basic Income Grant (BIG, a welfare scheme involving direct cash payments to the poor), Ferguson argues that it is possible for practices to look "neoliberal" while also being potentially "'pro-poor' (as the phrase has it)" (174). The BIG program rests on a neoliberal vision of individual risk management, but it also removes "the policing, paternalism, and surveillance of the traditional welfare state" (174). Ferguson's point is that we must distinguish "neoliberalism-as-rationality" (173) from neoliberalism as a "class project" (170). Similarly, by questioning the immutable link between the valorization of the enterprising subject and the creation of consumer-oriented cities, the image of the enterprising slum no longer exhibits such straightforward connections with power. Thus, while urban mythologies and the urban brands they prop up are always power laden, they are mythologies that can both reinforce *and* challenge dominant ideologies. Rather than showing how a mythology is linked with certain class interests or governing logics, it might be more productive to interpret new urban narratives as a phenomenon in their own right that contains their own "polyvalent" (Ferguson 2009, 174) political possibilities.

The image of the improvisational city contains similar contradictory possibilities. On one hand, it hinges on a notion of self-actualization, entrepreneurialism, and individual resourcefulness outside the state—hallmarks of the neoliberal subject (Rose 1996), that "'responsibilized' citizen . . . [who] comes to operate as a miniature firm . . . rationally assessing risks, and prudently choosing from among different courses of action" (Ferguson 2009, 172). On the other hand, this image might challenge the idea of the fluid, ad hoc, and visually chaotic urban landscape as necessarily a space of impoverishment in need of outside intervention, if not demolition. Similarly, emphasis on slum residents' ingenuity in accessing shelter, electricity, and water might excuse the state from providing those amenities in the first place (Amin 2013), but such an emphasis also has the potential to legitimize their place in a city that seems increasingly hostile to their presence.

STREET UTOPIAS

In spring 2006, while standing on a bustling street in central Mumbai, I witnessed how universalizing architectural discourses circulate on the ground, as well as the particularities they produce. Architects and design students in a small group were presenting the preliminary results of a visual survey to a visiting official from the BMC. The group had received a small grant from the BMC to map how pedestrian movement, street vending, vehicle movement, and shopkeepers' use of public space changed throughout the day. As the official listened carefully, the architects pointed out the bewildering variety of micropractices that produced this public space. They instructed him to observe the thousands of pedestrians effortlessly weaving their way through narrow streets, the dozens of hawkers who strategically sit between concrete planters, clusters of mobile vendors who work in the middle of the road but out of pedestrians' pathways, shopkeepers whose extensions blur the boundaries between the formal and informal, flower vendors stationed on the path to a nearby temple, and men on bicycles parked under an overpass offering cold drinks to thirsty passersby.

They also pointed out how hawking and walking are interlinked. They showed how the density of the crowd and the commerce on the streets' edge discouraged all but the occasional taxi or truck, so these disruptions fortunately were infrequent. And they showed how the street–sidewalk distinction was not the primary way space was divided. Rather than a problem, they argued, this reinvention of public space might actually be productive. Mumbai's streets mirror the "shared space" street design (sometimes called *woonerf*) celebrated by proponents of "new urbanism" by "blurring the boundary between street and sidewalk" (Baker 2004). Indeed, not only did the architects challenge classic modernist principles, but they also deployed transnationally circulating ideas of mixed-use urbanism, design, and sustainability as a way of intervening in the "local."

This intervention was not altogether successful. The visiting official concluded that the streets are too congested, too narrow, used by too many people, and for far too many different purposes. He confidently offered a solution: a massive elevated pedestrian walkway. With a sweeping gesture of his arm, he visualized the walkway's arc, soaring above the swirl of street activity from the exit of the station to a nearby arterial road. The architects and I watched the theatrics in stunned silence, unsure of how to respond. Indeed, it was two years before the first of thirty-two (and counting) pedestrian "skywalks" was constructed in Mumbai.[6] So at the time, the idea of pedestrian bridges sounded preposterous. Why was the solution to congestion in the sky when there was one on the ground? we wondered. Was the skywalk meant to benefit pedestrians or discipline them? It wasn't quite clear.

But perhaps these questions missed the point. Literally and figuratively soaring above the city, projects like pedestrian flyovers operate on a logic of urban fantasy and globally scaled aspiration; the dream to rise above the "mess" of the street, as one official says (Siddhaye 2011), often does not need technical justification.[7] No skywalk had yet been built, but they were shaping the reality of the city. In other words, unactualized structures have a presence in the tactile environment of the city. The imminent arrival of skywalks shaped how people interpreted streets, their use, and the potential design interventions that can transform them.

In this instance, the official's imaginary of a skywalk-filled city encountered the architects' alternative imaginary of a Jacobsian "sidewalk ballet" (Jacobs [1961] 1992). Might the improvisational city perspective serve this function as well? Might it too inform the spatial imaginaries, cultural practices, and political claims that produce streets? It is too early to tell, but it is at least worth retaining as a possibility.

Clearly the improvisational perspective tells an imperfect story of the city. It can ignore power inequalities and contains a troubling aura of universality. But rather than emphasize what it overlooks, I have attempted to explore the significance of this perspective as an important new spatial imaginary. In light of the unprecedented architectural, cultural, media, and academic attention to Mumbai's landscape of informality, contestations over the street, such as the hawker controversy I have described in this book, are necessarily enmeshed in new transnational processes. The fact of global entanglement itself is not new, but its stakes are. To many architectural writers, designers, students, and scholars, urban landscapes dotted with squatters, slums, and informal markets are understood to contain a particular sensibility of innovation that now represents a kind of futurity. The megacity is increasingly framed as a new "urban paradigm" and used as a potential model for urbanism in the "developed" West. Understanding the configurations of space, power, and practice in cities such as Mumbai has never been more important.

While the new attention to the urbanism of cities such as Mumbai is promising, it has often been limited by conformity to either a celebratory or a dystopic lens. This likely has to do with the political projects in which these analyses are embroiled. Some writers, bloggers, architects, filmmakers, and scholars are simply following professional trends, while many others have been drawn to the ad hoc urbanity of the Global South in order to find a lost urbanity at home, discover examples of sustainable practices, or simply think outside of Western-centric urban analysis.

In *The Slow Boil*, I have sought to go beyond the improvisational city perspective—which sees only entrepreneurialism—as well as its dystopic inverse—which sees only structural inequality. Clearly streetscapes contain both power imbalances and astonishing ingenuity. Urban analysis must find a way to not have to choose one perspective at the expense of the other in order to highlight the way this tension itself produces urban life—for the subaltern "informals" out on the street as much as for the "formal" citizens with whom they are inextricably linked.

NOTES

CHAPTER 1

1. The city's official name changed from Bombay to Mumbai in 1995. While historical documents published before 1995 refer to the city as "Bombay," for consistency, I refer to the city as Mumbai when speaking of both pre- and post-1995 eras.

2. According to a survey in 1997, roughly 5 percent of hawkers are operating with a license, very often one that has been renewed over the years (Tata Institute of Social Sciences and Youth for Unity and Voluntary Action 1998). However, because licenses are not transferable, the percentage of hawkers who work within the regulations may be smaller (Bhowmik 2003, n.d.). There are a few important exceptions to the criminalization of hawking in Mumbai. At least since the 1960s, people from the *Chamar* or *Mochi* communities—Dalits, historically "untouchables"—have had special permission to open small shoe repair stalls throughout the city.

3. The literature on the politics and experience of street vending, once limited, is now expansive (Mcgee 1973; Austin 1994; Bhowmik n.d.; Jellinek 1997; Robertson 1997; Cross 1998; Duneier 1999; Street Vendor Project 2006; Donovan 2008; Vahed 1999; Cross and Morales 2007).

4. Research on the link between urban transformations, whether in the name of "beautification," modernization, or "world-class city" making, and the removal of the visible presence of the poor is vast (Cross 1998; Delaney 1999; Rajagopal 2001; Popke and Ballard 2004; Herzfeld 2006; Mitchell and Staeheli 2006; Ghertner 2011b; Schindler 2014).

5. See also Ferguson (2009) for a related discussion of scholarly denunciations of neoliberalism.

6. Writing on Mumbai's incomplete embrace of the late-1990s privatization agenda then sweeping the globe, Lisa Björkman (2015, 60) argues, "In the end the privatization storm blew over in Mumbai. Or, as Gupta [an informant] pointed out, perhaps it never really arrived to begin with."

7. See Loukaitou-Sideris and Ehrenfeucht (2009). While street vendors have historically represented disorder, the meaning of this disorder has played out differently in different contexts. In New York, the 1920s "pushcart evil" (Bluestone 1991) indexed white Anglo-Saxon Protestants' anxieties over Jewish, Italian, and Irish immigrants, while in colonial Durban, South Africa, street vendors represented a sign of racialized disturbance (Vahed 1999).

8. In Hindi, the rough equivalent of inside-outside is *andar-bahar*. In Bengali, it would be *ghore-baire*. See Kaviraj (1997, 93) and Chatterjee (1993, 120) for discussions of the cultural politics of the "inner/outer distinction" in colonial India.

9. Echoing the shift from "persons to places" (Joyce 2003, 67), street encroachment and congestion were framed differently prior to the 1880s. Rather than "public nuisances," they were framed as problems of taxation and in terms of potential for public disturbance (Morley 1859). In the era preceding the founding of the BMC in 1865, urban governance was "mainly concerned with the police, administration of justice and the collection of taxes" (Ramanna 2002, 83; see also Edwardes 1923, 25–27). Until the 1880s, authorities were primarily concerned with what small-scale traders were selling rather than how and where they sold it. Mariam Dossal writes that "petty traders, such as butter and betelnut vendors, milk and onion sellers, tinmen and turners, sand and snuff sellers, were subjected to regular and expensive visits from the tax gatherer" (1991, 67).

10. The original seven islands of Bombay were transferred from Portuguese to British rule in 1661. However it was during "the 'imperial globalization' of the nineteenth and early twentieth centuries" (Kidambi 2007, 1) that this sleepy outpost acquired its "recognizably modern characteristics." Early historical monographs on the city, such as Da Cunha (1900) and Wacha (1920), emphasize the city's deep connections to global commerce from the early 1800s. As a banking hub and site of India's largest cotton market, Mumbai's prominent place in Indian Ocean and transoceanic trade in the early nineteenth century linked it with port cities around the world, including Shanghai, Karachi, Calcutta, and London (King 1976; Farooqui 2006). For a more extensive discussion of the history of Mumbai, see Wacha (1920), Dossal (1991), Prakash (2010), and Fernandes (2013).

11. Fernand Braudel (1992, 75–80) provides an account of the ubiquitous and—to the authorities—perplexing presence of peddlers in early modern Europe. While indexing an archaic practice, they readily adapted to new forms of transportation and played an important role in opening new markets.

12. The literature on transnational city-making practices under nineteenth-century British and French colonialism is large (Rabinow 1989; Çelik 1997; Roy 2001; Glover 2008; McFarlane 2008).

13. Jyoti Hosagrahar (2005), Swati Chattopadhyay (2005), and William Glover (2008) provide rich accounts of the spatial manifestations of colonial modernity in nineteenth-century urban India.

14. For a discussion of the blurred boundary between shop and street in colonial India, a recurring theme in travelers' accounts, see Glover (2008, 126–29).

15. Gandhi's dismissal of urban India, like that of many other nationalist leaders of the 1930s and 1940s, is well known: "I don't like Bombay, though. It looks as if it were the scum of London. I see here all the shortcomings of London but find none of its amenities" (quoted in Hazareesingh 2007, 124).

16. See also D. Arnold (2012) on early twentieth-century accounts of the seemingly unruly Indian streetscape: "The longed-for orderliness of Indian street-life in general, and its traffic in particular, thus became indicative of the regulatory needs of the modern nation" (123).

17. Prior to these cases, juridical involvement in urban spatial issues primarily focused on questions of use and tenure (Glover 2007). Courts were concerned, for instance,

with whether an open space was private property or had a history of public passage (e.g., *Municipal Board v. Khalil-Ul-Rahman* 1929), whether an unpaved (or "metaled") space adjacent to a road still fell under the category "road" (*Sudarshan Das Shastri v. Municipal Board of Agra* 1914), or whether a hawkers' stall constituted a "shop" and was thus subject to municipality rules governing it (*Abdul Gani Abdul Shakoor v. State* 1960). With some exceptions (*Pyare Lal v. New Delhi Municipal Corporation* 1967), these cases focused on how spaces should be categorized and practices regulated rather than on urban citizenship. From the 1980s onward, the Supreme Court's involvement in urban affairs focused instead on the constitutionality of evictions (Baviskar 2007a; Ghertner 2008; Bhan 2009).

18. The Indian Constitution includes socioeconomic directive principles such as economic justice and equality that are not necessarily political rights (Fortun 2001).

19. *Olga Tellis v. The Bombay Municipal Corporation* (1985) hinged on the frictions between democratic principles and urban transformation. As in the hawker case, it questioned the constitutionality of the 1888 BMC Act, which gives the municipality the right to evict people without notice. Interestingly, this case took the argument against the 1888 BMC Act a bit further than in *Bombay Hawkers' Union v. The Bombay Municipal Corporation* by questioning the continued legitimacy of colonial-era laws. In that case, the removal of encroachments and regulation over the use of the street was said to be "passed in an era when the pavement dwellers and slum dwellers did not exist and the consciousness of the modern notion of a welfare state was not present to the mind of the colonial legislature" (*Olga Tellis*). Despite the fact that people did live on Bombay's streets in 1888, this claim challenges an implicit sense of the law as an "abstraction" "objectified . . . [and] ascribed a life-force of its own" (Comaroff and Comaroff 2009, 33) outside historical or political context. Moreover, *Olga Tellis* argued that the demolished settlement—established in the 1960s by laborers constructing the adjacent road, and thus ironically a product of municipal development itself—now housed people who could not afford accommodation within any reasonable distance from their work. Thus, demolition of the homes would violate their right to life and livelihood, as it would prevent them from finding the work necessary to support their families. As the presiding justice explained, "the easiest way of depriving a person of his right to life would be to deprive him of his means of livelihood to the point of abrogation" (quoted in Mahalwar 1990, 252).

20. A major effort to reshape hawker regulation in India resulted in the National Policy on Street Vendors (Bhowmik 2003) in 2009. In 2014, the Street Vendors (Protection of Livelihood and Regulation of Street Vending) Bill was passed by the Rajya Sabha, the upper house of the parliament of India. This major new law calls for local governments to minimize evictions, survey street vendors, and provide licenses to street vendors in areas where "natural markets" occur.

21. In contrast to *Olga Tellis v. BMC*, initiated to protect squatters' rights, the new "citizen"-oriented PIL of the 1990s and 2000s focused on the government's complicity in enabling encroachment.

22. All names used in this book are pseudonyms. I have also changed the locations of all activities, practices, and events.

23. See Ocko and Gilmartin (2009) for a discussion of the historical development of the rule-of-law concept in India and in particular its juxtaposition with its discursive outside, the "rule of men" (66).

24. Ananya Roy (2003) provides an important account of the varied basis through which people make claims on the state in India. For instance, when women ticketless travelers in Kolkata say, "'We vote, and therefore why should we have to pay for what we cannot afford?'" (164), their claims are derived not only from a concept of abstract rights but also from a notion of entitlement (see also Chatterjee 2004 and Subramanian 2009).

25. For the sake of privacy, I did not record the content of the text word for word. What I include here is a paraphrased version.

26. The complex enmeshment of hawker and state practices undermines the assumption that "informal" economic activity takes place outside the purview of the state. That illegal street vending is enabled by state practices raises significant questions related to the explanatory potential of the informal economy concept, just as it questions taken-for-granted truths about the way state disciplinary power works. As James Ferguson (2007) writes, "The urban informal economy [has been] long understood as intrinsically resistant to, if not completely outside of, a state power conceived of as essentially regulatory" (84). A problem with the dominant view of informality is that it implicitly relies on the idea of a state that is dichotomous with its citizens or, as Julia Elyachar (2007) puts it, the idea that "the state is in one place and informality is in another" (69). Keith Hart (2006), who has been credited with developing the informal economy concept from his work in Accra in the early 1970s (Hart 1973), writes that the term was not meant to designate a distinct sector of activity but nevertheless was taken up this way because it fit with 1980s international lending agency development paradigms. For other studies critical of the informal economy concept, see Roitman (1990), Roy and AlSayyad (2004), and Fernández-Kelly and Shefner (2006).

CHAPTER 2

1. Cited in Chandavarkar (1994, 36).

2. After decades of relative inattention, a number of contemporary historians have provided detailed accounts of Bombay's early development in the nineteenth century (Chandavarkar 1994; Kidambi 2007; Tambe 2009; Dossal 2010; Prakash 2010; Chopra 2011; N. Rao 2013). Douglas Haynes (1991) provides a thorough account of the development of municipal governance and civic culture during this period. On the fragmented colonial state in nineteenth-century India, see Tambe and Fischer-Tiné (2009) and Beverley (2013). With some notable exceptions (Glover 2007; McFarlane 2008; Prakash 2010; Legg 2011; Fernandes 2012), little attention has been paid to how histories of spatial contestation might inform the present. See Hull (2011) and Sutherland (2011).

3. This is from Karmayog, an NGO electronic list. The contributor identified himself as "Amar." Posted on April 19, 2006.

4. In much urban studies writing, there is an assumption that the only way inequalities in the present can be "challenged" is "to think the city *once again* as a provisioning and

indivisible commons to which the poor have equal entitlement on a human rights basis" (Amin 2013, 278, 277, emphasis added).

5. For instance, the Mody Bay Reclamation was developed to provide land for state administration but ended up benefiting private interests: "Begun by the Government on its own account about twenty-five years ago, to obtain a good site for the Commissariat stores and offices, [it] was never used for that purpose. . . . Yet even in its present rough state it is made much use of. Two large factories for making ice have been built here by the Bombay Ice Manufacturing Co., Limited, and Mr. F.E. Cutler" (Maclean 1889, 267–68). Writes Walter Ducat in 1866, "Land Reclamations are perhaps the greatest favourites with capitalists," representing the excessive emphasis on developing commercial infrastructure at the expense of social services for the poor. "In their excitement and anxiety to provide Wharfs, Docks and Warehouse-room for the rising trade of the port, the public has apparently lost sight altogether of the not less evident want of land for dwelling houses, an evil which, strongly felt as it is now, must, unless some provision be made, keep pace with the advancement of Bombay" (184).

6. With voting rights linked to land and property ownership, only a small percentage of the population had a formal voice in local governance. In 1914, for instance, "one percent of the urban population only—11,500 citizens—had the right to vote" (Hazareesingh 2000, 802). Dossal (1991) describes how this manifested in small-scale traders' resentment toward the municipality: "Petty traders, such as butter and betelnut vendors, milk and onion sellers, tinmen and turners, sand and snuff sellers, were subjected to regular and expensive visits from the tax gatherer" (67).

7. For example, Banerjee-Guha (2007), Chatterjee (2009), Davis (2004), and Fernandes (2004).

8. For extensive discussions of debates over sanitation in nineteenth-century Bombay see, for instance, Edwardes 1902; Klein 1986; Arnold 1993; Chandavarkar 2004; McFarlane 2008.

9. This discussion of encroachments in the Fort is also cited in Edwardes (1902).

10. Cited in Chandavarkar (1994, 36).

11. See also King (1976). Recent urban historical scholarship has challenged the idea of a colonial urban dualism (Bissell 2011). Indeed, even after the establishment of the Native Town, visitors commented that few Europeans lived in the Fort (Graham 1813). In contrast to Calcutta, spatial segregation in colonial-era Bombay was based more on class than on race (Farooqui 2006). For instance, by the early twentieth century, even the formerly European enclave of Malabar Hill was considered to be overrun by wealthy Indians (Low 1907).

12. Cited in Chandavarkar (1994, 36).

13. As Nikhil Rao (2013, 27) discusses in his history of the Bombay City Improvement Trust, this administrative entity had a two-pronged urban renewal strategy consisting of "direct" and "indirect attack." Direct attack entailed demolition and street widening near slums to transform land prices, while indirect attack entailed the creation of new housing.

14. Debates around slums in Bombay were informed by a transnational discourse of urban public health (McFarlane 2008, 2011). The comparativism that McFarlane (2011) finds implicit in nineteenth-century governance was often explicit in journalists' accounts.

These comparisons also at times led to surprising conclusions. A visiting British journalist observed: "I was taken to see some of the dwellings in the condemned and congested district. I confess I was less impressed than perhaps my friends expected; for I have seen slum areas and municipal clearances nearer home, and for pure filth, foulness, degradation, and outward misery I am afraid that London has more painful sights to show than those which were brought before me in Bombay" (Low 1907, 28).

15. See Klein (1986) and C. Arnold (2012) for an account of the Bombay plague and its effects on housing. While the Improvement Trust was established to improve housing in the city, C. Arnold (2012, 113) argues that it "*increased* the crisis of housing for Bombay's poorer and working classes, reducing available housing and escalating the cost of that which remained."

16. Cited in Parpiani (2012, 66).

17. See also Curtis (1921, 572).

18. Cited in Ranganathan (2009, 325).

19. While the word *nuisance* had been used in prior official discourses surrounding the ordering and control of the streets—as discussed above, authorities in 1772 spoke of the "great nuisance" caused by small shops in the Fort (Edwardes 1902, 202)—it was only from the mid-nineteenth century that "nuisance," or, more specifically, "public nuisances," constituted a distinct legal and criminal category.

20. Eric Beverley (2011) provides a thorough outline of the interplay between "spaces of social control" and "spaces of autonomy" in Indian cities in the colonial era.

21. Writes Nikhil Rao (2013, 15), "Beginning in the late 1910s, demands for housing and basic urban services became the context in which a new lower-middle-class upper-caste identity constituted itself." Moreover, Rao argues that "the object of Bombay's upper-caste lower middle classes was not so much to fight colonial rule, as rather, to demand services from the municipal state."

22. By the 1910s, the *Bombay Chronicle* had "assumed the role of an active citizen seeking knowledge about, and answers to, the grave problems of urban life" (Hazareesingh 2000, 805). See also Hazareesingh 2007; Israel 1994.

23. See *Bombay Chronicle*, February 23, 1934.

24. As I discuss in Chapter 5, a public battle pitting "pedestrians" against "hawkers" reemerged in the mid-1980s (see *Bombay Hawkers' Union v. Bombay Municipal Corporation* 1985).

25. *Bombay Chronicle*, July 9, 1933.

26. See Rao and Haynes (2013) for a similar rethinking of the traditional periodization of South Asian urban history.

CHAPTER 3

1. For a description and analysis of India's informal waste industry of which Aamir is an integral, and yet hidden, part, see Gidwani and Chaturvedi (2011).

2. The architect Rahul Mehrotra (2007) calls these realms the "kinetic" and "static" city.

3. See also Wacquant (2002) for a related discussion of urban ethnography's potential to ignore structural inequality.

4. There is, of course, a parallel here with disciplinary debates over narrative styles in anthropology since the early 1980s (Clifford and Marcus 1986; Tsing 1993; Stewart 1996; Raffles 2002).

5. Mumbai's wholesale market used to be located in the historic Crawford Market. In 1996, nearly all wholesale trade in the city shifted to a vast new complex, the Agricultural Produce Market Committee market, in New Mumbai.

6. According to Robinson (2007, 841), "Muslim men are over-represented in street vending (more than 12 per cent as opposed to the national average of less than 8 per cent)." Furthermore, writes Basant (2007, 829), "vis-à-vis [other populations], a much larger proportion of Muslim workers . . . [are] engaged in street vending."

7. One crore equals Rs 10 million.

8. Ramesh's account of informal markets and settlements preceding and enabling the formal city echoes researchers' accounts of squatters as "developers" (Holston 1991; Sharma 2000; Apurtham 2008). For instance, Madhu Sarin (1979) describes a similar process in her study of the making of Chandigarh. She describes workers and street vendors transforming the landscape before construction of the planned city commenced.

CHAPTER 4

1. Prasad's multiple roles, skills, and diffuse sources of power are reminiscent of the "urban specialists" that Thomas Blom Hansen and Oskar Verkaaik describe. These are "individuals who by virtue of their reputation, skills and imputed connections provide services, connectivity and knowledge to ordinary dwellers in slums and popular neighborhoods" and whose power is partly derived from "extra-local connections to centres of power" (2009, 16).

2. This arrangement is made possible through what Barbara Harriss-White (2003) identifies as India's vast "shadow state" of *dalal*s (brokers): "technical fixers, gate-keepers . . . confidants, contractors and consultants" (89).

3. Echoing this intimate entanglement with the state, C. J. Fuller and John Harriss (2000) write that in India, "the *sarkar*—indifferently 'state' and 'government' in the commonest Indian vernacular term for them—appears on many levels and in many centres, and its lower echelons at least are always staffed by people with whom some kind of social relationship can or could exist; the 'faceless bureaucrats' actually do have faces" (15).

4. At the time of these conversations, Rs 1,200 was the equivalent of around $27.

5. Discussed in *Maharasthra Ekta Hawkers' Union v. Municipal Corporation, Greater Mumbai*, Supreme Court of India, September 12, 2003.

6. See also Appadurai (2001). Matthew Hull's *Government of Paper* (2012) shows how documents do important work as they circulate in and out of state spaces. Circulation often matters more than their actual content: "Documents often function less as instruments of documentation than as tools for building coalitions or oppositions among government functionaries, property owners, businessmen, and builders" (22). Kregg Hetherington (2009) discusses a similar negotiation between two competing notions of rights ("material" versus "abstract") within a liberal political framework in Paraguay: "In one of these views, property is governed by the idea that rights are a progressive result of human

labor on the land; in the other, property rights are understood as a result of legal recognition in an abstract code" (232). See Benjamin (2008) on "Occupancy Urbanism."

7. The word *hafta* also indexes the simultaneous banality and spectacularity of practices that are called "corrupt." Although bribery scandals involving politicians are a journalistic mainstay in India (Mazzarella 2006), accounts of hafta often also reflect an implicit acknowledgment of its ordinariness. Newspaper articles with titles such as "Rates for Plum Police Postings Dive," with the secondary caption reading "Dance Bar Ban Hits 'Hafta'—cops stand to lose Rs 180 cr a year—that's 37% of Mumbai police's budget of Rs 487 cr!" (Sen 2005) are not meant as sensational accounts of corruption but as descriptions of an ordinary, if unsavory, aspect of city life. Likewise, newspaper accounts occasionally note the "moral economy" (Olivier de Sardan 1999) of hafta. For instance, one story notes, "Every stall owner in the area has also maintained a record of how much hafta has been given and to whom. They have maintained books where the receiver signs on receipt of payment and if someone else comes (by mistake) to collect the money, the stall owner shows the diary saying, 'We have already paid money to other cops'" (Hafeez 2005).

8. In the mid-2000s, $1 was equivalent to Rs 45.

9. For instance, Fels (2008), Hasty (2005), Pierce (2006), and Shah (2009).

10. Mumbai newspapers occasionally describe upper-level BMC officials' efforts to counter these tipoffs—for instance: "The Brihanmumbai Municipal Corporation (BMC) initiated action almost immediately. It set up a central agency under deputy municipal commissioner V N Kalam Patil for the eviction drive as it felt the ward offices may not go all out. The process involved officials identifying the spot to be cleared and informing the concerned squad only at the last minute so that hawkers were not pre-warned. Even the cellphones of the eviction squad members were confiscated so that the area to be raided was not leaked" (Lewis 2005).

11. As urban planner Shirish Patel (2009) writes, "Mumbai in January 2005 had 4,413 police constables and 81 police inspectors living in slums. They were simultaneously officers of the law and illegal residents of the city."

12. Relatedly, Genevieve Lakier (2007) shows how in Nepal, political movements for an expanded democracy and the upholding of the rule of law may, ironically, utilize illiberal practices. She writes, "Even those who *desire* the panoptic authority of the modern state and its law to liberate them from an inequitable social order nonetheless achieve their aim by the evasion of the legal process" (267). This should not be understood as a contradiction but as an index of political contexts informed by diverse subjectivities and forms of power.

CHAPTER 5

1. Ashis Nandy (1995) writes, there is a long tradition of the middle class in India positioning itself as separate from society: "[In India] the westernized middle classes see themselves as guardians or custodians, trying desperately to protect the rest of the society—seen as inefficient, anarchic and irrational—through a hard-boiled law-and-order approach and the technology of the state, which is viewed as the major instrument

of modern rationality" (23–24). However, to the civic activists I write about in this chapter, the state is seen less as an instrument of modern rationality than as a hindrance to it.

2. The cartoonist RD Laxman has used the figure of the "ordinary man" in his work at least since the 1960s. This figure has long been a presence in Indian political commentary.

3. Everyday improvisation is often called *jugaad*. Since the late 2000s, there has been unprecedented talk of jugaad as a sign of local ingenuity and inventiveness, and perhaps even an ethic that offers an alternative path to development. See Jauregui (2014) for a rich ethnographic analysis of the concept.

4. There is a long history of philanthropic work in Mumbai. Parsi industrialists, a small minority who achieved significant financial success during the colonial era, played an especially prominent role: "The use of public philanthropy by the Indian mercantile elite [in the nineteenth century] ... [forged] the development of civic society" (Palsetia 2005, 198). For instance, wealthy Parsi merchants such as Jejeebhoy were among the first to explicitly support charitable work on behalf of the city as a whole rather than a specific community.

5. Amita Baviskar (2007b) discusses exclusionary environmental activism carried out in the name of the public interest that seeks to remove human-powered rickshaws from New Delhi's streets: "These concerns do not reflect the priorities of all street-users but mainly those of that section of Delhi's population that uses private vehicles, especially cars. Yet their interests get normalized and universalized as those of the 'public,' while the concerns and priorities of pedestrians and rickshaw riders and pullers (and cows and their owners), and all those who make money off them, are left by the wayside" (11).

6. This kind of political engagement framed in terms of individual initiative and self-actualization also informed other, largely middle-class, protests that captured media attention in India and abroad, such as the marches against terrorism in 2008 and the protests in support of the Jan Lokpal anticorruption bill in 2011.

7. For an extended discussion of "enterprising citizenship" in Indian popular culture and politics, see Anjaria and Anjaria (2013a).

8. It should be noted that there are no Chinese hawkers in Mumbai. It is possible that as a vendor of nonvegetarian food in this neighborhood, his foreignness, in the imagination of many residents, manifested in presumed racial difference.

9. See Singh and Parthasarathy (2010) and Singh (2012).

CHAPTER 6

1. Some consider the 2003 Venice Bienniale a significant turning point in the global representation of the urban megalopolis. Articles with titles such as "Putting Whole Teeming Cities on the Drawing Board" (Ourousoff 2006) document a shift in the discourse on cities from one on stand-alone buildings to the social and political worlds in which they are enmeshed: "The most promising trend this year is a renewed emphasis in architectural circles on urbanism as a field for creative exploration. Architects like Eyal Weisman (in London), Teddy Cruz (San Diego), Philipp Oswalt (Berlin) and Rem Koolhaas (Rotterdam and just about everywhere else) have been striving to bridge the gap between architectural fantasy and stark political and social realities.... The 10th Venice Biennale of Architecture, which opens this weekend, is the first to focus on entire cities rather than uncovering the

latest architectural trends. Organized by Ricky Burdett, the exposition examines the effect of design in cities as diverse as Cairo, Mumbai, São Paulo, Johannesburg, Mexico City and Caracas" (Ouroussof 2006).

2. Urbanist blogs such as the Atlantic Cities (http://www.theatlanticcities.com/), Planetizen (http://www.planetizen.com/), and Next City (http://nextcity.org) are particularly notable in this regard.

3. See Frederick Cooper (2001) for the important distinction between, on one hand, the novelty of particular global or transnational connections and, on the other, the novelty of globalization itself.

4. It is important to note that a sense of futurity informs both optimistic and "apocalyptic" (Angotti 2006) accounts of the megacity of the Global South. For instance, in sharp contrast to the improvisional city writers, Mike Davis (2004) argues that the dense informal landscapes of cities such as Lagos represent a foreboding global scenario.

5. See also Fernandes (2006) for a related critique of the "resilience" rhetoric in Mumbai.

6. Mumbai's skywalks were built by the MMRDA, a statewide agency responsible for infrastructural development that is independent of the BMC. Nevertheless, it seems from this encounter that BMC officials were aware of the MMRDA's future plans.

7. For a rich account of the diverse transnational processes that produce Mumbai's skywalks, see Harris (2013).

REFERENCES

Abdul Gani Abdul Shakoor v. State. 63 BOMLR 317, 1960. http://indiankanoon.org/doc/1869591/.

Abrams, Philip. "Notes on the Difficulty of Studying the State." *Journal of Historical Sociology* 1, no. 1 (1988): 58–89.

Aijaz, Rumi. "Form of Urban Local Government in India." *Journal of Asian and African Studies* 43, no. 2 (2008): 131–54.

Albuquerque, Teresa. *Urbs Prima in Indus: An Epoch in the history of Bombay, 1840–1865.* New Delhi: Promilla, 1985.

Almitra H. Patel Anr. v. Union of India and Ors. 2000. http://indiankanoon.org/doc/339109/.

American Institute of Architects New York. "Center for Architecture Announces Exhibition 'Jugaad Urbanism: Resourceful Strategies for Indian Cities.'" Press release, January 13, 2011. http://aiany.aiany.org/index.php?section=press-releases&prrid=224.

Amin, Ash. "Telescopic Urbanism and the Poor." *Cities* 17, no. 4 (2013): 476–92.

Anand, Nikhil, and Anne Rademacher. "Housing in the Urban Age: Inequality and Aspiration in Mumbai." *Antipode* 43, no. 5 (2011): 1748–72.

Anderson, Michael. "Public Nuisance and Private Purpose: Policed Environments in British India, 1860–1947." SOAS School of Law Research Paper 5. 1992.

Anderson, Philip. *The English in Western India; Being the Early History of the Factory at Surat, or Bombay, and the Subordinate Factories on the Western Coast.* Bombay: Smith, Taylor and Co., 1854.

Angotti, Tom. "Apocalyptic Anti-Urbanism: Mike Davis and His Planet of Slums." *International Journal of Urban and Regional Research* 30, no. 4 (2006): 961–67.

Anjaria, Jonathan Shapiro. "Guardians of the Bourgeois City: Citizenship, Public Space, and Middle Class Activism in Mumbai." *City and Community* 8, no. 4 (2009): 391–406.

———. "Ordinary States: Everyday Corruption and the Politics of Space in Mumbai." *American Ethnologist* 38, no. 1 (2011): 58–72.

———. "Is There a Culture of the Indian Street?" *Seminar* 6 (August 2012): 21–27.

Anjaria, Jonathan Shapiro, and Ulka Anjaria. "The Fractured Spaces of Entrepreneurialism in Post-Liberalization India." In *Enterprise Culture in Neoliberal India*, edited by Nandini Gooptu, 190–205. New York: Routledge, 2013a.

Anjaria, Ulka and Jonathan Shapiro Anjaria. "Slumdog Millionaire and Epistemologies of the City." In *The "Slumdog" Phenomenon: A Critical Anthology*, edited by Ajay Gehlawat, 53–68. London: Anthem, 2013b.

Annual Police Return Showing the State of Crime in the Town and Island of Bombay During the Year 1884. Bombay: Government Central Press, 1885.

193

Anwar, Nausheen H., and Sarwat Viqar. "Producing Cosmopolitan Karachi: Freedom, Security and Urban Redevelopment in the Post-Colonial Metropolis." *South Asian History and Culture* (2014): 1–21.

Appadurai, Arjun. "Spectral Housing and Urban Cleansing: Notes on Millennial Mumbai." *Public Culture* 12 no. 3 (2000): 627–51.

———. "Deep Democracy: Urban Governmentality and the Horizon of Politics." *Environment and Urbanization* 13, no. 2 (2001): 23–43

Arabindoo, Pushpa. "'City of Sand': Stately Re-Imagination of Marina Beach in Chennai." *International Journal of Urban and Regional Research* 35, no. 2 (2011): 379–401.

Aretxaga, Begoña. "Maddening States." *Annual Review of Anthropology* 32 (2003): 393–410.

Arnold, Caroline E. "The Bombay Improvement Trust, Bombay Millowners and the Debate over Housing Bombay's Millworkers, 1896–1918." *Essays in Economic and Business History* 30 (2012): 105–23.

Arnold, David. *Colonizing the Body: State Medicine and Epidemic Disease in Nineteenth-Century India*. Berkeley: University of California Press, 1993.

———. "The Problem of Traffic: The Street-Life of Modernity in Late-Colonial India." *Modern Asian Studies* 46, no. 1 (2012): 119–41.

Arputham, Jockin. "Developing New Approaches for People-Centred Development." *Environment and Urbanization* 20 (2008): 319–37.

Aubrey, D. *Letters from Bombay*. London: Remington, 1884.

Austin, Regina. "'An Honest Living': Street Vendors, Municipal Regulation, and the Black Public Sphere." *Yale Law Journal* 103, no. 8 (1994): 2119–31.

Bachelard, Gaston. *The Poetics of Space*. Translated by Maria Jolas. New York: Orion Press, 1964.

Bagaeen, Samer. "Brand Dubai: The Instant City; or the Instantly Recognizable City." *International Planning Studies* 12, no. 2 (2007): 173–97.

Baker, Henry D. *Special Consular Reports No. 72: British India, with Notes on Ceylon, Afghanistan, and Tibet*. Washington, DC: Government Printing Office, 1915.

Baker, Linda. "Why Don't We Do It on the Road?" *Salon*, May 20, 2004. http://dir.salon.com/story/tech/feature/2004/05/20/traffic_design/index.html.

Balakrishnan, S. "Move on Hawking Zones Slammed." *Times of India*, October 3, 2003. http://timesofindia.indiatimes.com/city/mumbai/Move-on-hawking-zones-slammed/articleshow/233679.cms.

Baliga, Linah. "Cops Pledge to Oust Hawkers Across Mumbai." *Times of India*, January 17, 2013. http://timesofindia.indiatimes.com/city/mumbai/Cops-pledge-to-oust-hawkers-across-Mumbai/articleshow/18053427.cms?intenttarget=no.

Banerjee-Guha, Swapna. "Post-Fordist Urban Space of Mumbai: The Saga of Contemporary Restructuration." In *Indian Cities in Transition*, edited by Annapurna Shaw, 260–82. New Delhi: Orient Longman, 2007.

Basant, Rakesh. "Social, Economic and Educational Conditions of Indian Muslims." *Economic and Political Weekly* 42, no. 10 (2007): 828–32.

Baud, Isa, and Navtej Nainan. "Negotiated Spaces for Representation in Mumbai: Ward

Committees, Advanced Locality Management and the Politics of Middle-Class Activism." *Environment and Urbanization* 20, no. 2 (2008): 483–99.

Baviskar, Amita. "Between Violence and Desire: Space, Power, and Identity in the Making of Metropolitan Delhi." *International Social Science Journal* 55, no. 175 (2003): 89–98.

———. "Demolishing Delhi: World-Class City in the Making." In *The Urban Poor in Globalising India: Dispossession and Marginalisation*, edited by Lalit Batra, 39–44. New Delhi: Vasudhaiva Kutumbakam Publications, 2007a.

———. "Cows, Cars and Rickshaws: Bourgeois Environmentalists and the Battle for Delhi's Street." Paper prepared for the workshop on the Middle Classes in India, the Institute of Economic Growth, University of Delhi Enclave, Delhi, India, 2007b.

Baviskar, Amita, and Nandini Sundar. "Democracy Versus Economic Transformation?" *Economic and Political Weekly* 43, no. 46 (2008): 87–89.

Baxi, Upendra. *Environment Protection Act: An Agenda for Implementation.* Bombay: N. M. Tripathi, 1987.

Bayat, Asef. "From 'Dangerous Classes' to 'Quiet Rebels': Politics of the Urban Subaltern in the Global South." *International Sociology* 15, no. 3 (2000): 533–57.

Benjamin, Solomon. "Occupancy Urbanism: Radicalizing Politics and Economy Beyond Policy and Programs." *International Journal of Urban and Regional Research* 32, no. 3 (2008): 719–29.

Berman, Marshall. *All That Is Solid Melts into Air: The Experience of Modernity.* New York: Simon and Schuster, 1982.

Betsky, Aaron. "Slumdog Entrepreneur." *Architect Magazine.* April 24, 2013. http://www.arc hitectmagazine.com/design/creativity-comes-at-a-cost-in-mumbais-dharavi-slum.aspx.

Beverley, Eric. "Colonial Urbanism and South Asian Cities." *Social History* 36, no. 4 (2011): 482–97.

———. "Frontier as Resource: Law, Crime, and Sovereignty on the Margins of Empire." *Comparative Studies in Society and History* 55, no. 2 (2013): 241–72.

Bhan, Gautam. "'This Is No Longer the City I Once Knew': Evictions, the Urban Poor and the Right to the City in Millennial Delhi." *Environment and Urbanization* 21, no. 1 (2009): 127–42.

———. "The Impoverishment of Poverty: Reflections on Urban Citizenship and Inequality in Contemporary Delhi." *Environment and Urbanization* 26, no. 2 (2014): 547–60.

Bhargava, Rajeev. "Are There Alternative Modernities?" In *Culture, Democracy, and Development in South Asia*, edited by N. N. Vohra, 9–26. New Delhi: Shipra Publications, 2001.

Bharucha, Nauzer. "From Mills to Malls, the Sky Is the Limit." *Times of India*, November 24, 2003.

Bhatia, Shailesh. "Hawking Not OK Please!" *Mid-Day*, March 25, 2007. http://archive. mid-day.com/news/2007 /mar/154114.htm.

Bhowmik, Sharit K. "National Policy for Street Vendors." *Economic and Political Weekly* 38, no. 16 (2003): 1543–46.

———. *Hawkers and the Urban Informal Sector: A Study of Street Vending in Seven Cities.* Report prepared for National Alliance of Street Vendors of India. N.d.

Birla, Ritu. *Stages of Capital: Law, Culture, and Market Governance in Late Colonial India.* Durham, NC: Duke University Press, 2009.

Bissell, William Cunningham. "Between Fixity and Fantasy: Assessing the Spatial Impact of Colonial Urban Dualism." *Journal of Urban History* 37, no. 2 (2011): 208–29.

Björkman, Lisa. "Becoming a Slum: From Municipal Colony to Illegal Settlement in Liberalization-Era Mumbai." *International Journal of Urban and Regional Research* 38, no. 1 (2013): 36–59.

———. *Pipe Politics, Contested Waters: Embedded Infrastructures of Millennial Mumbai.* Durham, NC: Duke University Press, 2015.

Bluestone, Daniel M. "The Pushcart Evil: Peddlers, Merchants, and New York City's Streets, 1890–1940." *Journal of Urban History* 18, no. 1 (1991): 68–92.

"BMC to Create Non-Hawking Zones Only, HC Told." *Indian Express*, April 19, 1999. http://www.indianexpress.com/ie/daily/19990420/ige20013.html.

"Bombay Fruit Merchants Meet." *Bombay Chronicle*, June 15, 1933.

Bombay Hawkers' Union and others v. Bombay Municipal Corporation and others 1985 3 SCC 528. http://indiankanoon.org/doc/231387/.

"Bombay's Lepers." *Bombay Chronicle*, December 23, 1933.

Booth, Robert. "Charles Declares Mumbai Shanty Town Model for the World." *Guardian*, February 5, 2009. http://www.theguardian.com/artanddesign/2009/feb/06/prince-charles-slum-comments.

Bose, Mihir. *The Magic of Indian Cricket, Revised Edition: Cricket and Society in India.* New York: Routledge, 2006.

Bose, Nirmal K. "Calcutta: A Premature Metropolis." *Scientific American* 213, no. 3 (1965): 90–102.

Boym, Svetlana. *The Future of Nostalgia.* New York: Basic Books, 2001.

Brand, Stewart. "Four Environmental Heresies." TED (Technology, Entertainment, Design) talk, 2009. http://www.ted.com/talks/stewart_brand_proclaims_4_environmental_heresies.html.

Braudel, Fernand. *The Wheels of Commerce: Civilization and Capitalism 15th–18th Century.* Vol. 2. Berkeley: University of California Press, 1992.

Brooks, Katherine. "David Van Der Leer, Architizer Judge, Talks Urban Studies, Stillspotting and the Beauty of Dutch Design." *Huffington Post*, April 4, 2013. http://www.huffingtonpost.com/2013/04/04/david-van-der-leer-architizer-a-awards-interview_n_3001093.html.

Bunsha, Dionne. "Targeting Hawkers." *Frontline*, 2002. http://www.hinduonnet.com/fline/fl1902/19020940.htm.

———. "On the Streets." *Frontline*, 2007. http://www.hinduonnet.com/fline/fl2413/stories/20070713004302000.htm.

Burdett, Ricky. "Mapping Scales of Urban Identity." *Architectural Design* 82, no. 6 (2012): 92–97.

Burdett, Ricky, and Deyan Sudjic. *The Endless City: The Urban Age Project by the London School of Economics and Deutsche Bank's Alfred Herrhausen Society.* London: Phaidon, 2010.

Burnett-Hurst, Alexander. *Labour and Housing in Bombay: A Study in the Economic Conditions of the Wage Earning Classes in Bombay.* London: P. S. King & Son, 1925.

Caldeira, Teresa. *City of Walls: Crime, Segregation, and Citizenship in São Paulo.* Berkeley, CA: University of California Press, 2000.

"Cancellation of Hawkers' Licenses." *Bombay Chronicle,* July 17, 1934.

Caton, Steven. *Lawrence of Arabia: A Film's Anthropology.* Berkeley: University of California Press, 1999.

Çelik, Zeynep. *Urban Forms and Colonial Confrontations: Algiers Under French Rule.* Berkeley: University of California Press, 1997.

Chakrabarty, Dipesh. *Provincializing Europe: Postcolonial Thought and Historical Difference.* Princeton, NJ: Princeton University Press, 2000.

———. *Habitations of Modernity: Essays in the Wake of Subaltern Studies.* Chicago: University of Chicago Press, 2002.

Chalfin, Brenda. "Sovereign and Citizens in Close Encounter: Airport Anthropology and Customs Regimes in Neoliberal Ghana." *American Ethnologist* 35, no. 4 (2008): 519–38.

Chandavarkar, Rajnarayan. *The Origins of Industrial Capitalism in India: Business Strategies and the Working Classes in Bombay, 1900–1940.* Cambridge: Cambridge University Press, 1994.

Chatterjee, Ipsita. "Social Conflict and the Neoliberal City: The Case of Hindu-Muslim Violence in India." *Transactions of the Institute of British Geographers* 34, no. 2 (2009): 143–60.

Chatterjee, Partha. *The Nation and Its Fragments: Colonial and Postcolonial Histories.* Princeton, NJ: Princeton University Press, 1993.

———. *The Politics of the Governed: Reflections on Popular Politics in Most of the World.* New York: Columbia University Press, 2004.

Chattopadhyay, Swati. *Representing Calcutta: Modernity, Nationalism, and the Colonial Uncanny.* London: Routledge, 2005.

Chesluk, Benjamin. "'Visible Signs of a City Out of Control': Community Policing in New York City." *Cultural Anthropology* 19, no. 2 (2004): 250–75.

Chopra, Preeti. *A Joint Enterprise: Indian Elites and the Making of British Bombay.* Minneapolis: University of Minnesota Press, 2011.

Citispace. *Hawking and Non-Hawking Zones in Greater Mumbai: Everything You Want to Know.* Mumbai: Citispace, 2004.

Clifford, James, and George E. Marcus, eds. *Writing Culture: The Poetics and Politics of Ethnography.* Berkeley: University of California Press, 1986.

Cole, Teju. *Open City: A Novel.* New York: Random House, 2012.

Comaroff, Jean. "Reflections on the Anthropology of Law, Governance, and Sovereignty." In *Rules of Law and Laws of Ruling: On the Governance of Law,* edited by Franz von Benda-Beckmann, Keebet von Benda-Beckmann, and Julia Eckert, 31–59. Surrey: Ashgate, 2013.

Comaroff, Jean, and John L. Comaroff, eds. *Law and Disorder in the Postcolony.* Chicago: University of Chicago Press, 2006.

Cooper, Frederick. "What Is the Concept of Globalization Good For? An African Historian's Perspective." *African Affairs* 100 (2001): 189–213.

Corbridge, Stuart, Glyn Williams, Manoj Srivastava, and René Véron. *Seeing the State: Governance and Governmentality in India*. Cambridge: Cambridge University Press, 2005.

Courage, Cara. "The Global Phenomenon of Tactical Urbanism as an Indicator of New Forms of Citizenship." In *Engage 32: Citizenship and Belonging*, edited by Karen Raney. London: Engage, the National Association for Gallery Education, 2013.

Coutard, Olivier, and Simon Guy. "STS and the City: Politics and Practices of Hope." *Science, Technology, and Human Values* 32, no. 6 (2007): 713–34.

Cross, John C. *Informal Politics: Street Vendors and the State in Mexico City*. Stanford, CA: Stanford University Press, 1998.

Cross, John, and Alfonso Morales, eds. *Street Entrepreneurs: People, Place, and Politics in Local and Global Perspective*. London: Routledge, 2007.

Curtis, George. "The Development of Bombay." *Journal of the Royal Society of Arts* 69 (1921): 559–77.

Cutler, J., & E. F. Griffin. *An Analysis of the Indian Penal Code: Including the Indian Penal Code Amendment Act, 1870 with Notes*. London: Butterworths, 1871.

Da Cunha, Joseph Gerson. *The Origin of Bombay*. Bombay, 1900.

Das, Veena. *Life and Words: Violence and the Descent into the Ordinary*. Berkeley: University of California Press, 2007.

Das, Veena, and Deborah Poole. "The State and Its Margins: Comparative Ethnographies." In *Anthropology in the Margins of the State*, edited by Veena Das and Deborah Poole, 3–34. Santa Fe, NM: School of American Research Press, 2004.

Dasgupta, Rana. "The Sudden Stardom of the Third World City." http://www.ranadasgupta.com/texts.asp?text_id=36, 2006.

Davis, Mike. "Planet of Slums: Urban Involution and the Informal Proletariat." *New Left Review* 26 (2004): 5–34.

de Certeau, Michel. *The Practice of Everyday Life*. Translated by Steven Rendall. Berkeley: University of California Press, 1984.

Delaney, Samuel. *Times Square Red, Times Square Blue*. New York: New York University Press, 1999.

Divakaruni, Chitra. "Put the Word in Context." *New York Times*, February 20, 2009. http://roomfordebate.blogs.nytimes.com/2009/02/20/the-real-roots-of-the-slumdog -protests/?_r=0.

Donovan, Michael G. "Informal Cities and the Contestation of Public Space: The Case of Bogotá's Street Vendors, 1988–2003." *Urban Studies* 45, no. 1 (2008): 29–51.

Dossal, Mariam. *Imperial Designs and Indian Realities: The Planning of Bombay City, 1845–1875*. Bombay: Oxford University Press, 1991.

———. *Theatre of Conflict, City of Hope: Bombay/Mumbai 1660 to Present*. Oxford: Oxford University Press, 2010.

Douglas, James. *Bombay and Western India: A Series of Stray Papers*. London: Sampson Low, Marston, 1893.

————. *Glimpses of Old Bombay and Western India, with Other Papers*. London: Sampson Low, Marston, 1900.

Douglas, Mary. *Purity and Danger: An Analysis of the Concepts of Pollution and Taboo*. London: Routledge & Kegan Paul, 1966.

Ducat, Walter. "Suburbs for Bombay." *Bombay Builder* 11, no. 9 (1866): 184–86.

Duneier, Mitchell. *Sidewalk*. New York: Farrar, Straus and Giroux, 1999.

Dupont, Véronique. "Dream of Delhi as a Global City." *International Journal of Urban and Regional Research* 35, no. 3 (2011): 533–54.

"Dwellings for the Labouring Poor." *Bombay Builder* 1, no. 11 (1866): 216–17.

Dwivedi, Sharada, and Rahul Mehrotra. *Bombay: The Cities Within*. Bombay: India Book House, 1995.

Echanove, Matias, and Rahul Srivastava. "Taking the Slum Out of 'Slumdog.'" *New York Times*, February 21, 2009.

Eckert, Julia. "Urban Governance and Emergent Forms of Legal Pluralism in Mumbai." *Journal of Legal Pluralism and Unofficial Law* 36, no. 50 (2004): 29–60.

Edwardes, Stephen M. *The Rise of Bombay: A Retrospect*. Bombay: Times of India Press, 1902.

————. *By-Ways of Bombay*. Bombay: D. B. Taraporevala, 1912.

————. *The Bombay City Police: A Historical Sketch 1672–1916*. London: Oxford University Press, 1923.

Elyachar, Julia. *Markets of Dispossession: NGOs, Economic Development, and the State*. Durham, NC: Duke University Press, 2007.

Engqvist, Jonatan, and Maria Lantz. *Dharavi: Documenting Informalities*. Stockholm, Sweden: Royal University College of Fine Art, 2008.

Farooqui, Amar. *Opium City: The Making of Early Victorian Bombay*. New Delhi: Three Essays Collective, 2006.

Fels, Mira. *Making Sense of Corruption in India: An Investigation into the Logic of Bribery*. Berlin: LIT Verlag, 2008.

Ferguson, James. *Expectations of Modernity: Myths and Meanings of Urban Life on the Zambian Copperbelt*. Berkeley: University of California Press, 1999.

————. "Formalities of Poverty: Thinking about Social Assistance in Neoliberal South Africa." *African Studies Review* 50, no. 2 (2007): 71–86.

————. "The Uses of Neoliberalism." *Antipode* 41, no. s1 (2009): 166–84.

Ferguson, James, and Akhil Gupta. "Spatializing States: Toward an Ethnography of Neoliberal Governmentality." *American Ethnologist* 29, no. 4 (2002): 981–1002.

Fernandes, Leela. "The Politics of Forgetting: Class Politics, State Power and the Restructuring of Urban Space in India." *Urban Studies* 41, no. 12 (2004): 2415–30.

Fernandes, Naresh. "India's Indestructible Heart." *New York Times*, July 12, 2006.

Fernández-Kelly, Patricia, and Jon Shefner, eds. *Out of the Shadows: Political Action and the Informal Economy in Latin America*. University Park: Pennsylvania State University Press, 2006.

"First Impressions of Art and Architecture in Bombay." *Bombay Builder* 1, no. 1 (1865):4–6.

"A Flourishing Slum." *Economist*, December 19, 2007. http://www.economist.com/node/10311293.

Fortun, Kim. *Advocacy After Bhopal: Environmentalism, Disaster, New Global Orders.* Chicago: University of Chicago Press, 2001.

Fuller, C. J., and John Harriss. "For an Anthropology of the Modern Indian State." In *The Everyday State and Society in Modern India.* Edited by C. J. Fuller and Véronique Bénéï, 1–30. New Delhi: Social Science Press, 2000.

Gaonkar, Dilip Parameshwar. "On Alternative Modernities." In *Alternative Modernities,* edited by Dilip Parameshwar Gaonkar, 1–16. Durham, NC: Duke University Press, 2001.

Gazetteer of Bombay City and Island. Vol. 3. Bombay: Times Press, 1910.

Ghertner, D. Asher. "Analysis of New Legal Discourse Behind Delhi's Slum Demolitions." *Economic and Political Weekly* 43, no. 20 (2008): 57–66.

———. "Gentrifying the State, Gentrifying Participation: Elite Governance Programs in Delhi." *International Journal of Urban and Regional Research* 35, no. 3 (2011a): 504–32.

———. "Rule by Aesthetics: World-Class City Making in Delhi." In *Worlding Cities: Asian Experiments and the Art of Being Global,* edited by Ananya Roy and Aihwa Ong, 279–306. Oxford: Blackwell, 2011b.

Gidwani, Vinay, and Bharati Chaturvedi. "Poverty as Geography: Motility, Stoppage and Circuits of Waste in Delhi." In *Urban Navigations: Politics, Space, and the City in South Asia,* edited by Jonathan Shapiro Anjaria and Colin McFarlane, 50–78. New Delhi: Routledge, 2011.

Giridharadas, Anand. "Horatio Alger Relocates to a Mumbai Slum." *New York Times,* January 17, 2009.

Glaeser, Edward. "Urban Ingenuity." *Royal Society of Arts* 157, no. 5546 (2011): 16–21.

Glover, William J. "Construing Urban Space as 'Public' in Colonial India: Some Notes from the Punjab." *Journal of Punjab Studies* 14, no. 2 (2007): 211–24.

———. *Making Lahore Modern: Constructing and Imagining a Colonial City.* Minneapolis: University of Minnesota Press, 2008.

Goldman, Michael. "Speculative Urbanism and the Making of the Next World City." *International Journal of Urban and Regional Research* 35, no. 3 (2011): 555–81.

Graham, Maria. *Journal of a Residence in India.* Edinburgh: George Ramsay and Company, 1813.

Graham, Stephen. *Cities Under Siege: The New Military Urbanism.* London: Verso, 2010.

"The Grant Road Nuisance." *Bombay Chronicle,* December 22, 1933.

Gregory, Steven. *Black Corona: Race and the Politics of Place in an Urban Community.* Princeton, NJ: Princeton University Press, 1999.

Gupta, Akhil. "Blurred Boundaries: The Discourse of Corruption, the Culture of Politics, and the Imagined State." *American Ethnologist* 22, no. 2 (1995): 375–402.

———. "Narratives of Corruption: Anthropological and Fictional Accounts of the Indian State." *Ethnography* 6, no. 1 (2005): 5–34.

Hafeez, Mateen. "At Nagpada, Police Marshals on a Different Beat." *Times of India,* December 20, 2005. http://mateenhafeez.blogspot.com/2005_12_01_archive.html.

Hamilton, Walter. *A Geographical, Statistical, and Historical Description of Hindostan, and the Adjacent Countries.* Vol. 2. London: John Murray, 1820.

Hansen, Thomas Blom. *Urban Violence in India: Identity Politics, "Mumbai," and the Post-colonial City.* New Delhi: Permanent Black, 2001.

Hansen, Thomas Blom, and Finn Stepputat, eds. *States of Imagination: Ethnographic Explorations of the Postcolonial State.* Durham, NC: Duke University Press, 2001.

Hansen, Thomas Blom, and Oskar Verkaaik. "Introduction—Urban Charisma: On Everyday Mythologies in the City." *Critique of Anthropology* 29, no. 1 (2009): 5–26.

"Harassing the Poor and Needy." *Bombay Chronicle*, May 25, 1933.

Hardiman, David. *Gandhi in His Time and Ours: The Global Legacy of His Ideas.* New York: Columbia University Press, 2004.

Harris, Andrew. "The Metonymic Urbanism of Twenty-First-Century Mumbai." *Urban Studies* 49, no. 13 (2012): 2955–73.

———. "Concrete Geographies: Assembling Global Mumbai Through Transport Infrastructure." *City* 17, no. 3 (2013): 343–60.

Harriss, John. "Antinomies of Empowerment: Observations on Civil Society, Politics and Urban Governance in India." *Economic and Political Weekly* 42, no. 26 (2007): 2716–24.

Harriss-White, Barbara. *India Working: Essays on Society and Economy.* Cambridge: Cambridge University Press, 2003.

Hart, Keith. "Informal Income Opportunities and Urban Employment in Ghana." *Journal of Modern African Studies* 11, no. 1 (1973): 61–89.

———. "Bureaucratic Form and the Informal Economy." In *Linking the Formal and Informal Economy*, edited by Basudeb Guha-Khasnobis, Ravi Kanbur, and Elinor Ostrum, 21–35. Oxford: Oxford University Press, 2006.

Harvey, David. "From Managerialism to Entrepreneurialism: The Transformation in Urban Governance in Late Capitalism." *Geografiska Annaler, Series B, Human Geography* 71, no. 1 (1989): 3–17.

———. "The Right to the City." *International Journal of Urban and Regional Research* 27 (2003): 939–41.

———. "Neo-Liberalism as Creative Destruction." *Geografiska Annaler, Series B: Human Geography* 88, no. 2 (2006): 145–58.

Hasty, Jennifer. "The Pleasures of Corruption: Desire and Discipline in Ghanaian Political Culture." *Cultural Anthropology* 20, no. 2 (2005): 271–301.

"Hateful and Degrading." *Bombay Chronicle*, May 31, 1933.

"Hawker Nuisance." *Bombay Chronicle*, September 1, 1933.

"Hawkers." *Bombay Chronicle*, June 30, 1934.

"The Hawkers." *Bombay Chronicle*, January 3, 1934.

"Hawkers and Footpaths." *Bombay Chronicle*, January 3, 1934.

"The Hawker's Nuisance." *Bombay Chronicle*, June 2, 1931.

Haynes, Douglas. *Rhetoric and Ritual in Colonial India: The Shaping of a Public Sphere in Surat City, 1852–1928.* Berkeley: University of California Press, 1991.

Hazareesingh, Sandip. "The Quest for Urban Citizenship: Civic Rights, Public Opinion, and Colonial Resistance in Early Twentieth-Century Bombay." *Modern Asian Studies* 34 (2000): 797–829.

————. "Colonial Modernism and the Flawed Paradigms of Urban Renewal: Uneven Development in Bombay, 1900-25." *Urban History* 28 (2001): 235–55.

————. *The Colonial City and the Challenge of Modernity: Urban Hegemonies and Civic Contestations in Bombay (1900–1925).* Hyderabad: Orient Longman, 2007.

Herzfeld, Michael. "Political Optics and the Occlusion of Intimate Knowledge." *American Anthropologist* 107, no. 3 (2005): 369–76.

————. "Spatial Cleansing: Monumental Vacuity and the Idea of the West." *Journal of Material Culture* 11, no. 1–2 (2006): 127–49.

————. *Evicted from Eternity: The Restructuring of Modern Rome.* Chicago: University of Chicago Press, 2009.

Hetherington, Kregg. "Privatizing the Private in Rural Paraguay: Precarious Lots and the Materiality of Rights." *American Ethnologist* 36, no. 2 (2009): 224–41.

Holston, James. *The Modernist City: An Anthropological Critique of Brasilia.* Chicago: University of Chicago Press, 1989.

————. "Autoconstruction in Working-Class Brazil." *Cultural Anthropology* 6, no. 4 (1991): 447–65.

Horniman, Benjamin. "Have a Thought for the Poor Pedestrian!" *Bombay Chronicle*, May 27, 1933.

Hosagrahar, Jyoti. *Indigenous Modernities: Negotiating Architecture and Urbanism.* London: Routledge, 2005.

Hull, Matthew S. "Communities of Place, Not Kind: American Technologies of Neighborhood in Postcolonial Delhi." *Comparative Studies in Society and History* 53, no. 4 (2011): 757–90.

————. *Government of Paper: The Materiality of Bureaucracy in Urban Pakistan.* Berkeley: University of California Press, 2012.

"In and Around Bombay." *Bombay Chronicle*, January 1, 1934.

"Is Bombay Clean?" *Bombay Chronicle*, December 30, 1933.

Israel, Milton. *Communications and Power: Propaganda and the Press in the Indian Nationalist Struggle.* Cambridge: Cambridge University Press, 1994.

Iyer, Kavitha. "Mumbai Turns Lab Rat for Urban Thinktank." *Daily News and Analysis*, December 9, 2012. http://www.dnaindia.com/mumbai/1775276/report-mumbai-turns-lab-rat-for-urban-thinktank.

Jacobs, Jane. *The Death and Life of Great American Cities.* New York: Random House, 1961.

Jameson, Frederic. *The Antinomies of Realism.* London: Verso, 2013.

Jauregui, Beatrice. "Provisional Agency in India: *Jugaad* and Legitimation of Corruption." *American Ethnologist* 41, no. 1 (2014): 76–91.

Jellinek, Lea. "Displaced by Modernity: The Saga of a Jakarta Street-Trader's Family from the 1940s to the 1990s." In *Cities in the Developing World: Issues, Theory, and Policy*, edited by Josef Gugler, 139–55. Oxford: Oxford University Press, 1997.

Jodhka, Surinder S. "Nation and Village: Images of Rural India in Gandhi, Nehru and Ambedkar." *Economic and Political Weekly* 37, no. 32 (2002): 3343–53.

Joyce, Patrick. *The Rule of Freedom: Liberalism and the Modern City.* London: Verso, 2003.

Jumani, Usha, and Joshi Bharati. *Legal Status of Hawkers in India*. Ahmedabad: Self Employed Women's Association, 1984.

Kanna, Ahmed. "Flexible Citizenship in Dubai: Neoliberal Subjectivity in the Emerging 'City-Corporation.'" *Cultural Anthropology* 25, no. 1 (2010): 100–29

Kaviraj, Sudipta. "Filth and the Public Sphere: Concepts and Practices About Space in Calcutta." *Public Culture* 10, no. 1 (1997): 83–113.

Kidambi, Prashant. *The Making of an Indian Metropolis: Colonial Governance and Public Culture in Bombay, 1890–1920*. Burlington, VT: Ashgate, 2007.

King, Anthony. *Colonial Urban Development: Culture, Social Power, and Environment*. London: Routledge, 1976.

Klein, Ira. "Urban Development and Death: Bombay City, 1870–1914." *Modern Asian Studies* 20, no. 4 (1986): 725–54.

Koolhaas, Rem, Stefano Boeri, Sanford Kwinter, Nadia Tazi, and Hans Ulrich Christ. *Mutations*. Bordeaux: Arc en Rêve Centre d'Architecture, 2000.

Koppikar, Smruti. "The Cookout: Mumbai's Roadside Kabob King Bade Miya Is Going Fine-Dining." *Outlook*, November 2, 2009. http://www.outlookindia.com/article/The -Cookout/262427.

Kulkarni, Vishwas. "Land Sharks: Colonial and Desi." *Mumbai Mirror*, January 10, 2010. http://www.mumbaimirror.com/others/sunday-read/Land-Sharks-Colonial-Desi/ articleshow/15983147.cms.

Kwinter, Sanford. "Notes on the Third Ecology." In *Ecological Urbanism*, edited by Mohsen Mostavi and Gareth Doherty, 94–105. Basel, Switzerland: Lars Müller, 2010.

Lakier, Genevieve. "Illiberal Democracy and the Problem of Law." In *Contentious Politics and Democratization in Nepal*, edited by Mahendra Lawoti, 214–72. New Delhi: Sage, 2007.

Lantz, Maria. "Who's Afraid of the Urban Poor?" In *Dharavi: Documenting Informalities*, edited by Jonatan Engqvist and Maria Lantz, 30–41. Stockholm, Sweden: Royal University College of Fine Art, 2008.

Legg, Stephen. *Spaces of Colonialism: Delhi's Urban Governmentalities*. Blackwell: Oxford University Press, 2011.

Lewis, Claire. "Hawker Network Beats BMC Eviction Drive." *Times of India*, April 29, 2005. http://timesofindia.indiatimes.com/city/mumbai/Hawker-network-beats-BMC -eviction-drive/articleshow/1093749.cms.

Leys, Colin. "What Is the Problem About Corruption?" *Journal of Modern African Studies* 3, no. 2 (1965): 215–230.

Lino e Silva, Moises, and Gareth Doherty. "Formally Informal: Daily Life and the Shock of Order in a Brazilian Favela." *Built Environment* 37, no. 1 (2011): 30–41.

Loukaitou-Sideris, Anastasia, and Renia Ehrenfeucht. *Sidewalks: Conflict and Negotiation over Public Space*. Cambridge, MA: MIT Press, 2009.

Low, Sidney. *A Vision of India*. New York: Dutton, 1907.

Lynch, Owen. "Potters, Plotters, Prodders in a Bombay Slum: Marx and Meaning or Meaning Versus Marx." *Urban Anthropology* 8, no. 1 (1979): 1–27.

Maclean, James Mackenzie. *A Guide to Bombay: Historical, Statistical, and Descriptive*. London: G. Street & Co, 1889.

MacLeod, Gordon. "From Urban Entrepreneurialism to a 'Revanchist City'? On the Spatial Injustices of Glasgow's Renaissance." *Antipode* 34, no. 3 (2002): 602–24.

Mahalwar, K. P. S. "Hawker's Right to Livelihood." *Central India Law Quarterly* 3 (1990): 250–54.

Maharashtra Ekta Hawkers Union and Anr. v. Municipal Corporation and Ors., Greater Mumbai 2003. http://indiankanoon.org/doc/1240612/

Masani, Rustom. *Evolution of Local Self Government in Bombay*. London: Oxford University Press, 1929.

Masselos, Jim. *The City in Action: Bombay Struggles for Power*. New Delhi: Oxford University Press, 2007.

Materials Towards a Statistical Account of the Town and Island of Bombay. Vol. 2. Bombay: Government Central Press, 1893.

Materials Towards a Statistical Account of the Town and Island of Bombay. Vol. 2: *Trade and Fortifications*. Bombay: Government Central Press, 1894.

Mazumdar, Ranjani. *Bombay Cinema: An Archive of the City*. Minneapolis: University of Minnesota Press, 2007.

Mazzarella, William. *Shoveling Smoke: Advertising and Globalization in Contemporary India*. Durham, NC: Duke University Press, 2003.

———. "Internet X-Ray: E-Governance, Transparency, and the Politics of Immediation in India." *Public Culture* 18, no. 3 (2006): 473–505.

McFarlane, Colin. "Governing the Contaminated City: Infrastructure and Sanitation in Colonial and Postcolonial Bombay." *International Journal of Urban and Regional Research* 32, no. 2 (2008): 415–35.

———. *Learning the City: Knowledge and Translocal Assemblage*. West Sussex: Wiley-Blackwell, 2011.

McFarlane, Colin, and Michael Waibel, eds. *Urban Informalities: Reflections on the Formal and Informal*. Surrey: Ashgate, 2012.

McGee, Terence G. *Hawkers in Hong Kong: A Study of Planning and Policy in a Third World City*. Hong Kong: Centre of Asian Studies, University of Hong Kong, 1973.

McKinsey & Company. *Vision Mumbai: Transforming Mumbai into a World-Class City: A Summary of Recommendations*. 2003.

McLaren, Christine. "Learning from Landlink." January 9, 2013. http://blogs.guggenheim.org/lablog/learning-from-landlink/.

Mehrotra, Rahul. "Conservation and Change: Questions for Conservation Education in Urban India." *Built Environment* 33, no. 3 (2007): 342–56.

Mehta, Suketu. *Maximum City: Bombay Lost and Found*. New York: Knopf, 2005.

Merry, Sally Engle. "Law, Culture, and Cultural Appropriation." *Yale Journal of Law and the Humanities* 10, no. 2 (1998): 575–603.

———. "Spatial Governmentality and the New Urban Social Order: Controlling Gender Violence Through Law." *American Anthropologist* 103, no. 1 (2001): 16–29.

Metcalfe, Thomas. *An Imperial Vision: Indian Architecture and Britain's Raj*. Oxford: Oxford University Press, 2002.

Mitchell, Don. "The End of Public Space? People's Park, Definitions of the Public, and Democracy." *Annals of the Association of American Geographers* 85, no. 1 (1995): 108–33.

———. "The S.U.V. Model of Citizenship: Floating Bubbles, Buffer Zones, and the Rise of the 'Purely Atomic' Individual." *Political Geography* 24, no. 1 (2005): 77–100.

Mitchell, Don, and Lynn A. Staeheli. "Clean and Safe? Property Redevelopment, Public Space and Homelessness in Downtown San Diego." In *The Politics of Public Space*, edited by Setha Low and Neil Smith, 143–76. New York: Routledge, 2006.

Mitchell, Timothy. "The Limits of the State: Beyond Statist Approaches and Their Critics." *American Political Science Review* 85, no. 1 (1991): 77–96.

Modak, N. V. "The City's Public Works." In *The Bombay Municipality at Work*, edited by Clifford Manshardt, 55–70. Bombay: D. B. Taraporevala & Sons, 1935.

Moray, Raju. "Trampling over Footpaths." *Indian Express*, September 9, 1998.

Moretti, Franco. *Signs Taken for Wonders: On the Sociology of Literary Forms*. London: Verso, 1983.

Morley, William H. "Papers on the Police of Bombay." In *An Analytical Digest of All the Reported Cases Decided in the Supreme Courts of Judicature in India, in the Courts of the Hon. East-India Company, and on Appeal from India, by Her Majesty in Council*. London: W.H. Allen and Co., 1859.

Moskin, Julia. "Six Arrested on Permit-Fraud Charges." *New York Times*, June 30, 2009a. http://www.nytimes.com/2009/07/01/dining/01permit.html.

———. "Turf War at the Hot Dog Cart." *New York Times*, July 1, 2009b. http://www.ny times.com/2009/07/01/dining/01truck.html.

Municipal Board v. Khalil-Ul-Rahman. AIR 1929 All 382 http://indiankanoon.org/doc /787840/.

Nair, Janaki. *The Promise of the Metropolis. Bangalore's Twentieth Century*. Delhi: Oxford University Press, 2005.

Nandy, Ashis. *The Savage Freud and Other Essays on Possible and Retrievable Selves*. New Delhi: Oxford University Press, 1995.

National Public Radio. "Why Are Squatter Cities the 'Cities of Tomorrow'?" *TED Radio Hour*, June 11, 2012. http://www.npr.org/2012/06/15/154803946/why-are-squatter -cities-the-cities-of-tomorrow.

"Native Papers." *Times of India*, July 23, 1890.

Neuwirth, Robert. *Shadow Cities: A Billion Squatters, a New Urban World*. New York: Routledge, 2005.

"The New Bombay: Embryonic Street Improvements." *Times of India*, November 19, 1901.

Ocko, Jonathan, and David Gilmartin. "State, Sovereignty, and the People: A Comparison of the 'Rule of Law' in China and India." *Journal of Asian Studies* 68, no. 1 (2009): 55–133.

Oldenburg, Philip. "Middlemen in Third-World Corruption: Implications of an Indian Case." *World Politics* 39, no. 4 (1987): 508–35.

Olga Tellis & Ors. v. Bombay Municipal Corporation & Ors, etc. 1985. 3 SCC 545. http:// indiankanoon.org/doc/709776/.

Olivier de Sardan, J. P. "A Moral Economy of Corruption in Africa." *Journal of Modern African Studies* 37, no. 1 (1999): 25–52.

Orr, J. P. *Density of Population in Bombay: A Lecture Delivered Before the Bombay Co-operative Housing Association.* Bombay: British India Press, 1914.

Ortner, Sherry. "Resistance and the Problem of Ethnographic Refusal." *Comparative Studies in Society and History* 37, no. 1 (1995): 173–93.

Ouroussoff, Nicolai. "Putting Whole Teeming Cities on the Drawing Board." *New York Times*, September 10, 2006.

Palsetia, Jesse S. "Merchant Charity and Public Identity Formation in Colonial India: The Case of Jamsetjee Jejeebhoy." *Journal of Asian and African Studies* 40, no. 3 (2005): 197–217.

Parpiani, Maansi. "Urban Planning in Bombay (1898–1928): Ambivalences, Inconsistencies and Struggles of the Colonial State." *Economic and Political Weekly* 47, no. 28 (2012): 64–70.

Parry, Jonathan. "The 'Crisis of Corruption' and 'The Idea of India': A Worm's-Eye View." In *Morals of Legitimacy: Between Agency and System*, edited by Italo Pardo, 27–56. New York: Berghahn Books, 2000.

Patel, Gautam. "Alien Versus Predator." *Mumbai Mirror*, March 8, 2013. http://www.mumbaimirror.com/columns/columnists/gautam-patel/Alien-versus-predator/articleshow/18862305.cms.

Patel, Shirish. "Plotting for the People?" *Indian Express*, June 18, 2009. http://www.indianexpress.com/news/plotting-for-the-people/477884/0.

Paxson, Heather. *The Life of Cheese: Crafting Food and Value in America.* Berkeley: University of California Press, 2013.

"Pedestrians Combine!" *Bombay Chronicle*, May 29, 1933.

"Pedestrians' Trials in Bombay." *Bombay Chronicle*, September 14, 1933.

Phadke, Shilpa, Shilpa Ranade, and Sameera Khan. "Why Loiter? Radical Possibilities for Gendered Dissent." In *Dissent and Cultural Resistance in Asia's Cities*, edited by Melissa Butcher and Selvaraj Velayutham, 187–203. New York: Routledge, 2009.

Pierce, Steven. "Looking like a State: Colonialism and the Discourse of Corruption in Northern Nigeria." *Comparative Studies of Society and History* 48, no. 4 (2006): 887–914.

"The Plague." *Indian Engineering.* Calcutta: C.J.A. Pritchard, February 13, 1897.

Popke, E. Jeffrey, and Richard Ballard. "Dislocating Modernity: Identity, Space and Representations of Street Trade in Durban, South Africa." *Geoforum* 35, no. 1 (2004): 99–110.

Prakash, Gyan. *Mumbai Fables.* Princeton, NJ: Princeton University Press, 2010.

Punj, Neera. "The Chalta Hai Attitude Puts Me Off." *DNA*, August 5, 2007. http://www.dnaindia.com/mumbai/report_the-chalta-hai-attitude-puts-me-off_1113632-all.

Pyare Lal etc v. New Delhi Municipal Corporation. AIR 133. http://indiankanoon.org/doc/1330298/.

Quayson, Ato. *Oxford St., Accra: City Life and the Itineraries of Transnationalism.* Durham, NC: Duke University Press, 2014.

Rabinow, Paul. "Governing Morocco: Modernity and Difference." *International Journal of Urban and Regional Research* 13, no. 1 (1989): 32–46.

Raffles, Hugh. *In Amazonia: A Natural History.* Princeton, NJ: Princeton University Press, 2002.

Raghunathji, Krishnanath. "Bombay Beggars and Criers." *Indian Antiquary* 9 (October 1880): 247–50.

———. "Bombay Beggars and Criers." *Indian Antiquary* 11 (February 1882): 44–47.

"A Railway Nuisance." *Bombay Chronicle,* April 19, 1934.

Rajagopal, Arvind. "The Violence of Commodity Aesthetics: Hawkers, Demolition Raids, and a New Regime of Consumption." *Social Text* 19, no. 3 (2001): 91–113.

Rajyashree, K. S. "Languages for Survival and Work in the Bombay Slum of Dharavi." In *Working with Language: A Multidisciplinary Consideration of Language Use in Work Contexts,* edited by Hywel Coleman, 369–92. Berlin, Germany: Mouton de Gruyter, 1989.

Ramanathan, Uma. "Illegality and the Urban Poor." *Economic and Political Weekly,* July 22, 2006, 3193–97.

Ramanna, Mridula. *Western Medicine and Public Health in Colonial Bombay, 1845–1895.* New Delhi: Orient Longman, 2002.

Ranganathan, Murali. *Govind Narayan's Mumbai: An Urban Biography from 1863.* London: Anthem Press, 2009.

Rao, Nikhil. *House, But No Garden: Apartment Living in Bombay's Suburbs, 1898–1964.* Minneapolis: University of Minnesota Press, 2013.

Rao, Nikhil, and Douglas Haynes. "Beyond the Colonial City: Re-Evaluating the Urban History of India, ca. 1920–1970." *South Asia: Journal of South Asian Studies* 36, no. 3 (2013): 317–35.

Rao, Shashank. "Hawkers Look to Take Over Rs 8–cr Andheri Auto Deck." *Midday,* July 11, 2015.

Rao, Ursula. "Tolerated Encroachment: Resettlement Policies and the Negotiation of the Licit/Illicit Divide in an Indian Metropolis." *Cultural Anthropology* 28, no. 4 (2013): 760–79.

Roach, Mary. "Honk Honk *BRIING BRIING* (Look Out!) Make Way for the Bike Riders." *Bicycling* (July 2013): 56–58, 95–98.

Roberts, Emma. *Notes of an Overland Journey Through France and Egypt to Bombay.* London: W.H. Allen & Co., 1841.

Roberts, Gregory David. *Shantaram.* New York: St. Martin's Press, 2004.

Robertson, Alexander. "Misunderstanding Corruption." *Anthropology Today* 22, no. 2 (2006): 8–11.

Robertson, Claire C. *Trouble Showed the Way: Women, Men and Trade in the Nairobi Area, 1890–1990.* Bloomington: Indiana University Press, 1997.

Robinson, Rowena. "Indian Muslims: The Varied Dimensions of Marginality." *Economic and Political Weekly* 42, no. 10 (2007): 839–43.

Rodrigues, Dulcinea Correa. *Bombay Fort in the Eighteenth Century.* Bombay: Himalaya Publishing House, 1994.

Roitman, Janet. "The Politics of Informal Markets in Sub-Saharan Africa." *Journal of Modern African Studies* 28, no. 4 (1990): 671–96.

Rose, Nikolas. "Governing 'Advanced' Liberal Democracies." In *Foucault and Political Rea-*

son, edited by Andrew Barry, Thomas Osborne, and Nikolas Rose, 37–64. Chicago: University of Chicago Press, 1996.

Rosenberg, David. "Epic Shanty Towns from Around the World." *Slate.com*, July 10, 2013. http://www.slate.com/blogs/behold/2013/07/10/noah_addis_future_cities_looks_at_squatter_communities_around_the_world.html.

Roy, Ananya. "Traditions of the Modern: A Corrupt View." *Traditional Dwellings and Settlements Review* 12, no. 2 (2001): 7–21.

———. *City Requiem, Calcutta: Gender and the Politics of Poverty*. Minneapolis: University of Minnesota Press, 2003.

———. "Why India Cannot Plan Its Cities: Informality, Insurgence and the Idiom of Urbanization." *Planning Theory* 8, no. 1 (2009): 76–87.

———. "The Agonism of Utopia: Dialectics at a Standstill." *Traditional Dwellings and Settlements Review* 23, no. 1 (2011a): 15–24.

———. "Slumdog Cities: Rethinking Subaltern Urbanism." *International Journal of Urban and Regional Research* 35, no. 2 (2011b): 223–38.

Roy, Ananya, and Nezar AlSayyad, eds. *Urban Informality: Transnational Perspectives from the Middle East, Latin America, and South Asia*. Lanham, MD: Lexington Books, 2004.

The Sanitary Record. Vol. 19. London: Sanitary Publishing Co., May 7, 1897.

The Sanitary Record. Vol. 22. London: Sanitary Publishing Co., November 18, 1898.

Sarin, Madhu. "Urban Planning, Petty Trading, and Squatter Settlements in Chandigarh, India." In *Casual Work and Poverty in Third World Cities*, edited by Ray Bromley and Chris Gerry, 133–60. New York: Wiley, 1979.

Saunier, Pierre-Yves, and Shane Ewen, eds. *Another Global City: Historical Explorations into the Transnational Municipal Moment, 1850–2000*. New York: Palgrave Macmillan, 2008.

Schindler, Seth. "The Making of 'World-Class' Delhi: Relations Between Street Hawkers and the New Middle Class." *Antipode* 46, no. 2 (2014): 557–73.

Scott, James. *Seeing like a State: How Certain Schemes to Improve the Human Condition Have Failed*. New Haven, CT: Yale University Press, 1998.

Searle, Llerena Guiu. "Conflict and Commensuration: Contested Market Making in India's Private Real Estate Development Sector." *International Journal of Urban and Regional Research* 38, no. 1 (2014): 60–78.

Sen, Jai. *The Unintended City: An Essay on the City of the Poor*. Calcutta: Cathedral Relief and Social Services, 1975.

Sen, Somit. "Rates for Plum Police Postings Dive." *Times of India*, August 18, 2005.

Sengupta, Somini. "Extreme Mumbai, Without Bollywood's Filtered Lens." *New York Times,* November 11, 2009. http://www.nytimes.com/2008/11/16/movies/16seng.html?pagewanted=all.

Sennett, Richard. *Flesh and Stone: The Body and the City in Western Civilization*. New York: Norton, 1996.

Sethi, Aman. *A Free Man: A True Story of Life and Death in Delhi*. New York: Norton, 2013.

Shah, Alpa. "Morality, Corruption, and the State: Insights from Jharkhand, Eastern India." *Journal of Development Studies* 45, no. 3 (2009): 295–313.

Shanbaug, Amit. "How Dheeraj Gupta Launched a Successful Vada Pao Chain Jumbo King." *Economic Times*, 2014. http://economictimes.indiatimes.com/news/emerging -businesses/entrepreneurship/how-dheeraj-gupta-launched-a-successful-vada-pav -chain-jumbo-king/articleshow/36940801.cms.

Sharma, Aradhana, and Akhil Gupta. "Introduction." In *The Anthropology of the State Reader*, edited by Aradhana Sharma and Akhil Gupta, 1–41. Malden: Blackwell, 2006.

Sharma, Kalpana. *Rediscovering Dharavi: Stories from Asia's Largest Slum.* New Delhi: Penguin, 2000.

Sharma, R. N. "The Politics of Urban Space." *Seminar* (July 2000). http://www.india -seminar.com/2000/491/491%20r.n.%20sharma.htm.

———. "Mega Transformation of Mumbai: Deepening Enclave Urbanism." *Sociological Bulletin* 59, no. 1 (2010): 69–91.

Shatkin, Gavin. "Contesting the Indian City: Global Visions and the Politics of the Local." *International Journal of Urban and Regional Research* 38, no. 1 (2014): 1–13.

Shepherd, William Ashton. *Bombay to Bushire and Bussora; Including an Account of the Present State of Persia, and Notes on the Persian War.* London: Richard Bentley, 1857.

Shore, Cris, and Dieter Haller. "Sharp Practice: Anthropology and the Study of Corruption." In *Corruption: Anthropological Perspectives*, edited by Dieter Haller and Cris Shore, 1–28. London: Pluto Press, 2005.

Siddhaye, Ninad. "The Skywalk: A Road above Hell." *Daily News and Analysis.* October 27, 2011 http://www.dnaindia.com/mumbai/report_the-skywalk-a-road-above -hell_1603873.

Simmel, Georg. "The Metropolis and Mental Life." In *The Sociology of Georg Simmel*, edited by Kurt H. Wolff, 409–24. New York: Free Press, 1950.

Simone, AbdouMaliq. *For the City Yet to Come: Changing African Life in Four Cities.* Durham, NC: Duke University Press, 2004.

Singh, Binti. "Parallel Structures of Decentralization in the Mega City Context of Urban India: Participation or Exclusion?" *Space and Polity* 16, no. 1 (2012): 111–27.

Singh, Binti, and D. Parthasarathy. "Civil Society Organization Partnership in Urban Governance: An Appraisal of the Mumbai Experience." *Social Bulletin* 59, no. 1 (2010): 92–110.

Singh, Gurjeet. "Group Actions and the Law: A Case Study of Social Action Litigation and Consumer Protection in India." *Journal of Consumer Policy* 18, no. 1 (1995): 25–54.

"Slum Dwellers Protest." *Daily News and Analysis*, January 23, 2009. http://www.dnaindia .com/india/1224332/report-slum-dwellers-protest-over-slumdog-millionaire-title.

Smith, Neil. *The New Urban Frontier: Gentrification and the Revanchist City.* London: Routledge, 1996.

———. "New Globalism, New Urbanism: Gentrification as Global Urban Strategy." *Antipode* 34, no. 3 (2002): 427–50.

———. "After Tompkins Square Park: Degentrification and the Revanchist City." In *The Blackwell City Reader*, edited by Gary Bridge and Sophie Watson, 201–9. Oxford: Blackwell, 2010.

Smith, Rachel. "Active Streets in India's Dharavi Slum." 2013. http://thisbigcity.net/active -streets-in-indias-dharavi-slum.

Sodan Singh, etc. etc. v. New Delhi Municipal Committee & Anr, etc. 4 SCC 155. http://indiankanoon.org/doc/165273/.

Soja, Edward W. *Postmodern Geographies: The Reassertion of Space in Critical Social Theory.* London: Verso, 1989.

"Sort of Municipal 'Loot.'" *Bombay Chronicle,* May 23, 1931.

Spies, Martina. "Dharavi: A Settlement, Not a Slum." Urb.im, March 31, 2012. http://urb.im/mm/120331dh.

Stevenson, Seth. "Trying Really Hard to Like India." *Slate,* September 30, 2004. http://www.slate.com/articles/life/welltraveled/features/2004/trying_really_hard_to_like_india/learning_to_like_india_a_fivestep_approach.html.

Stewart, Kathleen. *A Space on the Side of the Road: Cultural Poetics in an "Other" America.* Princeton, NJ: Princeton University Press, 1996.

Street Vendor Project. "Peddling Uphill: A Report on the Conditions of Street Vendors in New York City." New York: Street Vendor Project of the Urban Justice Center, 2006.

"Street Vendors," *Seminar.* Factfile (July 2000).

Subramanian, Ajantha. *Shorelines: Space and Rights in South India.* Palo Alto, CA: Stanford University Press, 2009.

Subramanian, Divya. "One for the Road, and Then Some." *Daily News and Analysis,* October 28, 2006. http://www.dnaindia.com/mumbai/report-one-for-the-road -and-then -some-1060761.

Subramanian, Reetika. "Download an App, Take an Illegal Hawker to Task." *Hindustan Times,* January 18, 2013. http://www.hindustantimes.com/India-news/Mumbai/Download-an-app-take-an-illegal-hawker-to-task/Article1–992646.aspx.

Sudarshan Das Shastri v. Municipal Board Of Agra And Anr. ILR 37 All 9 http://indiankanoon.org/doc/902992/, 1914.

Sunavala, Nergish. "BMW Guggenheim Lab." *Time Out Mumbai,* November 23, 2012. http://www.timeoutmumbai.net/around-town/features/bmw-guggenheim-lab.

Sundar, Nandini. "Toward an Anthropology of Culpability." *American Ethnologist* 31, no. 2 (2004): 145–63.

Sutherland, Heather. "Whose Makassar? Claiming Space in a Segmented City." *Comparative Studies in Society and History* 53, no. 4 (2011): 791–826.

Tambe, Ashwini. *Codes of Misconduct: Regulating Prostitution in Late Colonial Bombay.* Minneapolis: University of Minnesota Press, 2009.

Tambe, Ashwini, and Harald Fischer-Tiné, eds. *The Limits of British Colonial Control in South Asia: Spaces of Disorder in the Indian Ocean Region.* Abingdon, UK: Routledge, 2009.

Tata Institute of Social Sciences and Youth for Unity and Voluntary Action. *Census Survey of Hawkers on BMC Lands.* Mumbai: TISS-YUVA, 1998.

Thacker, Andrew. *Moving Through Modernity: Space and Geography in Modernism.* Manchester: Manchester University Press, 2003.

"Times View." *Times of India,* July 15, 2015.

"Town and Fort of Bombay." *Alexander's East India and Colonial Magazine* 9 (1835): 244–245.

Trouillot, Michel-Rolph. "The Anthropology of the State in the Age of Globalization." *Current Anthropology* 42, no. 1 (2001): 125–38.

Tsing, Anna. *In the Realm of the Diamond Queen*. Princeton, NJ: Princeton University Press, 1993.

———. "Inside the Economy of Appearances." *Public Culture* 12, no. 1 (2000): 115–44.

———. *Friction: An Ethnography of Global Connection*. Princeton, NJ: Princeton University Press, 2005.

Vahed, Goolam. "Control and Repression: The Plight of Indian Hawkers and Flower Sellers in the Durban CBD, 1910–1948." *International Journal of African Historical Studies* 32, no. 1 (1999): 19–48.

Valentine, Gill. "Food and the Production of the Civilised Street." In *Images of the Street: Planning, Identity and Control in Public Space*, edited by Nicholas Fyfe, 192–204. London: Routledge, 1998.

Verma, Divya. "100 March for Hawker Free Juhu Church Road." *Mid Day*, November 17, 2005.

Vidler, Anthony. *The Scenes of the Street: Transformations in Ideal and Reality, 1750–1871*. Cambridge, MA: MIT Press, 1978.

"Vote, for Yourself!" *Juhu Citizen*, April 2004. http://www.juhucitizen.org/issues/april04 .htm.

Wacha, Dinshaw. *Shells from the Sands of Bombay: Being My Recollections and Reminiscences, 1860–1875*. Bombay: K. T. Anklesaria, 1920.

Wacquant, Loïc. "Scrutinizing the Street: Poverty, Morality, and the Pitfalls of Urban Ethnography." *American Journal of Sociology* 107, no. 6 (2002): 1468–1532.

———. *Urban Outcasts: A Comparative Sociology of Advanced Marginality*. Cambridge: Polity Press, 2008.

Weinstein, Liza. *The Durable Slum: Dharavi and the Right to Stay Put in Globalizing Mumbai*. Minneapolis: University of Minnesota Press, 2014.

Whitehead, Judy, and Nitin More. "Revanchism in Mumbai? Political Economy of Rent Gaps and Urban Restructuring in a Global City." *Economic and Political Weekly* 42, no. 25 (2007): 2428–34.

Wohl, R. Richard, and Anselm L. Strauss. "Symbolic Representation and the Urban Milieu." *American Journal of Sociology* 63 (1958): 523–32.

Yardley, Jim. "In One Slum, Misery, Work, Politics and Hope." *New York Times*, December 29, 2011. http://www.nytimes.com/2011/12/29/world/asia/in-indian-slum-misery -work-politics-and-hope.html?pagewanted=all.

Yeoh, Brenda. *Contesting Space in Colonial Singapore: Power Relations and the Urban Built Environment*. Singapore: Singapore University Press, 2003.

———. "The Global Cultural City? Spatial Imagineering and Politics in the (Multi)cultural Marketplaces of South-east Asia." *Urban Studies* 42, nos. 5-6 (2005): 945–58.

Zeiderman, Austin. "Cities of the Future? Megacities and the Space/Time of Urban Modernity." *Critical Planning* (Summer 2008): 23–39.

Zérah, Marie-Hélène. "Middle Class Neighbourhood Associations as Political Players in Mumbai." *Economic and Political Weekly* 42, no. 47 (2007): 61–68.

INDEX

2008 Mumbai terrorist attacks, 105

Advanced Locality Management (ALM),
29, 152–154
Agricultural produce market committee,
73–76, 78–79, 98–99, 189
Amin, Ash, 9, 163–164, 174, 179, 186–
187n4
architectural exhibits, 164–167, 191–192n1
Appadurai, Arjun, 97, 116

Baviskar, Amita, 29, 138, 149, 191n5
Big Bazaar, 72, 78, 100, 102–103. *See also*,
supermarkets
Björkman, Lisa, 13, 15, 183n6
BMW Guggenheim Urban Lab, 164–168
Bombay Chronicle, 55, 58–59, 188n22
Bombay City Improvement Trust, 48–51,
188n13, 188n15
Bombay First and McKinsey & Company
"Vision Mumbai" report, 4, 16
*Bombay Hawkers' Union v. Bombay
Municipal Corporation*, 25–26, 185n19
Bombay High Court, 114; three-member
committee, 34, 122, 156
Brihanmumbai Municipal Corporation
(BMC), 3–4, 30–36, 42, 46–63, 80,
190n10; BMC Acts, 20, 25–26, 47, 52,
179; everyday encounters with 107–
112, 118–125; encroachment removal,
56–57, 80, 85–86, 89–90, 112; hawker
survey, 115, 183n2, 185n19; *pautis*, 114–
116, 126, 154–155; *See also* evictions
Braudel, Fernand, 184n11

Chakrabarty, Dipesh 24–25, 118, 169
Chandavarkar, Raj, 44, 53, 60

Chandigarh, 189n8
Chatterjee, Partha, 27, 30, 131–132, 138,
158, 184n8
citizens' groups, 3–5, 8, 29–31, 36, 135–
159; *see also* civic activism
citizenship, 3, 5, 13–17, 26–33, 57–60,
110, 131–133, 136–137, 158, 187n6
civic activism, 8, 17, 27–28, 57–59, 62,
115–116, 135–159
colonial urbanism, 19–24, 39–63, 184n8,
187n7, 187n11; and public health,
188n14, 188n15
the Constitution of India, 25–27, 159,
185n15
corruption, 7–8, 57, 81–82, 90, 107–133,
154, 190n7; theories of, 117–119;
scenes of, 107–111, 119, 123–125;
anti-corruption protest, 129, 136–137,
191n6
Crawford Market, 52, 189n5

Das, Veena, 32–33, 113
Demolition, *see evictions*
development, 78, 100, 103–105
Dharavi, 161, 169, 173–177
disciplinary power, 110, 114, 116, 121
Dossal, Mariam, 47, 184n9, 187n6
Dubai, 91, 101, 170
Durban, 19, 183n7

economic liberalization, 4, 11, 13, 138–
140, 173, 183n6
encroachment, 2, 39 42–46, 49–50, 65–68,
79–80, 95, 185n19
entrepreneurialism, 79, 94–97, 103, 140,
172–177; and citizenship, 139, 152,
and governance, 12, 40, 171

213

ALSO PUBLISHED IN THE SOUTH ASIA IN MOTION SERIES

The Demands of Recognition: State Anthropology and Ethnopolitics in Darjeeling
Townsend Middleton (2015)

The South African Gandhi: Stretcher-Bearer of Empire
Ashwin Desai and Goolam Vahed (2015)

Printed and bound by CPI Group (UK) Ltd, Croydon, CR0 4YY

23/04/2025

14660939-0001